Asael Dror

Modifying Windows

Osborne McGraw-Hill
Berkeley New York St. Louis San Francisco Auckland Bogotá Hamburg London Madrid Mexico City
Milan Montreal New Delhi Panama City Paris São Paulo Singapore Sydney Tokyo Toronto

Osborne **McGraw-Hill**
2600 Tenth Street
Berkeley, California 94710
U.S.A.

For information on software, translations, or book distributors outside of the U.S.A., please write to Osborne **McGraw-Hill** at the above address.

Modifying Windows

Copyright © 1994 by McGraw-Hill, Inc. All rights reserved. Printed in the United States of America. Except as permitted under the Copyright Act of 1976, no part of this publication may be reproduced or distributed in any form or by any means, or stored in a database or retrieval system, without the prior written permission of the publisher, with the exception that the program listings may be entered, stored, and executed in a computer system, but they may not be reproduced for publication.

1234567890 DOC 9987654

ISBN 0-07-881993-8

Information has been obtained by Osborne **McGraw-Hill** from sources believed to be reliable. However, because of the possibility of human or mechanical error by our sources, Osborne **McGraw-Hill**, or others, Osborne **McGraw-Hill** does not guarantee the accuracy, adequacy, or completeness of any information and is not responsible for any errors or omissions or the results obtained from use of such information.

Series Design: Seventeenth Street Studios

*To my grandmother Bracha Elboim
and the memory of my grandfather Zvi Elboim,
with love.*

Contents

Acknowledgments, vii
Preface, ix
Introduction, xi

1 Un-Common Dialogs   1

Common Dialogs,   3
Un-Common Dialogs,   4
Customization via Parameters,   4
   Help Please,   11
Hooking Common Dialog Messages,   17
   The WM_INITDIALOG Message,   25
Modifying the Dialog's Resource
   Template,   30
Modifying the Common Dialogs: What and
   Where,   39
   Getting Carried Away with Modifications,
   40

2 Dynamic Link Libraries   43

Three Ways to Link Your Modules,   44
   Static Linking,   45
   Dynamic Linking,   51
   Explicit Dynamic Linking,   58
Instances, Tasks, and Modules,   65
The Mechanism of Dynamic Linking,   68
Anatomy of a DLL,   69
   The Initialization Routine,   70
   The Termination Routine,   71
   DLL Initialization and Termination
     Example,   72

The Advantages of DLLs and When to Use
   Them,   73
Callback Routines,   75
   Setting Up DS,   76
   Asynchronous Operation,   78
   Reentrancy Issues,   78

3 Advanced Windows Debugging   81

The Debugging Version of
   Windows,   82
Seeing is Believing,   85
Your Own Message in Lights,   89
Real Windows Developers Use a Debugging
   Terminal,   94
The Kernel Debugger,   95

4 Superclassing and Subclassing   97

Overview,   98
Superclassing,   99
Subclassing,   105
   Subclassing a Class,   106
   Subclassing a Window,   111
   Getting a Window Handle,   118
   Staying Out of the Way,   118
   EXE or DLL,   119
   When Can We Terminate?,   120
   A Better Mousetrap?,   125

5 Hooks   129

Overview,   131
Using Hooks,   131

    Order, Please!,   135
    Performance Issues,   135
Hook Types,   136
System Queue Hooks,   136
    Keyboard Hook,   136
    Mouse Hook,   137
    Hardware Event Hook,   138
Message Transfer Hooks,   144
    Call Window Procedure Hook,   144
    Get Message Hook,   145
Message Filter Hooks,   145
    Task Message Filter Hook,   146
    System Message Filter Hook,   147
Journal Hooks,   148
    Journal Record Hook,   148
    Journal Playback Hook,   149
Computer-Based Training (CBT),   157
Shell Hook,   160
Debug Hook,   161

6   Installable Device Drivers: Conventional and Unconventional Uses   165

Device Drivers: An Overview,   166
    Device Drivers,   167
    Virtual Device Drivers,   168
    The Device Driver Kit,   169
Installable Device Drivers,   169
    APIs for Communicating with an Installable Device Driver,   171
    Installable Device-Driver Messages,   173
    Messages Sent by Windows to Installable Device Drivers,   173
    Driver Installation Messages,   178
    Installing an Installable Device Driver,   188
    Control Panel's Drivers Program,   190
    APIs for Getting Information about Installable Device Drivers,   191
Resident Dynamic Link Libraries,   197

7   Toolhelp   205

Background,   206
    Toolhelp's Purpose,   206
Using Toolhelp,   207
    Standard APIs,   207
    List-Walking APIs,   215
    Callback Support APIs,   221

8   Dynamic Link Interceptors   235

Link-Time DLIs,   237
Patching DLIs,   237
    Patching the Application on Disk,   238
    Patching the Application in Memory,   238
    Patching the DLL in Memory,   238
Replacement DLIs,   239
    DLI Implementation,   240
    Exported Functions,   240
    Modifying a Code Segment,   242
    DLI Initialization,   244
    Windows Exit Procedure (WEP),   245
    Pitfalls and Problems,   252
DLI Applications,   252

INDEX   263

Acknowledgments

This book was made possible with the help and support of two individuals, Robert Lafore and Jeff Pepper, and I cannot thank them too profusely.

Robert Lafore, the book's developmental editor, is the person responsible for keeping me under control (not an easy task!). He made sure the book would help make the reader a Windows guru, rather than require the reader to be a Windows guru in order to understand the book.

Jeff Pepper, Editor-in-Chief at Osborne/McGraw-Hill, believed in the importance of this book from day one. He also understood that the book is more of a software development project than a literary project, with all the implied schedule delays.

I would like to thank the rest of the Osborne team who made this book possible: Vicki Van Ausdall, for her patience and tolerance for all the new formatting elements I added at short notice; Alexa Maddox, for keeping the development process running flawlessly; copyeditor Kathy Krause, for *all* the commas in the book; project editors Janet Walden and Cindy Brown and the Osborne production team, who did an incredible job of turning the manuscript into a book in record time.

Finally, I would like to thank the gang from Microsoft, headed by David Weise, who took time off developing Windows in order to review the book for technical accuracy.

Asael Dror

Preface

If you visit your local computer book store, you will find hundreds of books that teach you the first steps of programming Windows. But, what happens after you know the basics and want to learn more advanced techniques and approaches? Unfortunately, this type of information is virtually unavailable.

Seeing the need for advanced Windows programming know-how, I set out two years ago to fill the gap with a technical newsletter for advanced Windows developers. Called the *Windows Developer Letter*, my newsletter covers advanced programming techniques and presents new approaches to getting more power out of Windows. However, at $300 a year, the *Windows Developer Letter* can reach only a small portion of the Windows developers audience. Thus, this book was born.

This book is based on a series of articles that appeared in the *Windows Developer Letter*. It discusses how to modify and customize Windows to develop powerful and unique software applications and tools. The book is not a reprint of the Microsoft manuals, nor a repeat of information readily available elsewhere. Rather, this book provides new insights, presents powerful new techniques, and goes into the nuts and bolts details and pitfalls of advanced Windows development. If you are a Windows programmer who would like to become a Windows guru, this is the book for you!

Finally, if you like this book, I believe you would love the newsletter. To subscribe to the *Windows Developer Letter*, call Wisdom Software, Inc. at (415) 824-8482, or see the enclosed coupon at the back of this book for more information.

Introduction

Why Modify Windows?

This book is targeted at Windows developers who want to go beyond normal, run-of-the-mill applications. It will introduce new approaches you may not have believed possible in Windows 3.1, and show you better ways to achieve the tasks you perform today. At the same time, it will give you an insight into how Windows *really* works.

Why modify Windows? To make your applications more powerful and more distinctive, and to create entire classes of applications not possible with conventional programming. Here are some examples of what you will learn.

Creating Add-on Products

Add-on software is a new breed of product. Add-on programs are not standalone applications, but rather enhancements to other applications. For example, a dictionary program may be implemented as an add-on to a word processor such as Microsoft Word for Windows. As the PC software market matures, it becomes harder and harder to sell new mainstream applications (such as a new word processor), but the large installed base of such applications creates an important marketing opportunity. If you create an add-on program that improves or adds an important feature to an application, you have a large and easily accessible installed base to whom to sell your product. When you develop an add-on product, you usually do not have access to the source code of the base product. Your goal of adding features to an existing product requires modifying the existing Windows application. We will discuss and demonstrate ways to do this.

Modifying the System

In the same way that add-on products enhance the features of a Windows application, system add-ons enhance the features of Windows itself. Unless you have rights to the Windows source code, this requires modifying Windows internals. An example of a system add-on is a product that improves the performance of Windows by replacing some of the Windows APIs with functionally equivalent, but more efficient, ones. This book will show you how to do this.

Writing Tools and Utilities

Developing low-level tools and utilities such as macro-recorders, system monitors, profilers, debuggers, etc. requires the ability to monitor and modify many of the system's events, including messages and API calls. We will discuss and show examples of the various ways that can be achieved.

Reusing Existing Code

By using existing code, rather than writing your own from scratch, you can save significant development time. If somebody already wrote and debugged the code, you can sometimes use the same code again for your own use. For example, if you need a dialog box to query the user for the name of a file to be opened, you can write your own dialog box, or you can use the GetOpenFile-Name common dialog instead. The latter approach makes life much easier. In real life, however, when you reuse code, you commonly need something "very similar, but just slightly different" than the existing code. In such situations there are three choices:

1. Rewrite the code from scratch so it will behave *exactly* the way you want it to.
2. Use the existing code the way it is, even if it's *not exactly* what you want.
3. Modify the existing code so it does *exactly* what you want *without* the need to rewrite the parts that are working as you require.

In this book you will learn how to implement the third choice.

How This Book Is Organized

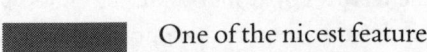

One of the nicest features of Windows is that there is no fundamental distinction between Windows' own elements (such as APIs and windows) and the application's. The real difference is that Windows' elements come with Windows, while other APIs and windows are bought by the end user separately. If Microsoft wants to extend or modify Windows, all they have to do is add or replace a DLL—and so can you!

In this book you will explore ways to modify and extend the different elements of Windows. This applies to both Windows' own elements and third party applications.

The book takes a gradual approach to the modification process, starting with the high-level elements of the system, and slowly working our way down to the lowest levels.

The highest level element you will modify is the Common Dialog Box. This is an extremely useful technique for everyday Windows programming situations. On the next level down, you will modify window procedures and messages. Using superclassing, subclassing, and hooks, you can modify any window, any window class, or any message in the system. These are powerful techniques that not only save you work, but also enable you to develop many application and system add-on products.

Finally, you will explore how to modify the actual APIs—the application's or Windows'. Many of the techniques discussed have been published originally in the *Windows Developer Letter*. Those techniques have never been published elsewhere and are know only to a select few. While API modifications are not something you would use daily, when you need them they represent the ultimate in power and control.

Learn As You Go

The focus of this book is modifying Windows, but before you modify, you need an understanding of what you are going to modify. Many of the techniques used in this book rely on some of Windows' most advanced features. Consequently, in addition to showing you how to modify Windows, this book will explore:

- *Dynamic Link Libraries* (DLLs)
- *Toolhelp*—what it is and how to use it
- *The kernel debugger*—probably the most powerful yet most underutilized tool in the SDK

- *Installable device drivers*—their original purpose, and how to go way beyond it!

What You Need to Get Started

Surprisingly little is required to get started with this book. I will assume you are a Windows developer, programming in C. While the book discusses very powerful and advanced techniques, the thorough background discussions and the liberal use of examples should make it comprehensible to anyone with a year or so of Windows programming experience. Knowledge of 80x86 architecture and assembly language will come in handy for the last few chapters, but is not essential.

The software you need includes a C compiler and the Windows 3.1 Software Development Kit (SDK). Actually, you may not even need the SDK, since some compiler vendors are bundling the SDK (or its equivalent) with their C compilers. While all the examples in the book were developed with Microsoft C 7 and the Windows 3.1 SDK, porting them to a different compiler is easy. A diskette with the source and executable code for all the examples in the book is available from Wisdom Software, Inc. (415-824-8482). See the enclosed coupon at the back of this book for details.

Chapter 1

Un-Common Dialogs

ONE of the chores a Windows application performs is querying the user for information. Controls, such as menus, buttons, list boxes, and so on, are some of the standard methods of receiving input from the user. When an application needs to query the user for elaborate information, a collection of controls are commonly grouped together in a dialog box that is used to acquire the required information.

Some information gathering operations are common to many different Windows applications and are performed in a similar manner in many applications. For example, word processors, spreadsheets, databases, and other applications all need to open files, and they commonly use a dialog to query the user for the name of the file to be opened. Similarly, many applications have dialog boxes for saving a file with an indicated filename, printing, setting up a printer, selecting a font, selecting a color, and more.

Before Windows 3.1, every application used its own dialogs to perform those common chores. This had two disadvantages:

1. From the user's viewpoint, the same logical operation (such as opening a file) was performed in different ways in different applications. One of the main goals of a CUI is to have a *Common User Interface* for all Windows applications, so as to decrease the effort required to learn a new application. Performing the same logical function differently in different applications does not fit in with the CUI philosophy.

2. From the developer's viewpoint, every new application required that the same dialogs be developed from scratch. This included writing (and debugging and maintaining) the code for the dialog box procedure as well as defining the dialog box template in a resource file.

CHAPTER 1
UN-COMMON DIALOGS

Common Dialogs

Windows 3.1 includes a Dynamic Link Library (DLL), called COMMDLG.DLL, that contains a set of APIs which perform many of the common chores that applications used to perform via a dialog box. (COMMDLG.DLL is one of the "redistributable" components of the SDK. This means that you can distribute COMMDLG.DLL with your applications, so that the applications can be used under Windows 3.0. See the SDK for the legal mumbo jumbo.)

The following table summarizes the chores performed by the common dialogs DLL.

Function	Dialog Box's Chore	API
Color	Select a color	ChooseColor
Font	Select a font	ChooseFont
Open	Select a file or files to be opened	GetOpenFileName
Save As	Select the filename for saving a file	GetSaveFileName
Print	Select printing options	PrintDlg
Print Setup	Select the printer and its options	PrintDlg
Find	Get the string to be found and get search options	FindText
Replace	Get the string to be found, the replacement string, and options	ReplaceText

COMMDLG.DLL contains both the dialog procedures and the resources required for the common dialogs. All an application has to do is fill in a structure of parameters and call a single API. The API handles the dialog box and returns the requested information. The common dialog boxes are modal, except for the Find and Replace dialog boxes, which are modeless.

To use the common dialog box APIs listed above, an application needs to `#include` COMMDLG.H in its source code, link with the COMMDLG.LIB library, and make sure it has at least 8K of stack available for use by the common dialog APIs.

Additional `#include` files that may be needed in some applications are DLGS.H and COLORDLG.H, which contain the element IDs used in the templates (you'll see why you may need these later). If any of the common dialog APIs fail, the CommDlgExtendedError API can be used to return an extended error code for the last error. CDERR.H contains those extended error codes.

MODIFYING WINDOWS

CommDlgExtendedError

Returns the error code of the last common dialog API

```
DWORD CommDlgExtendedError(VOID);
```

Returns:
The error code of last common dialog's call (see CDERR.H), or zero if the last call was successful.

Because common dialogs are new in Windows 3.1, their documentation is, let's just say, not quite mature. However, due to the tremendous number of options available with common dialogs, we'll concentrate on how to do things rather than dwell on the details of every possible parameter and flag. Using the GetOpenFileName API as an example, we'll show how to modify and extend the common dialogs.

Un-Common Dialogs

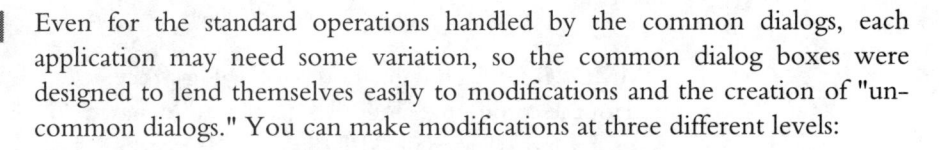

Even for the standard operations handled by the common dialogs, each application may need some variation, so the common dialog boxes were designed to lend themselves easily to modifications and the creation of "un-common dialogs." You can make modifications at three different levels:

1. Customization via parameters
2. Hooking common dialog messages
3. Resource template modification

We'll look at each of those levels separately.

Customization via Parameters

As mentioned earlier, each common dialog API receives a structure of parameters. By controlling the variables and flags in this structure, an application can customize the appearance and behavior of the dialog box.

CHAPTER 1
UN-COMMON DIALOGS

As an example, we will look at the Open file common dialog (the GetOpenFileName API).

GetOpenFileName
Selects a filename

```
BOOL GetOpenFileName(lpofn);

OPENFILENAME FAR * lpofn;
```

Returns:
If the user successfully selected a file, TRUE; else FALSE. (If GetOpenFileName returns FALSE, use CommDlgExtendedError to get the error code.)

The OPENFILENAME structure (which is used by both the Open and the Save As common dialogs) is defined as follows:

```
typedef struct tagOFN
    {
    DWORD       lStructSize;        // size of OFN structure
    HWND        hwndOwner;          // owner of dialog box, or NULL
    HINSTANCE   hInstance;          // for template
    LPCSTR      lpstrFilter;        // description and pattern stringz
                                    // pairs, null terminated, or NULL
    LPSTR       lpstrCustomFilter;  // additional filters, or NULL
    DWORD       nMaxCustFilter;     // size of CustomFilters buffer
    DWORD       nFilterIndex;       // index of filter to use in File
                                    // Name list box
    LPSTR       lpstrFile;          // buffer to contain selected file
                                    // specs
                                    // the input (if not NULL) is the
                                    // default filename
    DWORD       nMaxFile;           // size of strFile
    LPSTR       lpstrFileTitle;     // buffer to contain filename
                                    // (no path)
    DWORD       nMaxFileTitle;      // size of FileTitle
    LPCSTR      lpstrInitialDir;    // NULL == current dir
    LPCSTR      lpstrTitle;         // dialog box title, NULL == "Open"
                                    // or "Save As"

    DWORD   Flags;                  // possible values are:
        // OFN_ALLOWMULTISELECT
```

```
            // OFN_CREATEPROMPT         prompt if file does not exist
            // OFN_ENABLEHOOK
            // OFN_ENABLETEMPLATE
            // OFN_ENABLETEMPLATEHANDLE  use hInstance
            // OFN_EXTENSIONDIFFERENT
            // OFN_FILEMUSTEXIST
            // OFN_HIDEREADONLY          hide "Read Only" check box
            // OFN_NOCHANGEDIR
            // OFN_NOREADONLYRETURN
            // OFN_NOTESTFILECREATE
            // OFN_NOVALIDATE
            // OFN_OVERWRITEPROMPT
            // OFN_PATHMUSTEXIST
            // OFN_READONLY              "Read Only" check box initially
                                         // checked

            // OFN_SHAREAWARE
            // OFN_SHOWHELP              show "Help" push button,
                                         // hwndOwner must be valid

    UINT    nFileOffset;        // offset of filename (not path)
                                // in strFile
    UINT    nFileExtension;     // offset of filename extension in
                                // strFile
    LPCSTR  lpstrDefExt;        // default filename extension
    LPARAM  lCustData;          // data to hook function
                                // hook function
    UINT    (CALLBACK *lpfnHook)(HWND, UINT, WPARAM, LPARAM);

    LPCSTR  lpTemplateName;     // resource file for dialog box
                                // template
}   OPENFILENAME;
```

Although GetOpenFileName is intended to be used by the "Open file" option of an application, you can easily adapt it to select a file for other purposes. The following example is a simple dispatcher program. It allows the user to select a file to be executed. The file selection is done via the GetOpenFileName API's common dialog box.

RUN EXAMPLE PROGRAM

The following program uses the GetOpenFileName API to select a file to be executed. This is similar to selecting File, Run, Browse from the Program Manager. In our example, when the user selects the Run option from the menu, we fill the ofn structure and call the GetOpenFileName API. The elements of the structure we fill include

- **lStructureSize**, is initialized with the size of the structure. This is standard practice in many APIs that receive parameters via structures. This value allows the API to determine which version of the API the application assumes it's calling.
- **hwndOwner**, is the dialog box's owner: our main window.
- **lpstrFilter**, contains the "List Files of Type" filters. It contains both the filters' descriptions and their corresponding patterns. In our example there are two filters: "Programs", defined as "*.exe;*.com;*.pif;*.bat", and "All files", defined as "*.*".
- **lpstrTitle**, is the title of the dialog box. We use the title "Run" instead of the default title "Open".

The Flags are set to OFN_FILEMUSTEXIST (since we cannot run a nonexistent file), OFN_HIDEREADONLY (to hide the "Read Only" check box in the dialog box), and OFN_NOCHANGEDIR.

After a few more simple assignments, such as NULLs and 0s for options we don't utilize, and similar trivialities, we are ready to call GetOpenFileName.

GetOpenFileName handles the entire dialog, and if it returns with a TRUE return code we have a filespec in the FileName variable. We use that filespec as the parameter for WinExec.

Note that for the sake of simplicity, this example, like most of the examples in this book, does not perform elaborate error checking and recovery. This is done to keep the examples focused on the points being demonstrated. When developing commercial applications, you'll want to add extensive error-checking and recovery code.

MAKEFILE

```
all: run.exe

run.res: run.rc run.h makefile
    rc -r run.rc

run.obj: run.c run.h makefile
    cl -c -DSTRICT -AS -GA2 -Ox -W3 run.c

run.exe: run.obj run.def run.res makefile
    link run,,,libw commdlg slibcew, run.def
    rc run.res
```

RUN.C

```c
// run a program - an example of using common dialogs
//
// from Modifying Windows by Asael Dror
//

#include <windows.h>
#include <commdlg.h>

#include "run.h"

HINSTANCE hInst;                                    // current instance

                                                    // application E.P.
int PASCAL WinMain(HINSTANCE hInstance, HINSTANCE hPrevInstance,
            LPSTR LPCmdLine, int nCmdShow)

  {
  MSG msg;
  if (hPrevInstance)                        // one inst only!
     return(FALSE);

  if (!InitApplication(hInstance))          // init app
     return(FALSE);

  if (!InitInstance(hInstance, nCmdShow))         // init instance
     return(FALSE);

                                                // msg loop
  while (GetMessage(&msg, NULL, 0, 0))       // get any msg/any wnd
     {
     TranslateMessage(&msg);                 // translate virt keys
     DispatchMessage(&msg);                  // dispatch message
     }
  return(msg.wParam);
  }

BOOL InitApplication(HINSTANCE hInstance)         // init app
  {
                                               // reg main wnd class
  WNDCLASS wc;

                                               // fill wnd class str
  wc.style = 0;
  wc.lpfnWndProc = MainWndProc;               // window proc
  wc.cbClsExtra = 0;
```

```c
    wc.cbWndExtra = 0;
    wc.hInstance = hInstance;                   // class owner
    wc.hIcon = LoadIcon(NULL, IDI_APPLICATION); // def app icon
    wc.hCursor = LoadCursor(NULL, IDC_ARROW);   // standard cursor
    wc.hbrBackground = (HBRUSH)(COLOR_WINDOW + 1); // wnd bckgnd clr
    wc.lpszMenuName = "MainMenu";
    wc.lpszClassName = "RunClass";              // window class name

    return(RegisterClass(&wc));                 // register wnd class
    }

                                                // instance init
BOOL InitInstance(HINSTANCE hInstance, int nCmdShow)
    {
    HWND  hWnd;                                 // window handle

    hInst = hInstance;                          // save in static var

    hWnd = CreateWindow (                       // main window
            "RunClass",                         // class name
            "RUN",                              // title bar text
            WS_OVERLAPPEDWINDOW | WS_VISIBLE,   // normal & visible
            CW_USEDEFAULT,                      // default x
            nCmdShow,                           // default y,
                                                // show as requested
            CW_USEDEFAULT,                      // default width
            CW_USEDEFAULT,                      // default height
            HWND_DESKTOP,                       // no parent
            NULL,                               // use class menu
            hInstance,                          // inst of mod for win
            NULL);                              // not used
    if (!hWnd) return(FALSE);
    UpdateWindow(hWnd);                         // send WM_PAINT msg
    return (TRUE);                              // OK
    }


LRESULT __export CALLBACK MainWndProc(
                        HWND hWnd,              // window handle
                        UINT message,           // message
                        WPARAM wParam,          // param
                        LPARAM lParam)          // param
    {
    OPENFILENAME ofn;
    char FileName[256] = "";

    switch (message)
        {
```

MODIFYING WINDOWS

```
      case WM_DESTROY:
         PostQuitMessage(0);                      // bye bye, rc = 0
         break;

      case WM_COMMAND:
         switch (wParam)
            {
            case IDM_RUNPGM:
               ofn.lStructSize = sizeof(ofn);
               ofn.hwndOwner = hWnd;
               ofn.lpstrFilter =
               "Programs\0*.exe;*.com;*.pif;*.bat\0All files\0*.*\0";
               ofn.lpstrCustomFilter = NULL;
               ofn.nFilterIndex = 0;
               ofn.lpstrFile = FileName;
               ofn.nMaxFile = sizeof(FileName);
               ofn.lpstrFileTitle = NULL;
               ofn.lpstrInitialDir = NULL;
               ofn.lpstrTitle = "RUN";
               ofn.Flags = OFN_FILEMUSTEXIST | OFN_HIDEREADONLY |
                           OFN_NOCHANGEDIR;
               ofn.lpstrDefExt = NULL;

               if (GetOpenFileName(&ofn))
                  WinExec(FileName, SW_SHOWNORMAL);

               break;

            default:                              // default proc and ret
               return (DefWindowProc(hWnd, message,
                                  wParam, lParam));
            }
      break;

      default:                                    // default proc and ret
         return (DefWindowProc(hWnd, message,
                            wParam, lParam));
      }
   return(0);
   }
```

RUN.H

```
LRESULT __export CALLBACK MainWndProc(HWND, UINT, WPARAM, LPARAM);
BOOL InitApplication(HINSTANCE);
```

```
BOOL InitInstance(HINSTANCE, int);

#define IDM_RUNPGM 100
```

RUN.RC

```
#include <windows.h>
#include "run.h"

MainMenu   MENU    PRELOAD
            {
                MENUITEM    "&Run", IDM_RUNPGM
            }
```

RUN.DEF

```
NAME            RUN

DESCRIPTION     'Run a program'

EXETYPE         WINDOWS

STUB            'WINSTUB.EXE'

CODE PRELOAD MOVEABLE DISCARDABLE
DATA PRELOAD MOVEABLE MULTIPLE

HEAPSIZE        1024
STACKSIZE       8192
```

Figure 1-1 shows the common dialog displayed by this program.

Help Please

An easy way to embellish a common dialog box is to add a Help button to it. You can do this with the OFN_SHOWHELP flag, which all the common dialog boxes support.

When OFN_SHOWHELP is set, the common dialog will send (not post) the owner window (as indicated by hWndOwner) a message when the user

Figure 1-1
Common dialog displayed by the Run program

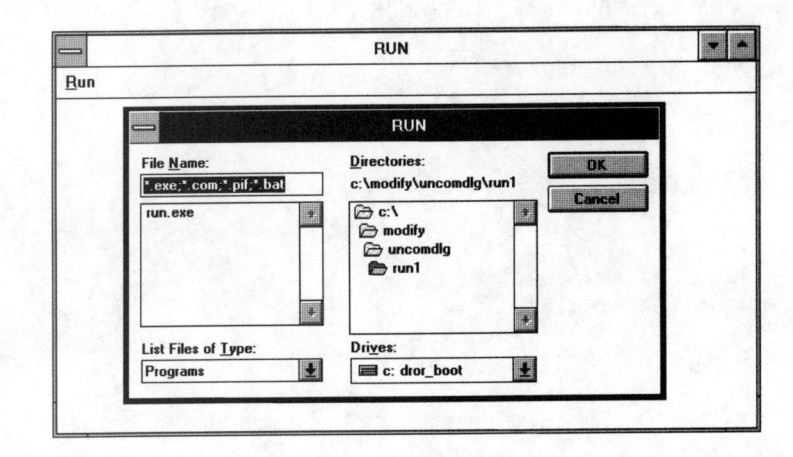

pushes the Help button. The numerical value of this message—that is, the message ID—is determined at run time by the message registration mechanism.

MESSAGE REGISTRATION

When different applications communicate via messages, they need to obtain a unique system-wide ID for their messages. The RegisterWindowMessage API supports this by returning a unique message number for a message description input string. By using the same message description input string, different applications can receive the same unique message ID.

RegisterWindowMessage

Register a unique system-wide message

```
UINT RegisterWindowMessage(lpszMsgDesc);

LPCSTR lpszMsgDesc;    // message description string
```

Returns:
If successful, this API returns the message number corresponding to the message description string. The message number is in the range 0xC000 to 0xFFFF. If unsuccessful, this API returns 0.

The common dialogs use a variety of registered messages. (Considering that the message description strings used by the common dialogs have a #define in COMMDLG.H, it makes little sense to use the registration mechanism rather than simply assign those few messages a fixed predetermined value like all other Windows messages—but that's the way it is.)

In our case, the help message is a registered message whose message description string is `#define HELPMSGSTRING` in COMMDLG.H.

RUN EXAMPLE PROGRAM WITH HELP

The following program is a revised version of the dispatcher program, with help added. When the program receives the help message from the Open file dialog box, it displays a help message via a message box. Note that since the message box is application modal and a dialog box is up, we should use the dialog as the parent. However, since we do not have the dialog box's handle handy, we can solve the problem by creating the message box as task modal, which disables all the current task's top level windows.

MAKEFILE

```
all: run.exe
run.res: run.rc run.h makefile
    rc -r run.rc

run.obj: run.c run.h makefile
    cl -c -DSTRICT -AS -GA2 -Ox -W3 run.c

run.exe: run.obj run.def run.res makefile
    link run,,,libw commdlg slibcew, run.def
    rc run.res
```

RUN.C

```
// run a program - an example of using common dialogs
//
// from Modifying Windows by Asael Dror
//

#include <windows.h>
#include <commdlg.h>

#include "run.h"
```

MODIFYING WINDOWS

```
HINSTANCE hInst;                                        // current instance
UINT HelpMsgID;

                                                        // application E.P.
int PASCAL WinMain(HINSTANCE hInstance, HINSTANCE hPrevInstance,
               LPSTR LPCmdLine, int nCmdShow)


  {
  MSG msg;
  if (hPrevInstance)                    // one inst only!
     return(FALSE);

  if (!InitApplication(hInstance))      // init app
     return(FALSE);

  if (!InitInstance(hInstance, nCmdShow))       // init instance
     return(FALSE);

                                                // msg loop
  while (GetMessage(&msg, NULL, 0, 0))  // get any msg/any wnd
     {
     TranslateMessage(&msg);            // translate virt keys
     DispatchMessage(&msg);             // dispatch message
     }
  return(msg.wParam);
  }

BOOL InitApplication(HINSTANCE hInstance)       // init app
  {
                                                // reg main wnd class
  WNDCLASS wc;

                                                // fill wnd class str
  wc.style = 0;
  wc.lpfnWndProc = MainWndProc;         // window proc
  wc.cbClsExtra = 0;
  wc.cbWndExtra = 0;
  wc.hInstance = hInstance;             // class owner
  wc.hIcon = LoadIcon(NULL, IDI_APPLICATION);   // def app icon
  wc.hCursor = LoadCursor(NULL, IDC_ARROW);     // standard cursor
  wc.hbrBackground = (HBRUSH)(COLOR_WINDOW + 1); // wnd bckgnd clr
  wc.lpszMenuName = "MainMenu";
  wc.lpszClassName = "RunClass";        // window class name

  return(RegisterClass(&wc));           // register wnd class
  }
```

CHAPTER 1
UN-COMMON DIALOGS

```c
                                            // instance init
BOOL InitInstance(HINSTANCE hInstance, int nCmdShow)
  {
  HWND  hWnd;                               // window handle

  hInst = hInstance;                        // save in static var

  HelpMsgID = RegisterWindowMessage(HELPMSGSTRING);

  hWnd = CreateWindow (                     // main window
         "RunClass",                        // class name
         "RUN",                             // title bar text
         WS_OVERLAPPEDWINDOW | WS_VISIBLE,  // normal & visible
         CW_USEDEFAULT,                     // default x
         nCmdShow,                          // default y,
                                            // show as requested
         CW_USEDEFAULT,                     // default width
         CW_USEDEFAULT,                     // default height
         HWND_DESKTOP,                      // no parent
         NULL,                              // use class menu
         hInstance,                         // inst of mod for win
         NULL);                             // not used
  if (!hWnd) return(FALSE);
  UpdateWindow(hWnd);                       // send WM_PAINT msg
  return (TRUE);                            // OK
  }


LRESULT __export CALLBACK MainWndProc(
                        HWND hWnd,          // window handle
                        UINT message,       // message
                        WPARAM wParam,      // param
                        LPARAM lParam)      // param

  {
  OPENFILENAME ofn;
  char FileName[256] = "";

  switch (message)
     {
     case WM_DESTROY:
        PostQuitMessage(0);                 // bye bye, rc = 0
        break;
     case WM_COMMAND:
        switch (wParam)
           {
           case IDM_RUNPGM:
              ofn.lStructSize = sizeof(ofn);
              ofn.hwndOwner = hWnd;
```

MODIFYING WINDOWS

```
                    ofn.lpstrFilter =
                      "Programs\0*.exe;*.com;*.pif;*.bat\0All files\0*.*\0";
                    ofn.lpstrCustomFilter = NULL;
                    ofn.nFilterIndex = 0;
                    ofn.lpstrFile = FileName;
                    ofn.nMaxFile = sizeof(FileName);
                    ofn.lpstrFileTitle = NULL;
                    ofn.lpstrInitialDir = NULL;
                    ofn.lpstrTitle = "RUN";
                    ofn.Flags = OFN_FILEMUSTEXIST | OFN_HIDEREADONLY |
                                OFN_NOCHANGEDIR | OFN_SHOWHELP;
                    ofn.lpstrDefExt = NULL;

                    if (GetOpenFileName(&ofn))
                        WinExec(FileName, SW_SHOWNORMAL);

                    break;

                default:                          // default proc and ret
                    return (DefWindowProc(hWnd, message,
                                          wParam, lParam));
                }
            break;

        default:                                  // default proc and ret
            if (message == HelpMsgID)
                MessageBox(NULL, "Help is never there when you need it!",
                           "Help",
                            MB_ICONINFORMATION | MB_OK | MB_TASKMODAL);

            return (DefWindowProc(hWnd, message,
                                  wParam, lParam));
        }
    return(0);
    }
```

RUN.H

```
LRESULT __export CALLBACK MainWndProc(HWND, UINT, WPARAM, LPARAM);
BOOL InitApplication(HINSTANCE);
BOOL InitInstance(HINSTANCE, int);

#define IDM_RUNPGM 100
```

RUN.RC

```
#include <windows.h>
#include "run.h"

MainMenu    MENU    PRELOAD

    {

 MENUITEM    "&Run",  IDM_RUNPGM
            }
```

RUN.DEF

```
NAME            RUN

DESCRIPTION     'Run a program'

EXETYPE         WINDOWS

STUB            'WINSTUB.EXE'

CODE PRELOAD MOVEABLE DISCARDABLE
DATA PRELOAD MOVEABLE MULTIPLE

HEAPSIZE        1024
STACKSIZE       8192
```

Figure 1-2 shows the common dialog with the Help button added.

Generally, customization via parameters and flags allows us to perform only the modifications that the authors of the common dialog APIs expected and decided to support. For more elaborate modification, two additional modification mechanisms exist: hooking common dialog messages and modifying the resource template.

Hooking Common Dialog Messages

The common dialog hook (not to be confused with the hooks discussed in Chapter 5) allows us to intercept messages before they are received by the common dialog's dialog procedure. (This is somewhat similar to subclassing, which we will discuss in Chapter 4.)

To use a common dialog hook, we need to tell the common dialog API that a hook routine is being used. This is done by setting the ENABLEHOOK flag

Figure 1-2
Common dialog with Help button

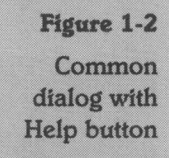

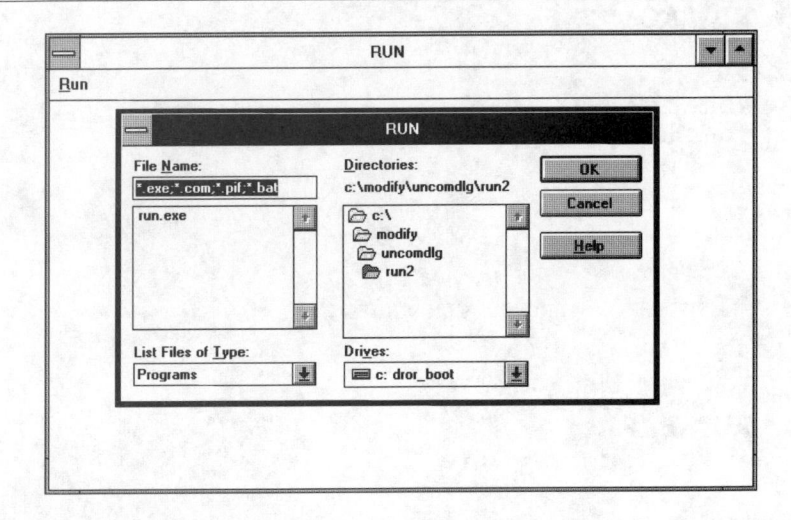

(OFN_ENABLEHOOK in the case of Open file) in the API's parameter structure. We also need to supply the API with the address of the common dialog hook callback routine. This address is passed in the `lpfnHook` element of the parameter structure.

The common dialog hook callback routine has the following format:

Common Dialog Hook Callback Routine

```
UINT CALLBACK _ _export CommonDialgosHookCallbackRoutine (
    HWND       hDlg,    // dialog's handle
    UNIT       message, // message ID
    WPARAM     wParam,  // parameter - message specific
    LPARAM     lParam); // parameter - message specific
```

Returns:
For the WM_INITDIALOG message, a return value of TRUE indicates that the common dialog API should set the focus; a return value of FALSE indicates that the callback routine has taken care of setting the focus.

For all other messages, a return value of TRUE causes the message to be discarded, and a return value of FALSE causes the messages to be passed on to the dialog procedure for default processing.

When a common dialog hook is used, the callback routine is called with each message destined for the common dialog's dialog procedure. The hook routine can react to the message, as well as determine whether the message should be passed on to the dialog procedure for default processing. The decision whether to pass the message on to the dialog procedure, a process known as message filtration, is performed via the hook routine's return code: TRUE causes the message to be discarded; FALSE passes the message on to the dialog procedure for its default processing.

On entry to the common dialog hook callback routine, the DS register points to the common dialog's data segment. To access our program's data segment, we need to set DS to our program's data segment. For the Microsoft C 7.0 compiler, this is most easily achieved by compiling with the -GA switch, which sets DS equal to SS on entry to an __export routine. We will discuss this issue further in the next chapter.

For the callback routine to communicate with the dialog's controls, it needs to know their element IDs. Fortunately, the SDK contains an #include file, DLGS.H, that contains the #define of all the control IDs used by the common dialogs. Furthermore, the SDK contains the source code for the resource files (the template) of all the dialog boxes of the common dialog APIs, as well as their bitmaps. (They are all nicely hidden in the SDK's \SAMPLES\COMMDLG subdirectory.)

COMMON DIALOG MESSAGE HOOKING EXAMPLE PROGRAM

The following program uses a common dialog message hook to sound a beep whenever the "OK" button or the "Cancel" button is pushed in the "Run" dialog box. Furthermore, our handling of the Help button has been improved. In the previous example, "Help" for all the common dialog boxes was handled identically. In the current example, the Help button is handled in the callback routine and is therefore specific to that dialog box. Since the handle to the dialog window is readily available in the callback routine (it's one of the parameters), we use it as the MessageBox's parent and make the MessageBox application modal (the default) rather than task modal as we did in the previous example. Finally, we return TRUE in response to the Help button being pushed, since the callback routine performs all the required actions for this event.

MAKEFILE

```
all: run.exe
```

```
run.res: run.rc run.h makefile
   rc -r run.rc

run.obj: run.c run.h makefile
   cl -c -DSTRICT -AS -GA2 -Ox -W3 run.c

run.exe: run.obj run.def run.res makefile
   link run,,,libw commdlg slibcew, run.def
   rc run.res
```

RUN.C

```c
// run a program - an example of using un-common dialogs
//
// from Modifying Windows by Asael Dror
//

#include <windows.h>
#include <commdlg.h>
#include <dlgs.h>

#include "run.h"

HINSTANCE hInst;                                        // current instance

                                                        // application E.P.
int PASCAL WinMain(HINSTANCE hInstance, HINSTANCE hPrevInstance,
               LPSTR LPCmdLine, int nCmdShow)

  {
  MSG msg;
  if (hPrevInstance)                    // one inst only!
     return(FALSE);

  if (!InitApplication(hInstance))      // init app
     return(FALSE);

  if (!InitInstance(hInstance, nCmdShow))        // init instance
     return(FALSE);

                                                 // msg loop
  while (GetMessage(&msg, NULL, 0, 0))   // get any msg/any wnd
     {
     TranslateMessage(&msg);                     // translate virt keys
     DispatchMessage(&msg);                      // dispatch message
```

```
        }
    return(msg.wParam);
    }

BOOL InitApplication(HINSTANCE hInstance)        // init app
    {
                                                 // reg main wnd class
    WNDCLASS wc;

                                                 // fill wnd class str
    wc.style = 0;
    wc.lpfnWndProc = MainWndProc;                // window proc
    wc.cbClsExtra = 0;
    wc.cbWndExtra = 0;
    wc.hInstance = hInstance;                    // class owner
    wc.hIcon = LoadIcon(NULL, IDI_APPLICATION);  // def app icon
    wc.hCursor = LoadCursor(NULL, IDC_ARROW);    // standard cursor
    wc.hbrBackground = (HBRUSH)(COLOR_WINDOW + 1); // wnd bckgnd clr
    wc.lpszMenuName = "MainMenu";
    wc.lpszClassName = "RunClass";               // window class name

    return(RegisterClass(&wc));                  // register wnd class
    }


                                                 // instance init
BOOL InitInstance(HINSTANCE hInstance, int nCmdShow)
    {
    HWND  hWnd;                                  // window handle

    hInst = hInstance;                           // save in static var

    hWnd = CreateWindow (                        // main window
            "RunClass",                          // class name
            "RUN",                               // title bar text
            WS_OVERLAPPEDWINDOW | WS_VISIBLE,    // normal & visible
            CW_USEDEFAULT,                       // default x
            nCmdShow,                            // default y,
                                                 // show as requested
            CW_USEDEFAULT,                       // default width
            CW_USEDEFAULT,                       // default height
            HWND_DESKTOP,                        // no parent
            NULL,                                // use class menu
            hInstance,                           // inst of mod for win
            NULL);                               // not used
    if (!hWnd) return(FALSE);
    UpdateWindow(hWnd);                          // send WM_PAINT msg
    return (TRUE);                               // OK
```

MODIFYING WINDOWS

```c
    }

LRESULT __export CALLBACK MainWndProc(
                            HWND hWnd,            // window handle
                            UINT message,         // message
                            WPARAM wParam,        // param
                            LPARAM lParam)        // param
{
    OPENFILENAME ofn;
    char FileName[256] = "";

    switch (message)
       {
       case WM_DESTROY:
          PostQuitMessage(0);                     // bye bye, rc = 0
          break;
       case WM_COMMAND:
          switch (wParam)
             {
             case IDM_RUNPGM:
                ofn.lStructSize = sizeof(ofn);
                ofn.hwndOwner = hWnd;
                ofn.lpstrFilter =
                "Programs\0*.exe;*.com;*.pif;*.bat\0All files\0*.*\0";
                ofn.lpstrCustomFilter = NULL;
                ofn.nFilterIndex = 0;
                ofn.lpstrFile = FileName;
                ofn.nMaxFile = sizeof(FileName);
                ofn.lpstrFileTitle = NULL;
                ofn.lpstrInitialDir = NULL;
                ofn.lpstrTitle = "RUN";
                ofn.Flags = OFN_FILEMUSTEXIST | OFN_HIDEREADONLY |
                            OFN_NOCHANGEDIR | OFN_SHOWHELP |
                            OFN_ENABLEHOOK;
                ofn.lpstrDefExt = NULL;
                ofn.lpfnHook = GetOpenFileNameHook;

                if (GetOpenFileName(&ofn))
                   WinExec(FileName, SW_SHOWNORMAL);

                break;

             default:                             // default proc and ret
                return (DefWindowProc(hWnd, message,
                                  wParam, lParam));
             }
       break;
```

```
        default:                              // default proc and ret
            return (DefWindowProc(hWnd, message,
                                wParam, lParam));
        }
    return(0);
    }


                // common dialog message hook callback routine
UINT CALLBACK __export GetOpenFileNameHook(
                        HWND hDlg,
                        UINT message,
                        WPARAM wParam,
                        LPARAM lParam)

{
switch (message)
    {
    case WM_INITDIALOG:
        return TRUE;

    case WM_COMMAND:
            switch (wParam)
                {
                case IDOK:
                    MessageBeep(MB_OK);
                    break;

                case IDCANCEL:
                    MessageBeep(MB_ICONASTERISK);
                    break;

                case pshHelp:
                    MessageBox(hDlg,
                            "Help is never there when you need it!",
                            "Help", MB_ICONINFORMATION | MB_OK);

                    return TRUE;

                default:
                    break;
                }
        break;

    default:
        return FALSE;
```

```
        }
    return FALSE;
    }
```

RUN.H

```
LRESULT __export CALLBACK MainWndProc(HWND, UINT, WPARAM, LPARAM);
BOOL InitApplication(HINSTANCE);
BOOL InitInstance(HINSTANCE, int);
UINT CALLBACK __export GetOpenFileNameHook(HWND, UINT,
                                           WPARAM, LPARAM);


#define IDM_RUNPGM 100
```

RUN.RC

```
#include <windows.h>
#include "run.h"

MainMenu    MENU    PRELOAD
            {
            MENUITEM    "&Run", IDM_RUNPGM
            }
```

RUN.DEF

```
NAME            RUN

DESCRIPTION     'Run a program'

EXETYPE         WINDOWS

STUB            'WINSTUB.EXE'

CODE PRELOAD MOVEABLE DISCARDABLE
DATA PRELOAD MOVEABLE MULTIPLE
```

```
HEAPSIZE        1024
STACKSIZE       8192
```

The WM_INITDIALOG Message

As a rule, a common dialog hook routine receives all messages before the common dialog procedure does. However, there is one exception—the WM_INITDIALOG message. WM_INITDIALOG is passed to the common dialog hook routine *after* the dialog box procedure processes it. This allows the dialog to initialize all its controls *before* the common dialog hook routine receives the message. Consequently, when the common dialog hook procedure receives the WM_INITDIALOG message, the controls of the dialog are already set up, giving the callback routine an ideal opportunity to "change things" just before the dialog is displayed. Some of the "things" that can be changed at this time include the size and location of controls, hiding controls, adding and initializing new controls, and so on.

Since the WM_INITDIALOG is commonly used by the callback routine to change the controls inside the dialog box, the code returned by the callback routine when it is called with the WM_INITDIALOG message has a different meaning than when the callback routine is called with other messages (i.e., discard or process message). For the WM_INITDIALOG message, a return code of TRUE from the common dialog callback routine indicates that the common dialog API should set the focus. A return code of FALSE indicates that the callback routine has already set the focus itself. (This is the reason the previous example program had to handle the WM_INITDIALOG message. If we did not handle the message explicitly, the callback routine would return FALSE and the focus would not have been set!)

COMMON DIALOG MESSAGE HOOKING EXAMPLE PROGRAM

The following modification of our example program demonstrates the use of WM_INITDIALOG, and improves (at least in my opinion) on the behavior of the "Open file" common dialog box by setting the initial value of the "File Name" edit control to null. This replaces the "normal" behavior of setting this value to the pattern of the filter (i.e., "*.exe;*.com;*.pif;*.bat"). Setting the initial value of the edit control is done with a SetWindowText call, when the callback routine is called with the WM_INITDIALOG message. The handle to the edit control's window is retrieved by a GetDlgItem call with `edt1` (defined in DLG.H) as the element's ID.

MAKEFILE

```
all: run.exe

run.res: run.rc run.h makefile
   rc -r run.rc

run.obj: run.c run.h makefile
   cl -c -DSTRICT -AS -GA2 -Ox -W3 run.c

run.exe: run.obj run.def run.res makefile
   link run,,,libw commdlg slibcew, run.def
   rc run.res
```

RUN.C

```c
// run a program - an example of using un-common dialogs
//
// from Modifying Windows by Asael Dror
//

#include <windows.h>
#include <commdlg.h>
#include <dlgs.h>

#include "run.h"

HINSTANCE hInst;                                    // current instance

                                                    // application E.P.
int PASCAL WinMain(HINSTANCE hInstance, HINSTANCE hPrevInstance,
             LPSTR LPCmdLine, int nCmdShow)

  {
  MSG msg;
  if (hPrevInstance)                    // one inst only!
     return(FALSE);

  if (!InitApplication(hInstance))      // init app
     return(FALSE);

  if (!InitInstance(hInstance, nCmdShow))        // init instance
     return(FALSE);
```

CHAPTER 1
UN-COMMON DIALOGS

```c
                                            // msg loop
   while (GetMessage(&msg, NULL, 0, 0))     // get any msg/any wnd
      {
      TranslateMessage(&msg);               // translate virt keys
      DispatchMessage(&msg);                // dispatch message
      }
   return(msg.wParam);
   }

BOOL InitApplication(HINSTANCE hInstance)   // init app
   {
                                            // reg main wnd class
   WNDCLASS wc;

                                            // fill wnd class str
   wc.style = 0;
   wc.lpfnWndProc = MainWndProc;            // window proc
   wc.cbClsExtra = 0;
   wc.cbWndExtra = 0;
   wc.hInstance = hInstance;                // class owner
   wc.hIcon = LoadIcon(NULL, IDI_APPLICATION); // def app icon
   wc.hCursor = LoadCursor(NULL, IDC_ARROW);   // standard cursor
   wc.hbrBackground = (HBRUSH)(COLOR_WINDOW + 1); // wnd bckgnd clr
   wc.lpszMenuName = "MainMenu";
   wc.lpszClassName = "RunClass";           // window class name

   return(RegisterClass(&wc));              // register wnd class
   }


                                            // instance init
BOOL InitInstance(HINSTANCE hInstance, int nCmdShow)
   {
   HWND  hWnd;                              // window handle

   hInst = hInstance;                       // save in static var

   hWnd = CreateWindow (                    // main window
         "RunClass",                        // class name
         "RUN",                             // title bar text
         WS_OVERLAPPEDWINDOW | WS_VISIBLE,  // normal & visible
         CW_USEDEFAULT,                     // default x
         nCmdShow,                          // default y,
                                            // show as requested
         CW_USEDEFAULT,                     // default width
         CW_USEDEFAULT,                     // default height
         HWND_DESKTOP,                      // no parent
```

MODIFYING WINDOWS

```
                   NULL,                        // use class menu
                   hInstance,                   // inst of mod for win
                   NULL);                       // not used
    if (!hWnd) return(FALSE);
    UpdateWindow(hWnd);                         // send WM_PAINT msg
    return (TRUE);                              // OK
    }


LRESULT __export CALLBACK MainWndProc(
                             HWND hWnd,         // window handle
                             UINT message,      // message
                             WPARAM wParam,     // param
                             LPARAM lParam)     // param

{
OPENFILENAME ofn;
char FileName[256] = "";

switch (message)
   {
   case WM_DESTROY:
      PostQuitMessage(0);                       // bye bye, rc = 0
      break;


   case WM_COMMAND:
      switch (wParam)
         {
         case IDM_RUNPGM:
            ofn.lStructSize = sizeof(ofn);
            ofn.hwndOwner = hWnd;
            ofn.lpstrFilter =
            "Programs\0*.exe;*.com;*.pif;*.bat\0All files\0*.*\0";
            ofn.lpstrCustomFilter = NULL;
            ofn.nFilterIndex = 0;
            ofn.lpstrFile = FileName;
            ofn.nMaxFile = sizeof(FileName);
            ofn.lpstrFileTitle = NULL;
            ofn.lpstrInitialDir = NULL;
            ofn.lpstrTitle = "RUN";
            ofn.Flags = OFN_FILEMUSTEXIST | OFN_HIDEREADONLY |
                        OFN_NOCHANGEDIR | OFN_SHOWHELP |
                        OFN_ENABLEHOOK;
            ofn.lpstrDefExt = NULL;
            ofn.lpfnHook = GetOpenFileNameHook;

            if (GetOpenFileName(&ofn))
               WinExec(FileName, SW_SHOWNORMAL);
```

CHAPTER 1
UN-COMMON DIALOGS

```c
            break;

        default:                        // default proc and ret
            return (DefWindowProc(hWnd, message,
                                  wParam, lParam));
        }
    break;


    default:                            // default proc and ret
        return (DefWindowProc(hWnd, message,
                              wParam, lParam));
    }
  return(0);
}


            // common dialog message hook callback routine
UINT CALLBACK __export GetOpenFileNameHook(
                HWND hDlg,
                UINT message,
                WPARAM wParam,
                LPARAM lParam)

{
HWND hWndFileNameEditCtl;

switch (message)
    {
    case WM_INITDIALOG:
        hWndFileNameEditCtl = GetDlgItem(hDlg, edt1);
        SetWindowText(hWndFileNameEditCtl,"");
        return TRUE;

    case WM_COMMAND:
        switch (wParam)
            {
            case pshHelp:
                MessageBox(hDlg,
                        "Help is never there when you need it!",
                        "Help", MB_ICONINFORMATION | MB_OK);

                return TRUE;

            default:
                break;
```

MODIFYING WINDOWS

```
                }
            break;

        default:

            return FALSE;
        }
    return FALSE;
}
```

RUN.RC

```
#include <windows.h>
#include "run.h"

MainMenu    MENU    PRELOAD
            {
            MENUITEM    "&Run", IDM_RUNPGM
            }
```

RUN.DEF

```
NAME            RUN

DESCRIPTION     'Run a program'

EXETYPE         WINDOWS

STUB            'WINSTUB.EXE'

CODE PRELOAD MOVEABLE DISCARDABLE
DATA PRELOAD MOVEABLE MULTIPLE

HEAPSIZE        1024
STACKSIZE       8192
```

Figure 1-3 shows the output of our modified example.

Modifying the Dialog's Resource Template

Our example program still does not have a way to query the user for parameters for the program to be executed, nor a way to specify that the program should

CHAPTER 1
UN-COMMON DIALOGS

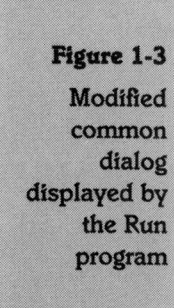

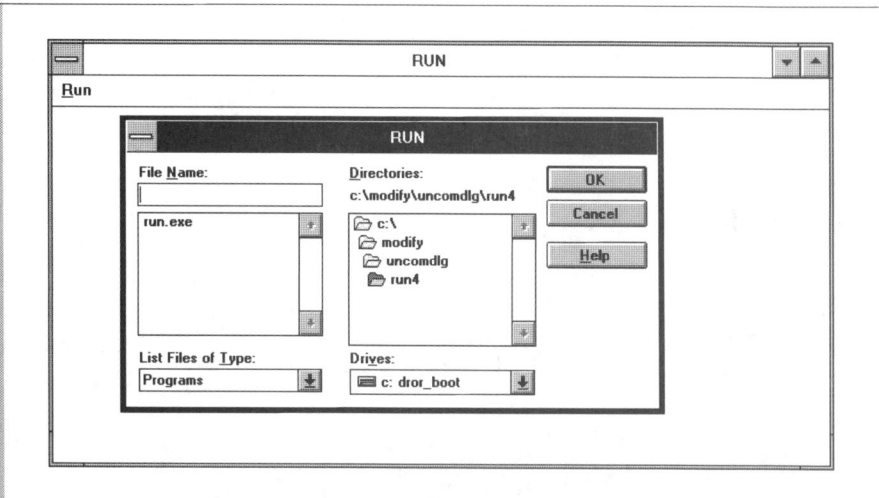

Figure 1-3
Modified common dialog displayed by the Run program

be run minimized. To add these niceties, we need to add a "Parameters" edit control and a "Run Minimized" check box to the dialog box. Although we could add those controls in the callback routine when processing the WM_INITDIALOG message, it would be much easier if we could somehow just modify the dialog's template in the resource files. We can! A special flag instructs the common dialog APIs to use an external template rather than the template included in the DLL. As mentioned earlier, the SDK contains the source code for the common dialogs' templates, so we actually have an excellent starting point for creating our own templates.

To instruct the API to use an external template, set the ENABLETEMPLATE flag (OFN_ENABLETEMPLATE in the case of the "Open file" common dialog) in the structure passed to the API. Furthermore, we need to specify the ID of the dialog box template in the `lpTemplateName` parameter and set `hInstance` to the data instance that contains the template. (If the dialog template is already in memory, we can pass its handle via `hInstance`, make `lpTemplateName = NULL`, and use the ENABLETEMPLATEHANDLE flag instead of ENABLETEMPLATE.)

COMMON DIALOG TEMPLATE MODIFICATION EXAMPLE PROGRAM

The following program is the final version of our Run example. It contains a "Parameters" edit control as well as a "Run Minimized" check box. Furthermore, the entire dialog had to be sized to accomodate the added controls. The

MODIFYING WINDOWS

new controls handle all interaction with the user by themselves. The callback routine only needs to retrieve the information from the new controls when the dialog is about to be destroyed. This is done when the common dialog hook is called with the WM_DESTROY message.

MAKEFILE

```
all: run.exe

run.res: run.rc run.dlg run.h makefile
    rc -r run.rc

run.obj: run.c run.h makefile
    cl -c -DSTRICT -AS -GA2 -Ox -W3 run.c

run.exe: run.obj run.def run.res makefile
    link run,,,libw commdlg slibcew, run.def
    rc run.res
```

RUN.C

```
// run a program - an example of using un-common dialogs
//
// from Modifying Windows by Asael Dror
//

#include <windows.h>
#include <commdlg.h>
#include <dlgs.h>

#include "run.h"

HINSTANCE hInst;                                    // current instance

UINT fuCmdShow;
char szParam[256];

                                                    // application E.P.
int PASCAL WinMain(HINSTANCE hInstance, HINSTANCE hPrevInstance,
            LPSTR LPCmdLine, int nCmdShow)

    {
```

```
   MSG msg;
   if (hPrevInstance)                      // one inst only!
      return(FALSE);

   if (!InitApplication(hInstance))        // init app
      return(FALSE);

   if (!InitInstance(hInstance, nCmdShow)) // init instance
      return(FALSE);

                                           // msg loop
   while (GetMessage(&msg, NULL, 0, 0))    // get any msg/any wnd
      {
      TranslateMessage(&msg);              // translate virt keys
      DispatchMessage(&msg);               // dispatch message
      }
   return(msg.wParam);
   }

BOOL InitApplication(HINSTANCE hInstance)  // init app
   {
                                           // reg main wnd class
   WNDCLASS wc;

                                           // fill wnd class str
   wc.style = 0;
   wc.lpfnWndProc = MainWndProc;           // window proc
   wc.cbClsExtra = 0;
   wc.cbWndExtra = 0;
   wc.hInstance = hInstance;               // class owner
   wc.hIcon = LoadIcon(NULL, IDI_APPLICATION);  // def app icon
   wc.hCursor = LoadCursor(NULL, IDC_ARROW);    // standard cursor
   wc.hbrBackground = (HBRUSH)(COLOR_WINDOW + 1); // wnd bckgnd clr
   wc.lpszMenuName = "MainMenu";
   wc.lpszClassName = "RunClass";          // window class name

   return(RegisterClass(&wc));             // register wnd class
   }

                                           // instance init
BOOL InitInstance(HINSTANCE hInstance, int nCmdShow)
   {
   HWND  hWnd;                             // window handle

   hInst = hInstance;                      // save in static var

   hWnd = CreateWindow (                   // main window
            "RunClass",                    // class name
```

```
                    "RUN",                          // title bar text
                    WS_OVERLAPPEDWINDOW | WS_VISIBLE, // normal & visible
                    CW_USEDEFAULT,                  // default x
                    nCmdShow,                       // default y,
                                                    // show as requested
                    CW_USEDEFAULT,                  // default width
                    CW_USEDEFAULT,                  // default height
                    HWND_DESKTOP,                   // no parent
                    NULL,                           // use class menu
                    hInstance,                      // inst of mod for win
                    NULL);                          // not used
    if (!hWnd) return(FALSE);
    UpdateWindow(hWnd);                             // send WM_PAINT msg
    return (TRUE);                                  // OK
    }


LRESULT __export CALLBACK MainWndProc(
                            HWND hWnd,              // window handle
                            UINT message,           // message
                            WPARAM wParam,          // param
                            LPARAM lParam)          // param

    {
    OPENFILENAME ofn;
    char FileName[256] = "";
    DWORD dwErrorCode;

    switch (message)
       {
       case WM_DESTROY:
          PostQuitMessage(0);                       // bye bye, rc = 0
          break;

       case WM_COMMAND:
          switch (wParam)
             {
             case IDM_RUNPGM:
                ofn.lStructSize = sizeof(ofn);
                ofn.hwndOwner = hWnd;
                ofn.lpstrFilter =
                "Programs\0*.exe;*.com;*.pif;*.bat\0All files\0*.*\0";
                ofn.lpstrCustomFilter = NULL;
                ofn.nFilterIndex = 0;
                ofn.lpstrFile = FileName;
                ofn.nMaxFile = sizeof(FileName);
                ofn.lpstrFileTitle = NULL;
                ofn.lpstrInitialDir = NULL;
                ofn.lpstrTitle = "RUN";
```

CHAPTER 1
UN-COMMON DIALOGS

```c
                ofn.Flags = OFN_FILEMUSTEXIST | OFN_HIDEREADONLY |
                           OFN_NOCHANGEDIR | OFN_SHOWHELP |
                           OFN_ENABLEHOOK | OFN_ENABLETEMPLATE;
                ofn.lpstrDefExt = NULL;
                ofn.lpfnHook = GetOpenFileNameHook;
                ofn.lpTemplateName = MAKEINTRESOURCE(FILEOPENORD);
                ofn.hInstance = hInst;

                if (GetOpenFileName(&ofn))
                   WinExec(_fstrcat(_fstrcat(FileName, " "),szParam),
                           fuCmdShow);
                else
                                            // intentionally left in
                                            // for debugging
                   dwErrorCode = CommDlgExtendedError();
                break;

             default:                       // default proc and ret
                return (DefWindowProc(hWnd, message,
                                      wParam, lParam));
            }
         break;

         default:                           // default proc and ret
            return (DefWindowProc(hWnd, message,
                                  wParam, lParam));
      }
   return(0);
   }


                // common dialog message hook callback routine

UINT CALLBACK __export GetOpenFileNameHook(
                       HWND hDlg,
                       UINT message,
                       WPARAM wParam,
                       LPARAM lParam)


   {
   HWND hWndFileNameEditCtl;

   switch (message)
      {
      case WM_INITDIALOG:
         hWndFileNameEditCtl = GetDlgItem(hDlg, edt1);
         SetWindowText(hWndFileNameEditCtl,"");
         return TRUE;
```

MODIFYING WINDOWS

```
        case WM_COMMAND:
            switch (wParam)
                {
                case pshHelp:
                    MessageBox(hDlg,
                               "Help is never there when you need it!",
                               "Help", MB_ICONINFORMATION | MB_OK);

                    return TRUE;

                default:
                    break;
                }
        break;

        case WM_DESTROY:
                                                // get Run Minimized state
            if (IsDlgButtonChecked(hDlg, IDCB_RunMin))
                fuCmdShow = SW_SHOWMINIMIZED;
            else
                fuCmdShow = SW_SHOWNORMAL;

                                                // get Parameters
            GetDlgItemText(hDlg, IDE_Param, szParam, sizeof(szParam));
        break;

        default:
            return FALSE;
        }
    return FALSE;
}
```

RUN.H

```
LRESULT __export CALLBACK MainWndProc(HWND, UINT, WPARAM, LPARAM);
BOOL InitApplication(HINSTANCE);
BOOL InitInstance(HINSTANCE, int);
UINT CALLBACK __export GetOpenFileNameHook(HWND, UINT,
                                            WPARAM, LPARAM);


#define IDM_RUNPGM 100
#define IDCB_RunMin 200
#define IDT_Param 300
#define IDE_Param 400
```

RUN.RC

```
#include <windows.h>
#include <dlgs.h>

#include "run.h"

rcinclude run.dlg

MainMenu    MENU    PRELOAD
            {
                MENUITEM    "&Run", IDM_RUNPGM
            }
```

RUN.DLG

```
FILEOPENORD DIALOG LOADONCALL MOVEABLE DISCARDABLE 30, 24,  280, 134
CAPTION "Open"
STYLE WS_CAPTION | WS_SYSMENU | WS_POPUP | DS_MODALFRAME
FONT 8, "Helv"
   {
   LTEXT "File &Name:", stc3,   6,   6,  76,  9
   CONTROL "", edt1, "edit", ES_LEFT | ES_AUTOHSCROLL | WS_BORDER |
           WS_TABSTOP | WS_CHILD | ES_OEMCONVERT, 6, 16, 90, 12
   CONTROL "", lst1, "listbox", LBS_SORT | LBS_HASSTRINGS |
           LBS_NOTIFY | LBS_DISABLENOSCROLL | WS_VSCROLL | WS_CHILD |
           WS_BORDER | WS_TABSTOP | LBS_OWNERDRAWFIXED, 6, 32, 90, 68

   LTEXT "&Directories:", -1, 110, 6, 92, 9
   LTEXT "", stc1, 110, 18, 92, 9, SS_NOPREFIX
   CONTROL "", lst2, "listbox", LBS_SORT | LBS_HASSTRINGS |

 LBS_NOTIFY | LBS_DISABLENOSCROLL | WS_VSCROLL | WS_CHILD |
           WS_BORDER | WS_TABSTOP | LBS_OWNERDRAWFIXED,
           110, 32, 92, 68

   LTEXT "List Files of &Type:", stc2, 6, 104, 90, 9
   CONTROL "", cmb1, "combobox", CBS_DROPDOWNLIST | CBS_AUTOHSCROLL |
           WS_BORDER | WS_VSCROLL | WS_TABSTOP | WS_CHILD,
```

```
                    6,  114,  90,  36

  LTEXT "Dri&ves:", stc4, 110, 104, 92, 9
    CONTROL "", cmb2, "combobox", CBS_SORT | CBS_HASSTRINGS |
          CBS_OWNERDRAWFIXED | CBS_DROPDOWNLIST | WS_CHILD |
          CBS_AUTOHSCROLL | WS_BORDER | WS_VSCROLL | WS_TABSTOP,
          110, 114, 92, 68

    DEFPUSHBUTTON "OK", IDOK, 208, 6, 50, 14, WS_GROUP
    PUSHBUTTON "Cancel", IDCANCEL, 208, 24, 50, 14, WS_GROUP
    PUSHBUTTON "&Help", pshHelp, 208, 46, 50, 14, WS_GROUP

    CHECKBOX "&Read Only", chx1, 0, 0, 0, 0,
            BS_AUTOCHECKBOX | WS_TABSTOP | WS_GROUP

     LTEXT "&Parameters:", IDT_Param, 208, 68, 84, 9
     CONTROL "", IDE_Param, "edit", ES_LEFT | ES_AUTOHSCROLL |
          WS_BORDER | WS_TABSTOP | WS_CHILD | ES_OEMCONVERT,
          208, 78, 64, 12

     CHECKBOX "Run &Minimized", IDCB_RunMin, 208, 98, 60, 12,
            BS_AUTOCHECKBOX | WS_TABSTOP | WS_GROUP
  }
```

RUN.DEF

```
NAME            RUN

DESCRIPTION     'Run a program'

EXETYPE         WINDOWS

STUB            'WINSTUB.EXE'

CODE PRELOAD MOVEABLE DISCARDABLE
DATA PRELOAD MOVEABLE MULTIPLE

HEAPSIZE        1024
STACKSIZE       8192
```

Figure 1-4 shows the output of our final Run program.

Figure 1-4
Final version of Run program

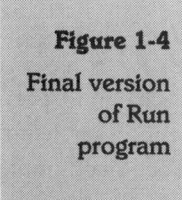

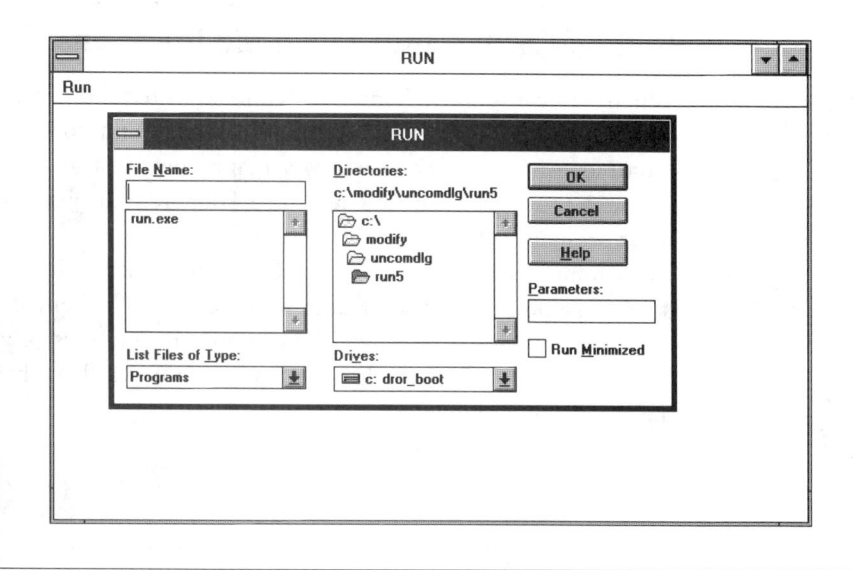

Modifying the Common Dialogs: What and Where

Although we have the source code for the dialog template, we don't have the source code for the common dialog APIs. Thus, we need to be careful that our changes to the template don't break the APIs. This means that we should make our changes in the most unobtrusive fashion possible. We can add new controls to the dialogs and initialize them as needed at WM_INITDIALOG time. We can also move and resize existing controls. However, we should not delete any of the existing controls or change their IDs, or the APIs may fail. If we want to delete an existing control, we should instead disable and hide it.

When we add controls in the template, we almost always need to add a callback routine to interact with those controls. Although many of the operations that can be done in the resource template can also be done via the callback hook (such as changing a control's size and location), the template is usually the easier approach. For modifications that must be determined at run time, such as removing (i.e., disabling and hiding) controls depending on the running environment, we need to use the callback routine approach.

Getting Carried Away with Modifications

Whenever we modify Windows, we need to remind ourselves not to go too far. When the object that we modify is huge and complex, changing even hundreds of lines of code is not a major modification. On the other hand, although the common dialogs are "nice," they're really just a collection of simple short programs. If we modify them too much, we can easily lose sight of why we chose to use them in the first place, rather than write our own. From the user's viewpoint, overmodification will lose the CUI effect that the common dialogs are supposed to achieve. From our viewpoint as developers, when we overmodify we can reach the point where it would have been easier to write the thing from scratch.

Chapter 2

Dynamic Link Libraries

IN the old DOS days, the routines a program called to perform various operations were all located in the same EXE file as the program. Under Windows, a program often calls routines that are not part of the program's EXE file, but rather reside in external libraries known as *Dynamic Link Libraries* (DLLs). Furthermore, some of a program's routines are not called directly by the program itself, but rather by Windows. Such routines are known as *callback* routines. This chapter focuses on DLLs, but we'll also touch on callback routines. And yes, a callback routine may sometimes reside in a DLL.

While DLLs and callback routines are used by all Windows programs, they are especially important in the context of modifying Windows. When we modify Windows we often append our code to the code we are modifying. The appended code is called as a callback routine by programs that are trying to call the original (now modified) code. Furthermore, since the modification code is not a standalone application, but rather an extension of another application (or of Windows itself), it most often belongs in a DLL rather than an EXE.

Three Ways to Link Your Modules

Dynamic link libraries have gotten a bad reputation as hard to use and difficult to understand. This is true only when you try to memorize a random collection of rules about their use. In this book we will look at how DLLs really work. Once you understand this, the details of how to use them will fall easily into place.

A prerequisite to understanding DLLs is understanding how different routines can be linked together. Under Windows there are three ways routines can be linked:

1. Statically at link time
2. Dynamically at load time
3. Dynamically at run time

Let's examine each type of linking.

Static Linking

In the early days of computer programming, a program consisted of one source file that contained one program. As the program became larger it became harder to develop and maintain as one entity, and so was split into multiple routines. The different routines were called by the main program as required. As more programs were developed, it became clear that some of those routines would be useful in many different programs. For example, a routine that displayed text on the screen would be useful in almost any program. Rather than include the source code of all those "useful routines" with every program and recompile the entire "library", each of the routines was compiled separately to form an OBJ file. A linker was added to the development process to combine those OBJs with your compiled program to create the final EXE. As the number of required OBJs grew, the concept of grouping those OBJs into an *object library* (LIB) was created. The linker could pull the required OBJs from the LIB, as well as combine individual OBJs to form the final EXE.

Using static linking, when a program calls an external procedure (or for that matter accesses any external data), the compiler does not know the address of that external routine (or data), and so indicates in the created OBJ file that the called address needs to be *fixed up* by the linker. The linker appends the required OBJ files together and fixes up the references to contain the routine's address. Thus, we now have one EXE file containing all the required routines ready to execute. This is summarized in Figure 2-1.

STATIC LINKING EXAMPLE PROGRAM

The following program uses static linking to call routines for displaying information via a message box. One routine displays its own message, while the other routine receives the message to be displayed via a parameter. (For now,

Figure 2-1
Static linking

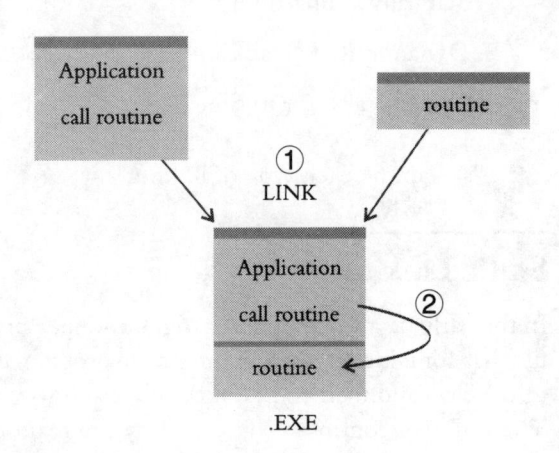

① The Linker combines the routine with the application to form the .EXE file.
② Application calls routine in the same module.

let's ignore the fact that the example also uses dynamic linking to communicate with the Windows' API—we'll discuss dynamic linking next). The program's output is shown in Figure 2-2.

```
MAKEFILE

all: main.exe

main.res: main.rc main.h makefile
    rc -r main.rc

main.obj: main.c main.h makefile
    cl -c -DSTRICT -AS -GA2 -Ox -W3 main.c

msgrtn.obj: msgrtn.c msgrtn.h makefile
    cl -c -DSTRICT -AS -GA2 -Ox -W3 msgrtn.c

main.exe: main.obj msgrtn.obj main.def main.res makefile
    link main msgrtn,,,libw slibcew, main.def
    rc main.res
```

MAIN.C

```c
// an example of different linking techniques
//
// from Modifying Windows by Asael Dror
//

#include <windows.h>
#include <commdlg.h>

#include "main.h"
#include "msgrtn.h"


HINSTANCE hInst;                                    // current instance

                                                    // application E.P.
int PASCAL WinMain(HINSTANCE hInstance, HINSTANCE hPrevInstance,
            LPSTR LPCmdLine, int nCmdShow)

  {
  MSG msg;

  if (!hPrevInstance)                               // if first instance
     if (!InitApplication(hInstance))               // init app
        return(FALSE);

  if (!InitInstance(hInstance, nCmdShow))           // init instance
     return(FALSE);

                                                    // msg loop
  while (GetMessage(&msg, NULL, 0, 0))              // get any msg/any wnd
     {
     TranslateMessage(&msg);                        // translate virt keys
     DispatchMessage(&msg);                         // dispatch message
     }
  return(msg.wParam);
  }

BOOL InitApplication(HINSTANCE hInstance)           // init app
  {
                                                    // reg main wnd class
  WNDCLASS wc;

                                                    // fill wnd class str
  wc.style = 0;
  wc.lpfnWndProc = MainWndProc;                     // window proc
```

MODIFYING WINDOWS

```c
   wc.cbClsExtra = 0;
   wc.cbWndExtra = 0;
   wc.hInstance = hInstance;             // class owner
   wc.hIcon = LoadIcon(NULL, IDI_APPLICATION); // def app icon
   wc.hCursor = LoadCursor(NULL, IDC_ARROW);   // standard cursor
   wc.hbrBackground = (HBRUSH)(COLOR_WINDOW + 1); // wnd bckgnd clr
   wc.lpszMenuName = "MainMenu";
   wc.lpszClassName = "MyClass";         // window class name

   return(RegisterClass(&wc));           // register wnd class
   }

                                         // instance init
BOOL InitInstance(HINSTANCE hInstance, int nCmdShow)
   {
   HWND  hWnd;                           // window handle

   hInst = hInstance;                    // save in static var

   hWnd = CreateWindow (                 // main window
           "MyClass",                    // class name
           "Linking Techniques",         // title bar text
           WS_OVERLAPPEDWINDOW | WS_VISIBLE, // normal & visible
           CW_USEDEFAULT,                // default x
           nCmdShow,                     // default y,
                                         // show as requested
           CW_USEDEFAULT,                // default width
           CW_USEDEFAULT,                // default height
           HWND_DESKTOP,                 // no parent
           NULL,                         // use class menu
           hInstance,                    // inst of mod for win
           NULL);                        // not used
   if (!hWnd) return(FALSE);
   UpdateWindow(hWnd);                   // send WM_PAINT msg
   return (TRUE);                        // OK
   }


LRESULT __export CALLBACK MainWndProc(
                          HWND hWnd,     // window handle
                          UINT message,  // message
                          WPARAM wParam, // param
                          LPARAM lParam) // param
   {

   char MainMsgText[] = "This is a message from the main routine";
```

```
   switch (message)
     {
     case WM_DESTROY:
        PostQuitMessage(0);                       // bye bye, rc = 0
        break;

     case WM_COMMAND:
        switch (wParam)
           {
           case IDM_RTNMSG:
              RTNMSG(hWnd);                       // call routine
              break;

           case IDM_MAINMSG:
              MainMSG(hWnd, MainMsgText);         // call routine
              break;

           default:                               // default proc & ret
              return (DefWindowProc(hWnd, message,
                                 wParam, lParam));
           }
     break;

     default:                                     // default proc & ret
        return (DefWindowProc(hWnd, message,
                           wParam, lParam));
     }
   return(0);
   }
```

MAIN.H

```
LRESULT __export CALLBACK MainWndProc(HWND, UINT, WPARAM, LPARAM);
BOOL InitApplication(HINSTANCE);
BOOL InitInstance(HINSTANCE, int);

#define IDM_RTNMSG 100
#define IDM_MAINMSG 200
```

MAIN.RC

```
#include <windows.h>
```

```
#include "main.h"

MainMenu    MENU    PRELOAD
                {
                MENUITEM    "&RTNMSG", IDM_RTNMSG
                MENUITEM    "&MainMSG", IDM_MAINMSG
                }
```

MAIN.DEF

```
NAME              MAIN

DESCRIPTION       'Static Linking Example'

EXETYPE           WINDOWS

STUB              'WINSTUB.EXE'

CODE PRELOAD MOVEABLE DISCARDABLE
DATA PRELOAD MOVEABLE MULTIPLE

HEAPSIZE          1024
STACKSIZE         8192
```

MSGRTN.C

```c
// example of different linking techniques
//
// from Modifying Windows by Asael Dror
//


#include <windows.h>
#include "msgrtn.h"

UINT WINAPI RTNMSG(HWND hWndParent)
{
   MessageBox(hWndParent, "This is a message from another routine",
      "Linking Techniques", MB_OK);

   return(0);
}
```

```
UINT WINAPI MainMSG(HWND hWndParent, PSTR MainMsgText)
{
   MessageBox(hWndParent, MainMsgText, "Linking Techniques", MB_OK);

   return(0);
}
```

MSGRTN.H

```
UINT WINAPI RTNMSG(HWND);
UINT WINAPI MainMSG(HWND, PSTR);
```

Dynamic Linking

In Windows (as well as in other operating systems), many of the routines used by the applications, including the functions Windows provides to the applications—the *Application Programming Interface* (APIs)—reside in a special type of library: a *Dynamic Link Library* (DLL). At link time, the linker does not actually include the code of these routines in the EXE, but instead includes a reference

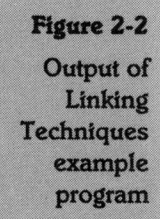

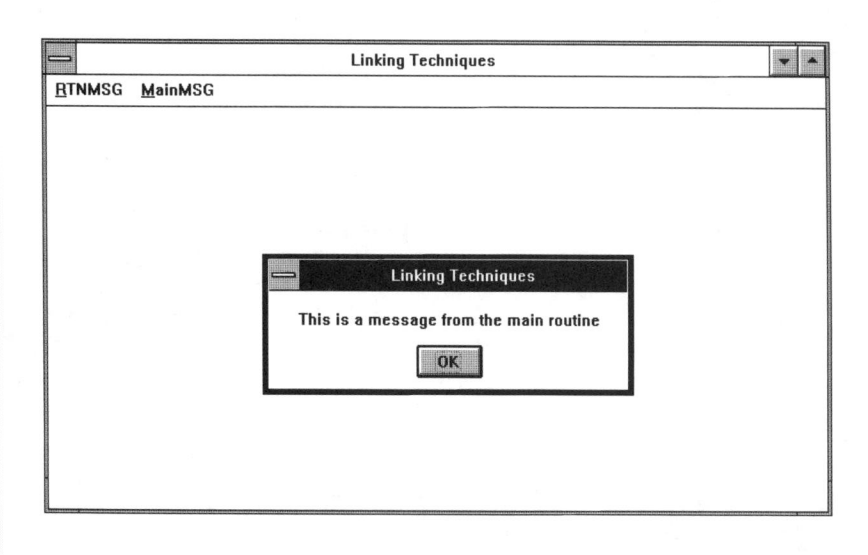

Figure 2-2
Output of Linking Techniques example program

to the routine. When the application is loaded, Windows loads the appropriate DLLs into memory and resolves (fixes up) the references to the actual addresses in memory of the routines in the DLL. This is called *implicit dynamic linking*, or *dynamic load-time linking*, and is shown in Figure 2-3.

THE EXPORT AND IMPORT BUSINESS

How does the linker know if an external routine (or external value) will be made available at run time via dynamic linking? How can it be sure that the routine was not mistakenly excluded from the linking process and an "unresolved external reference" error should be generated? Also, at run time how does the Windows loader know where to find the routine's code in the DLL? The answer to those questions is via the DEF file.

Exports For a DLL, the DEF file contains a list of all exported entry points (and variables) in the module. The description of exported entry points is performed by the EXPORTS statement, which specifies the name by which the routine

Figure 2-3
Dynamic load-time (implicit) linking

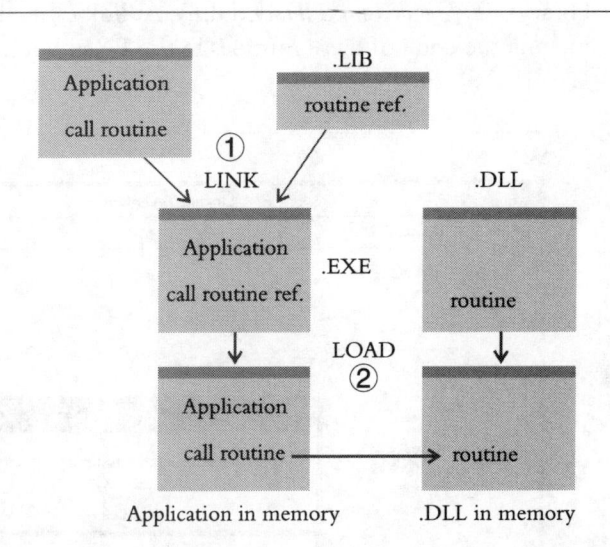

① The Linker combines a reference to the routine into the application's .EXE header.
② The Windows Loader sees that the application uses the DLL, and so loads the DLL into memory and fixes up the application to call the routine in memory.

will be known to the outside world (and, optionally, a different internal name). In addition, the EXPORTS statement may specify an ordinal number for the routine, allowing the routine to be imported by this ordinal number rather than the name. The linker uses the EXPORTS statements to create a number of tables in the DLL's header. One table specifies the location of all external entries in the DLL by ordinal number and is known as the *entry table*. Two additional tables are used for external names. One of those tables is called the *resident name table* and the other is called the *non-resident name table*. We will discuss the differences between the two later in this chapter.

Additional options of the EXPORTS statements include

- ◆ NODATA   Specifies that the routine will not be associated with the DLL's data segments. We will discuss this in more detail later in this chapter.

- ◆ RESIDENTNAME   Specifies that the routine's name will be included in the resident entry table

- ◆ NONAME   An undocumented option that removes the routine's name from the entry table, thus allowing linking by ordinal number only

An EXPORTS statement may look as follows:

```
EXPORTS
    FnName              @2
    WorldNM = MyName    @3
    Fn2                 @4    NODATA
```

We can see a listing of the EXPORTS in a DLL's header with the EXEHDR utility. Here is a portion of the output we get by running EXEHDR on one of Windows' own DLLs—KRNL386.EXE.

```
Microsoft (R) EXE File Header Utility  Version 3.00
Copyright (C) Microsoft Corp 1985-1992.  All rights reserved.

Library:                KERNEL
Description:            Microsoft Windows Kernel Interface
Version 3.10
Data:                   SHARED
Initialization:         Global
Initial CS:IP:          seg    1 offset aa1b
Initial SS:SP:          seg    0 offset 0000
DGROUP:                 seg    4
```

MODIFYING WINDOWS

```
Heap allocation:         0200 bytes
Runs in protected mode only

no. type address  file  mem   flags
  1 CODE 00001620 0c571 0c571 PRELOAD
  2 CODE 0000dbc0 02ab8 02ab8 PRELOAD, (movable),(discardable)
  3 CODE 000106a0 00c52 00c54 PRELOAD, (movable),(discardable)
  4 DATA 00011310 013d2 013d2 SHARED, PRELOAD


Exports:
ord seg offset name
342   1 a820   __GP exported, shared data
173 254 f000   __ROMBIOS exported
 19   1 02cb   GLOBALUNLOCK exported
184   1 139a   GLOBALDOSALLOC exported
127   1 06d7   GETPRIVATEPROFILEINT exported, shared data
166   2 028f   WINEXEC exported
122   1 81ff   ISTASKLOCKED exported
 99   1 0bc5   GETLPERRMODE exported
 88   1 836f   LSTRCPY exported
 81   1 046e   _LCLOSE exported
335   1 4b83   ISBADWRITEPTR exported
171   1 00e4   ALLOCDSTOCSALIAS exported
170   1 00d0   ALLOCCSTODSALIAS exported
137   1 0211   FATALAPPEXIT exported
183 254 0000   __0000H exported
 18   1 0278   GLOBALLOCK exported
161   2 29c9   LOCALCOUNTFREE exported
193 254 0040   __0040H exported
 42   1 9c8f   DISABLEDOS exported
198   1 039f   GLOBALUNFIX exported
120   1 72d4   UNDEFDYNLINK exported
159   1 0ec5   GLOBALHANDLENORIP exported
 85   1 0443   _LOPEN exported
141   1 8014   INITTASK1 exported
164   1 0324   GLOBALLRUNEWEST exported
130   3 0888   FILECDR exported
 55   3 08ee   CATCH exported
 26   1 0e39   GLOBALFREEALL exported
128   1 0709   GETPRIVATEPROFILESTRING exported, shared data
339   1 a70e   DIAGQUERY exported
```

Finally, we should note that while our discussion is focused on exporting entry points, which are addresses in our code, the same mechanism can be used to export addresses in the DLL's data in order to create system-wide accessible global variables. The class subclassing example in Chapter 4 uses this technique.

Imports For a routine using a DLL, the DEF file contains IMPORTS statements specifying the name of the module containing the routines and the name or ordinal number of the routine's entry point. It may also specify an internal name by which the routine will be called by the program. An example of IMPORTS statements is

```
IMPORTS
   ModName.FuName
   ModName.4
   MyName2 = ModName.WorldNM
```

In addition to using IMPORTS statements in the DEF file, a program can use an *import library* (LIB) to specify the same information as the IMPORTS statements. This is useful when you need to import a long list of imported routines, such as the Windows API. An import library can be created with the IMPLIB utility using the DLL's DEF file as input. Alternately, the DLL itself can act as the input to IMPLIB, since the information from its DEF file was incorporated by the linker into the DLL's header. While an import library has the same suffix as an object library (LIB) and is used in a similar manner by the linker, there is a major difference between the two. An object library contains the actual code for the routines, while an import library contains only the information about where the routines can be found at run time.

IMPLICIT DYNAMIC LINKING EXAMPLE

The following program uses implicit dynamic linking to perform the same functions as the previous example did with static linking. The MAIN.C, MAIN.H, and MAIN.RC files are identical to the previous example and so are not listed.

MAKEFILE

```
all: main.exe msgrtn.dll

msgrtn.obj: msgrtn.c msgrtn.h makefile
    cl -c -DSTRICT -AS -GD2 -Ox -W3 msgrtn.c

msgrtn.dll: msgrtn.obj msgrtn.def makefile
    link msgrtn, msgrtn.dll,,libw sdllcew, msgrtn.def
    rc msgrtn.dll

main.res: main.rc main.h makefile
    rc -r main.rc

main.obj: main.c main.h msgrtn.h makefile
    cl -c -DSTRICT -AS -GA2 -Ox -W3 main.c

main.exe: main.obj main.def main.res makefile
    link main,,,libw slibcew, main.def
    rc main.res
```

MAIN.DEF

```
NAME            MAIN

DESCRIPTION     'Dynamic Linking Example'

EXETYPE         WINDOWS

STUB            'WINSTUB.EXE'

CODE PRELOAD MOVEABLE DISCARDABLE
DATA PRELOAD MOVEABLE MULTIPLE

HEAPSIZE        1024
STACKSIZE       8192

IMPORTS
                MSGRTN.RTNMSG
                MSGRTN.MainMSG
```

MSGRTN.C

```c
// example of different linking techniques
//
// from Modifying Windows by Asael Dror
//


#include <windows.h>
#include "msgrtn.h"

UINT __export WINAPI RTNMSG(HWND hWndParent)
{
   MessageBox(hWndParent, "This is a message from another routine",
      "Linking Techniques", MB_OK);

   return(0);
}

UINT __export WINAPI MainMSG(HWND hWndParent, LPSTR MainMsgText)
{
   MessageBox(hWndParent, MainMsgText, "Linking Techniques", MB_OK);

   return(0);
}
```

MSGRTN.H

```c
UINT __export WINAPI RTNMSG(HWND);
UINT __export WINAPI MainMSG(HWND, LPSTR);
```

MSGRTN.DEF

```
LIBRARY        MSGRTN

DESCRIPTION    'Display MessageBox DLL'

EXETYPE        WINDOWS

STUB           'WINSTUB.EXE'
```

```
CODE PRELOAD MOVEABLE DISCARDABLE
DATA PRELOAD MOVEABLE SINGLE

EXPORTS
          RTNMSG            @1
          MainMSG           @2
```

If you compare this example with the static linking example, you will notice that the differences between the two programs fall into two categories:

1. The DEF files have been changed to export and import the routine's entry points as explained in the previous discussion.

2. The DLL's routines are now __export; the parameter to the DLL is LPSTR rather than PSTR; and the DLL is compiled with the −GD switch instead of −GA and linked with SDLLCEW.LIB rather than SLIBCEW.LIB. Finally, notice that its data segment is defined SINGLE. We will discuss the reasons for these changes soon.

Explicit Dynamic Linking

Normally, when we call a DLL we are using implicit dynamic linking (also called dynamic load-time linking). Our application calls the routine, and Windows transparently loads the DLL and fixes up our code to access the routine in memory. However, there is another way to call DLL routines. As our program executes, we can explicitly load a DLL into memory under our program's control, get the addresses of routines within the DLL, and call those routines directly. This is called *explicit dynamic linking* or *dynamic run-time linking*.

The first stage in explicit dynamic linking is loading the DLL into memory. This is achieved by calling the LoadLibrary API. (LoadLibrary actually calls LoadModule to perform the loading, and if you wish you can call LoadModule directly instead of LoadLibrary.)

LoadLibrary

Load a dynamic link library

```
HINSTANCE LoadLibrary(lpszLibFileName);

LPCSTR lpszLibFileName;    // DLL's file name
```

Returns:
If the DLL was loaded successfully, this function returns the instance of the DLL (>32). If not, it returns an error code (<= 32).

To get the address of an exported routine in the (previously loaded) DLL, we use the GetProcAddress API.

GetProcAddress

Get the address of a DLL's routine in memory

```
FARPROC GetProcAddress(hInstance, lpszProcName)

HINSTANCE hInstance;       // hInstance of DLL
                           // or hModule of DLL (undocumented)
LPCSTR lpszProcName;       // Routine's name or ordinal
                           // ordinals can be specified as
                           // "#n" or as
                           // MAKEINTRESOURCE(n) where n is
                           // the ordinal number
```

Returns:
If successful, the API returns the FAR address of the routine in memory. If not, it returns NULL.

MODIFYING WINDOWS

Finally, when we have no further need for the DLL, we should free it with the FreeLibrary (or FreeModule) API.

FreeLibrary

Free a DLL from memory

```
VOID FreeLibrary (hInstance);

HINSTANCE hInstance;    // hInstance of DLL
```

Returns:
VOID.

Explicit dynamic linking is summarized in Figure 2-4.

Figure 2-4 Dynamic run-time (explicit) linking

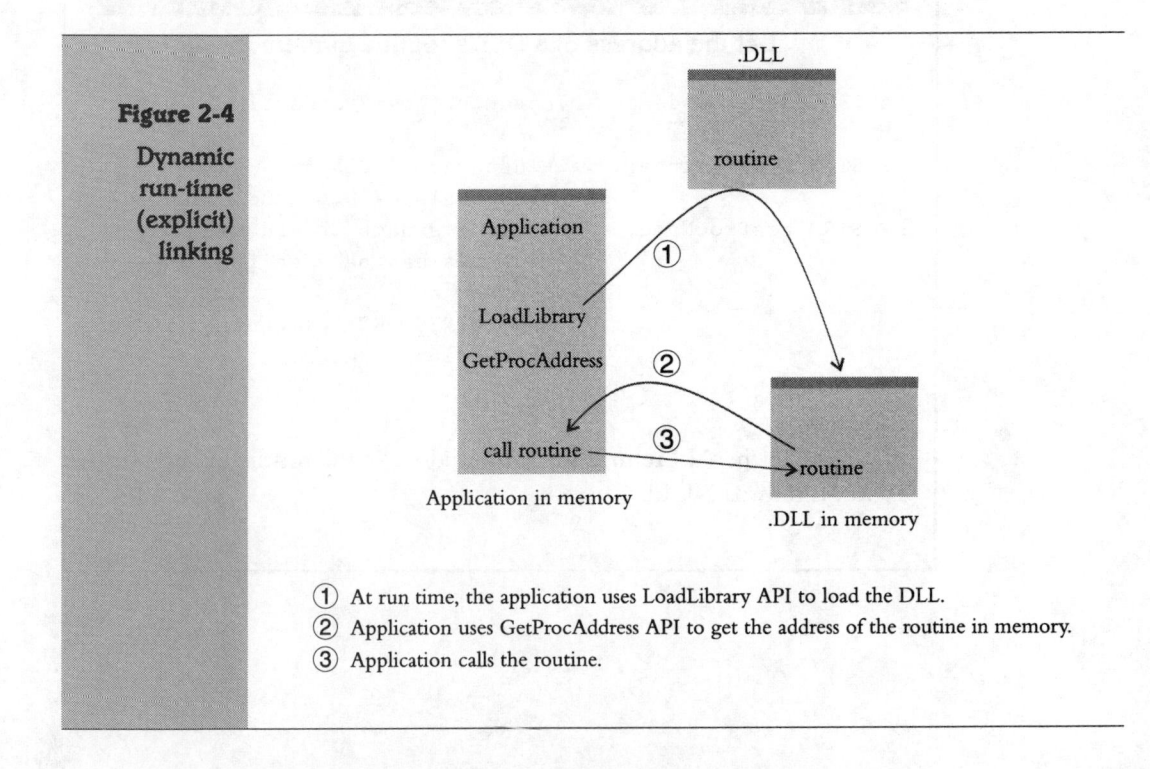

① At run time, the application uses LoadLibrary API to load the DLL.
② Application uses GetProcAddress API to get the address of the routine in memory.
③ Application calls the routine.

EXPLICIT DYNAMIC LOADING EXAMPLE PROGRAM

The following example is an explicit dynamic linking equivalent of the previous program; the only differences are in the MAIN.C, MAIN.H, and MAIN.DEF files.

MAIN.C

```c
// an example of different linking techniques
//
// from Modifying Windows by Asael Dror
//

#include <windows.h>
#include <commdlg.h>

#include "main.h"

HINSTANCE hInst;                            // current instance
HINSTANCE hDLLInst;                         // DLL's instance

LPRTNMSG lpRTNMSG;                          // address of RTNMSG routine
LPMAINMSG lpMainMSG;                        // address of MainMSG routine

                                            // application E.P.
int PASCAL WinMain(HINSTANCE hInstance, HINSTANCE hPrevInstance,
            LPSTR LPCmdLine, int nCmdShow)

   {
   MSG msg;

   if (!hPrevInstance)                      // if first instance
      if (!InitApplication(hInstance))      // init app
         return(FALSE);

   if (!InitInstance(hInstance, nCmdShow))  // init instance
      return(FALSE);

                                            // msg loop
   while (GetMessage(&msg, NULL, 0, 0))     // get any msg/any wnd
      {
      TranslateMessage(&msg);                // translate virt keys
      DispatchMessage(&msg);                 // dispatch message
      }
```

```
    return(msg.wParam);
    }

BOOL InitApplication(HINSTANCE hInstance)          // init app
    {
                                                   // reg main wnd class
    WNDCLASS wc;

                                                   // fill wnd class str
    wc.style = 0;
    wc.lpfnWndProc = MainWndProc;          // window proc
    wc.cbClsExtra = 0;
    wc.cbWndExtra = 0;
    wc.hInstance = hInstance;              // class owner
    wc.hIcon = LoadIcon(NULL, IDI_APPLICATION);  // def app icon
    wc.hCursor = LoadCursor(NULL, IDC_ARROW);    // standard cursor
    wc.hbrBackground = (HBRUSH)(COLOR_WINDOW + 1); // wnd bckgnd clr
    wc.lpszMenuName = "MainMenu";
    wc.lpszClassName = "MyClass";          // window class name

    return(RegisterClass(&wc));            // register wnd class
    }

                                           // instance init
BOOL InitInstance(HINSTANCE hInstance, int nCmdShow)
    {
    HWND  hWnd;                            // window handle

    hInst = hInstance;                     // save in static var

    hWnd = CreateWindow (                  // main window
            "MyClass",                     // class name
            "Linking Techniques",          // title bar text
            WS_OVERLAPPEDWINDOW | WS_VISIBLE,  // normal & visible
            CW_USEDEFAULT,                         // default x
            nCmdShow,                              // default y,
                                           // show as requested
            CW_USEDEFAULT,                 // default width
            CW_USEDEFAULT,                 // default height
            HWND_DESKTOP,                  // no parent
            NULL,                          // use class menu
            hInstance,                     // inst of mod for win
            NULL);                         // not used
    if (!hWnd) return(FALSE);
    UpdateWindow(hWnd);                    // send WM_PAINT msg
    return (TRUE);                         // OK
    }
```

CHAPTER 2
DYNAMIC LINK LIBRARIES

```c
LRESULT __export CALLBACK MainWndProc(
                        HWND hWnd,          // window handle
                        UINT message,       // message
                        WPARAM wParam,      // param
                        LPARAM lParam)      // param
{

   char MainMsgText[] = "This is a message from the main routine";

   switch (message)
      {
      case WM_CREATE:
                                    // load DLL
         hDLLInst = LoadLibrary("MSGRTN.DLL");

                                    // get address of RTNMSG routine
         lpRTNMSG = (LPRTNMSG) GetProcAddress(hDLLInst, "RTNMSG");

                                    // get address of MainMSG routine
         lpMainMSG = (LPMAINMSG) GetProcAddress(hDLLInst, "MainMSG");
         break;

      case WM_DESTROY:
                                    // free DLL
         FreeLibrary(hDLLInst);
         PostQuitMessage(0);                      // bye bye, rc = 0
         break;

      case WM_COMMAND:
         switch (wParam)
            {
            case IDM_RTNMSG:
               lpRTNMSG(hWnd);          // call RTNMSG routine
               break;

            case IDM_MAINMSG:
                                        // call MainMSG routine
               lpMainMSG(hWnd, MainMsgText);
               break;

            default:                    // default proc & ret
               return (DefWindowProc(hWnd, message,
                              wParam, lParam));
            }
         break;

      default:                          // default proc & ret
```

MODIFYING WINDOWS

```
            return (DefWindowProc(hWnd, message,
                            wParam, lParam));
    }
    return(0);
}
```

MAIN.H

```
LRESULT __export CALLBACK MainWndProc(HWND, UINT, WPARAM, LPARAM);
BOOL InitApplication(HINSTANCE);
BOOL InitInstance(HINSTANCE, int);

#define IDM_RTNMSG 100
#define IDM_MAINMSG 200

typedef UINT (__export WINAPI *LPRTNMSG) (HWND);
typedef UINT (__export WINAPI *LPMAINMSG) (HWND, LPSTR);
```

MAIN.DEF

```
NAME            MAIN

DESCRIPTION     'Dynamic Linking Example'

EXETYPE         WINDOWS

STUB            'WINSTUB.EXE'

CODE PRELOAD MOVEABLE DISCARDABLE
DATA PRELOAD MOVEABLE MULTIPLE

HEAPSIZE        1024
STACKSIZE       8192
```

Instances, Tasks, and Modules

In order to understand the interactions between DLLs and EXEs, we need understand the concepts of instances, tasks, and modules.

When we start a new Windows program, a new and unique *instance* of the program is created. The new instance is allocated its own automatic data segment, which is also known as the *instance data*. This data segment is used to store the instance's static variables, stack, and the local heap.

In addition to creating a new instance of the application, starting a new Windows program also creates a new *task*. A Windows 3.x task is an executable entity as well as the owner of resources. A task has its own image of the CPU registers (i.e., the values in the CPU hardware registers when the task is executed). The task can execute different pieces of code or different modules. Any resources acquired by the executing task, such as file handles and message queues, belong to the task, not the module in which the task was running when it acquired the resources.

A *module* is a piece of code (a code segment) either in an EXE or a DLL. (A module may also contain resources that are read-only data.) During its "life," a task may execute different modules. When a new program is started, Windows loads the program's code, a module; creates a new instance; and starts a new task in that module. Now let's imagine that a second copy of the same program is started. Windows creates an additional instance and a new task; however, there is no need to reload the program's code (the module) from disk, since it's already in memory, and code segments are read-only. Thus, both tasks can execute the same module. While multiple tasks can execute the same code (module), each task has its own data (instance). In the situation discussed above, we have two instances, two tasks, and one module, as is summarized below.

INSTANCE 1	INSTANCE 2
TASK A	TASK B
MODULE α	MODULE α

A DLL is not an executable entity, it's just code (and resources). This means that the DLL is a module but not a task. Tasks can execute it, but it does not have a life of its own.

A DLL has only one instance, hence only one instance data segment. (A DLL may also be created with no instance data at all!) No matter how may times a DLL is used, it will have only one instance. Thus, all tasks running in a DLL share the same data segment (or use their own).

When a task enters a DLL, it is running with its own stack and data (instance); i.e., (usually) DS == SS == task's instance data. If the DLL has no data segment (as defined in the DEF file), or if DATANONE is defined for some of its routines, a task executing such a routine will not have its DS changed, and so will execute using the data segment it used before entering the DLL.

For a task to be able to access the DLL's data segments (which contain static and global data, as well as the local heap), its DS register needs to be set to the DLL's data segment. The −GD switch tells the compiler to generate a prolog for each __export routine that loads DS with the segment selector of the DLL's data segment. This means that all tasks running in a DLL share the same data segment (the DLL's), and DS != SS (since SS = the task's instance data, where the task's stack is located).

By default, the __export keyword does not cause the compiler to emit EXPORTS instructions to the linker. Specifying the −GEe switch will cause the compiler to generate EXPORTS instructions for all __export routines. However, there are good reasons not to use the compiler's services and instead to manually put EXPORTS statements in the DEF file. For one thing, if you need to specify special attributes, such as RESIDENT or NODATA, you must use the manual EXPORTS statements. More important, if your routines are imported via ordinal numbers, you must use the DEF file's EXPORTS statements rather than letting the compiler do the work. This is essential, since you need to keep the ordinal values given to specific routines constant, and the compiler may change the value of the ordinals assigned to a routine each time you recompile.

Now we can understand why the __export keyword had to be added to the MSGRTN code when it was converted from static linking to dynamic linking. Since the dynamically linked MAIN and MSGRTN modules use different data segments (instances), we need to correctly set the DS on entry to MSGRTN so that we can access the DLL's data. This is also the reason for passing the parameter to the dynamic link routine (the message from MAIN) via a FAR pointer rather than a near one. The text of the message to be displayed is located in another segment (MAIN's data segment), so we need a FAR pointer to access it. (If we used a near pointer, the data would be accessed with the correct offset, but from the wrong segment!)

Finally, the C run-time library we use should not assume that DS == SS; that's why we need to link with SDLLCEW rather than SLIBCEW.

From our understanding of tasks, modules, and instances, we can conclude what happens to resources allocated in a DLL. Since resources belong to a task, any resources (such as global memory, file handles, or message queues) acquired in the DLL belong to the task that allocated them, not to the DLL. For example, if task

A opened a file via code in a DLL, task B *cannot* access that file using the same handle, even when task B is also running in the DLL. The file handle belongs to the task, not to the DLL. However, there are a few exceptions to this rule:

1. Local memory is allocated out of the local heap, which is part of the automatic (instance) data segment. Since all tasks that execute the DLL share the same instance (or data segment), they all share the same local memory.

2. Global memory allocated with the GMEM_SHARE (or the equivalent GMEM_DDESHARE) flag belongs to the module that allocated it, not the task. Thus, global memory allocated with the GMEM_SHARE flag inside a DLL belongs to the DLL.

GETTING A HANDLE

Before finishing our discussion of instances, tasks, and modules, let's review how we can acquire a handle to one of these entities. Such handles are required when calling APIs that manage instances, tasks, and modules, as well as their associated resources.

The `hInstance` is usually the easiest handle to obtain. It is passed as a parameter to each new program and to the DLL's initialization routine (discussed later).

Given a module name (the name specified in the DEF file's NAME or LIBRARY statement), GetModuleHandle returns the `hModule`. In addition (although this is undocumented), you can pass GetModuleHandle an `hInstance` [i.e., `MAKELP(0, hInstance)`] and get its associated `hModule`.

Since instances are associated with a module, some APIs that expect an `hInstance` will also take an `hModule` (such as GetProcAddress; see the preceding "GetProcAddress" box).

The `hTask` of the current task can be obtained with the GetCurrentTask API. This is useful for DLLs that need to keep task-specific data in the DLL's common data segment. (Note, however, that `hTasks` are reused by the system; consequently, your DLL may need to keep track of when a task for which it keeps data terminates. This can be done with Toolhelp, as we'll discuss in Chapter 7.)

The Mechanism of Dynamic Linking

Now that we have the necessary background knowledge, let's look at how dynamic linking actually works.

When a new module is loaded (either EXE or DLL), the Windows loader examines the module's header and loads any of the DLLs it is implicitly linked to. As each DLL is loaded, Windows loads any DLLs that it itself is implicitly linked to, and so on. The loading of the DLLs when a module is loaded is equivalent to performing LoadLibrary calls for the DLLs. However, in implicit linking, the order in which Windows will load the DLLs is undetermined.

When LoadLibrary is called (explicitly or implicitly) to load a DLL (or any module), Windows checks to see if the module is already in memory. If it's not already loaded, Windows loads the DLL (actually just the DLL's preload segments; other segments are loaded only when they are used), allocates its automatic data segment, sets the module use-count to one, and calls the DLL's initialization entry point. The *use-count* is used to keep track of how may users a module has. If LoadLibrary is called for a module that's already in memory, Windows *does not* reload the module, *nor* does it call its initialization entry point. Instead, the use-count for the module is incremented. You can retrieve the use-count of a particular module with the GetModuleUsage API.

GetModuleUsage
Get a module's use-count

```
INT GetModuleUsage(hInstance);

HINSTANCE hInstance;     // hModule

                         // or an hInstance of the module
```

Returns:
The module's current use-count.

Note that loading a module is performed by specifying the filename of the EXE or DLL to be loaded, while internally Windows keeps track of modules by their module name (as given in the NAME or LIBRARY statement of the DEF file) and module handle. Consequently, if the filename is different than the module name, Windows may get confused and reload a module that's already in memory. The solution is to keep the module name the same as the filename.

The next step in using a DLL is getting the addresses of the entry points (or variables) in the DLL. This may be performed when a module that uses the DLL is loaded (for implicit dynamic linking) or in response to a call to GetProcAddress. As we discussed earlier, the DLL's header contains three tables that are used to find the entry points in the DLL: the entry table, the resident name table, and the non-resident name table. The entry table and the resident name table are loaded and kept in memory as long as the DLL is loaded. When Windows needs to find the address of an entry point in the DLL via an ordinal number, it uses the entry table. When it needs to find an entry point via its name, the resident name table is used. Only if the entry is not found in the resident name table is the non-resident name table loaded and searched. Since entry name tables take up much more space and take more time to search than the entry table (which is organized by ordinal number), using ordinals is more efficient. Linking by name is usually performed only by explicitly linking applications, and (unless you have to link by name and performance is critical) you can usually keep the routine names in the non-resident name table. For implicitly linking applications, the linker will link by ordinal if the information is available either in the IMPORTS or EXPORTS statements.

Finally, when FreeLibrary is called (explicitly, or implicitly by the loading instance's termination), Windows decreases the DLL's (or module's) use-count. If decreasing the use-count causes the use-count to reach zero, then the DLL's termination routine (WEP) is called and the DLL is freed from memory.

Anatomy of a DLL

Now that we understand the mechanism, let's take a detailed look at the structure of a DLL.

A DLL may contain three types of externally accessible entry points:

1. Exported routines

2. An initialization routine

3. A termination routine

The exported routines are the services the DLL provides to the outside world and were the focus of discussion above. While the routines must be FAR, they do not have to follow the PASCAL calling convention. In addition, a DLL may contain routines that are called to perform any one-time initialization and any final termination of the DLL.

The Initialization Routine

When a DLL is loaded, Windows calls (via a far call) its initialization entry point. The address of the initialization entry point is specified by the assembler(!) END statement. Although it is named LibEntry by convention, any name can be used.

On entry to the initialization entry point, the following parameters are passed in registers:

DI = DLL's hInstance. (Remember that a DLL will have only one hInstance.)

DS = DLL's data segment selector (if any).

CX = Requested size (in bytes) of the initial local heap, as specified by the HEAPSIZE statement in the DEF file.

If the initialization succeeded, the routine returns TRUE in the AX register. Otherwise, it returns FALSE in AX. This will abort the DLL's loading (and for implicit linking, fail the application's loading).

What does a DLL's initialization routine do? This answer depends on your application. Any one-time initialization required when the DLL is loaded into memory can be performed in this routine, including the initialization of the local heap (if any). For example, in Chapter 5 we use the initialization routine to install hooks. In addition, the initialization routine is often used to initialize the value of static variables according to the run-time environment. Note, however, that for implicitly linked DLLs the initialization routine is called before the application has started to work, and so there is no message queue. Consequently, you should avoid APIs that require a message queue.

Where was the DLL's initialization routine (or the termination routine) in the previous example? Well...a default initialization routine was included by the C run-time library. This default initialization routine initializes the local heap as well as the C run-time library, and then calls our initialization routine (if any). If we want the C DLL's initialization routine to call our own initialization routine, we need to create a C language routine by the name of LibMain. Alternately, if we do not use the C run-time libraries (i.e., if we link with CNOCRTW.LIB), we can supply our own DLL initialization (and termination) routine. Since the DLL's entry point needs to be specified by an assembler END statement, and since parameters are passed to the initialization routine in registers, such a routine should be written in assembly language (we will see an example soon). Finally, note that though the documentation does not say so, at least in Windows 3.1 you can omit the initialization routine completely!

The Termination Routine

The termination routine, known as WEP (Windows Exit Procedure), is a FAR PASCAL routine called by Windows (by name, not ordinal number) just before the DLL is freed from memory, i.e., after a FreeLibrary (explicit or implicit) causes the DLL's use-count to reach zero. Just as it does with LibEntry, the C run-time library will supply a default WEP. We may want to use our own WEP to clean up after the DLL, performing such chores as unregistering hooks (see Chapter 5). If we want the C DLL's WEP routine to call our WEP routine, we need to create a C language routine by the name _WEP.

When the WEP is called, it receives as a parameter an INT nExitType (which can be either WEP_FREE_DLL or WEP_SYSTEM_EXIT). If the WEP is successful, it should return a return code of 1.

Under Windows 3.0, the WEP was intended only for device drivers, which used it to unhook interrupts and bring the hardware back to a known state. WEP's support in Windows 3.0 was extremely buggy and unstable. For example, Windows might call the WEP without calling the DLL's initialization routine, or the WEP might be called with no data segment allocated, or the WEP might have been called multiple times and many more nasties.

Fortunately, in Windows 3.1, support for hardware device drivers has been incorporated into installable device drivers (discussed in Chapter 6), and WEP support has gone through tremendous improvement. Consequently, Windows 3.1 applications can do almost anything in the WEP. Under Windows 3.1, WEP code may call other DLLs, including Windows APIs. All affected DLLs (i.e., all those whose use-count was decreased to zero) have their WEPs called before any of the DLLs are actually discarded. Furthermore, under Windows 3.1, the WEP need not be in a FIXED or PRELOAD segment, need not be RESIDENTNAME, and actually need not exist at all!

The WEP needs to terminate with a RETF 2 instruction, discarding the nExitType parameter passed to the WEP.

Finally, remember that for implicitly linked DLL's the WEP is called after the application has terminated, so there is no message queue.

DLL Initialization and Termination Example

The following assembly language example demonstrates a DLL's initialization and WEP routines. The initialization routine does nothing except initialize the local heap (if needed), while the WEP does nothing. We will use initialization routines and WEPs (both in assembler and C) throughout the book.

MAKEFILE

```
all: anatomy.dll

anatomy.obj: anatomy.asm makefile
    masm anatomy;

anatomy.dll: anatomy.obj anatomy.def makefile
    link /NOD anatomy, anatomy.dll, nul, libw, anatomy.def
    rc anatomy.dll
```

ANATOMY.ASM

```
;
; Dynamic Link Library - Initialization and WEP example
; from Modifying Windows by Asael Dror
;

        .286

_TEXT segment word public 'CODE'
    assume  cs:_TEXT,ds:nothing,es:nothing,ss:nothing

    extrn   LocalInit:FAR


LibEntry proc   FAR

; DLL Entry Point, called for Initialization when DLL is loaded
; On entry:
; DI = instance handle
; DS = DS (if any)
; CX = heap size (if any)
;
```

```
        or      cx, cx
        jnz     InitLocalHeap
        mov     ax, 1                   ; OK RC
        ret

InitLocalHeap:
        push    ds
        push    0
        push    cx
        call    LocalInit
        ret                             ; ret with RC from API

LibEntry endp

WEP     proc    far                     ; Window Exit Proc
        public  WEP
        mov     ax,1                    ; OK RC
        ret     2
WEP     endp

_TEXT   ends
        end     LibEntry                ; LibEntry is DLL's entry point
```

ANATOMY.DEF

```
LIBRARY            GENERIC
DESCRIPTION        'A Generic DLL'
EXETYPE            WINDOWS
STUB               'WINSTUB.EXE'

CODE PRELOAD MOVEABLE DISCARDABLE
DATA NONE

EXPORTS
        WEP        @1        RESIDENTNAME
```

The Advantages of DLLs and When to Use Them

Now that we know all about DLLs, let's review their advantages and when they should be used.

Keep in mind that Windows itself (except for the 386-Enhanced mode section) is basically a collection of DLLs. While many of Windows' modules, such as USER.EXE and VGA.DRV, do not have a DLL suffix, they are DLLs nevertheless. (Try running EXEHDR on them!)

Upgradablity Since a DLL's resources and code are not part of the application, replacing a DLL with a newer version will automatically upgrade all the programs that use the DLL. (Before replacing an existing DLL, make sure to use version checking to verify that the new DLL is actually newer than the existing one!) There is no need to recompile or relink any of the DLL's users. To drive home the importance of this delayed binding feature, imagine if all Windows applications used static linking to bind to the Windows API. A new release of Windows would require relinking all existing applications! When writing a new version of an existing DLL, special care should be given to working with old applications that assume they are still running with the old DLL. This includes not changing the names of external routines and variables, keeping the same ordinal numbers for the same functions, and supporting the old parameters and return values. Support for additional parameters can be achieved by including the version number (or structure size) as part of the parameters passed to the routine.

Customizablity In addition to containing code, DLLs may contain resources (which are read-only data). Using the resources and code in a DLL, an application can be customized for a given market without the need to have access to the application's source code. An example of such customization is translating the messages issued by an application to a different language.

Space Savings Using a DLL allows multiple routines to share the same copy of code and resources. This saves both disk and memory space.

Portability By placing low-level and version-dependent code in DLLs rather than in the application, we can keep our applications portable across different versions of Windows. For this reason, code that services interrupts, performs software interrupts, or issues direct I/O instructions should be kept in DLLs rather than in the application's EXE. Furthermore, FIXED segments (which are page fixing in 386 Enhanced mode) are only supported in DLLs. (We will discuss installable device drivers—a special type of DLL—in Chapter 6.)

Hardware Independence Using DLLs and delaying the binding between the application and the hardware device drivers to run time allows Windows applications to be hardware independent. An application does not need to know at link time which display driver will be used at run time. Furthermore, even the GDI does not know (or care) which display driver it will run with. This point is even more dramatic with printer drivers, which can be changed while Windows is running.

Delayed Binding In the same way that Windows uses delayed binding to be hardware independent, our application can use delayed binding to allow run-time adaptation and customization. For example, a spelling checker can use dynamic run-time linking to allow changing the dictionary it uses.

Data Sharing Since all tasks using a DLL share the same instance, DLLs can be used to share data between different tasks.

Task-Independent Code The natural place for code or resources that do not belong to a specific task but that can be used by any task in the system (such as the Windows API, fonts, system-wide hooks, callback routines, or global subclassing) is in an independent entity—a DLL—rather than a specific EXE.

Callback Routines

Callbacks are routines that are called by another entity, such as Windows or other applications, rather than directly by our own application. The most famous callback routine is a window procedure.

Because this book deals with modifying and extending Windows, we will use many types of hooks and interceptors, which are based on installing various callback routines at different levels of the system. Because of their nature, there are a few new issues associated with callback routines. We will take this opportunity to mention some of these issues, which will appear at various places throughout the book.

Setting Up DS

When the callback routine is called, DS must be set to the address of the correct data segment. The old technique for doing this was based on the compiler generating code similar to the code below for all **FAR** routines:

```
mov    ax, ds
nop
...
mov ds,ax
```

If such a function is not exported, this code is just a NOP, and no harm is done (except for the wasted cycles...). But if the function is exported, the loader would examine each exported routine looking for the entry sequence of:

```
mov    ax, ds
nop
```

If the loader found this signature, it would change it to:

```
nop
nop
nop
```

The modified code,

```
nop
nop
nop
...
mov ds,ax
```

would load DS from AX.

By passing the correct data selector value in AX when calling the routine, we could use the same routine's code (i.e., the module) with different data segments (i.e., by different instances). While for a DLL there is only one instance, a program can have multiple instances that all share the same code but have different data segments. For example, when Windows sends a message to a window procedure, it loads AX with the data selector that corresponds to the `hInstance` specified when the Window was created. In this way, the same window procedure can be used by multiple instances.

How do we set AX to the correct data selector before calling a routine? The answer is with MakeProcInstance.

FARPROC MakeProcInstance

Create a calling thunk for binding an exported routine with an instance

```
FARPROC MakeProcInstance(lpRtn,hInstance)

FARPROC lpRtn;         // address of routine
HINSTANCE hInstance;   // instance to bind to routine
```

Returns:
If successful, this function returns the address of a thunk; Else NULL.

Calling MakeProcInstance with an address of an exported routine and an `hInstance` returns the address of a thunk that contains code similar to this:

```
mov    ax, SEG corresponding to hInstance
jmp    lpRtn
```

Thus, when the routine is entered by calling the address returned by MakeProcInstance, AX is set to the specified `hInstance`'s data segment.

The newer versions of most compilers take a better approach. They take advantage of the fact that the stack is (usually) kept in the data segment; i.e., SS == DS. Thus, the prologs for routines that have the `__export` keyword and are compiled with the –GA switch (for MSC 7.0) simply load DS from SS on entry to an `__export` routine. There is no need for the loader to fix up the code, there are no unnecessary segment register loads, and there is no need for the MakeProcInstance API (except in special cases...).

Is a callback routine ever called from another task, so that SS != data segment? Yes! Some callback routines, such as system-wide hook callback routines (Chapter 5) and toolhelp callbacks (discussed in Chapter 7), are called with another task's SS. (Just the sort of routines that need to be placed in a DLL, as we previously discussed.)

One solution to this issue is to use the –GEd (MSC) switch, which tells the compiler that for `__export` routines, the prolog code should load DS with the segment selector of the data segment (DGROUP), just as it does for DLLs.

Asynchronous Operation

Because callback routines are called by other programs, they may be called at (almost) any time, and we cannot be sure exactly when they will be called. The routines and their data must always be ready to be called.

Reentrancy Issues

Some callback routines may be called again before they return from the previous call. Thus, the same routine is called while it is still executing. Special care in the handling of non-automatic variables is required in such routines.

Another reentrancy-related issue is that Windows itself is not reentrant; i.e., you cannot call most Windows APIs while they are in the middle of executing (and calling your callback routine). Fortunately, a few Windows APIs are reentrant.

We will deal with some of the more complex issues of callback routines as we come across them later in the book.

Chapter 3

Advanced Windows Debugging

WHEN debugging Windows applications, we use a variety of tools and techniques. Those include using a high-level debugger, and including code in our program to assist the debugging process by displaying, in a window, the program's progress and variable content information. However, as we venture into Windows' internals, many of those techniques become harder to use or completely useless. If we are modifying Windows itself, we need to minimize our reliance on debuggers and techniques that are based on the same Windows services that we are modifying!

In this chapter, we will explore ways to debug "low-level" Windows applications. These techniques are essential for debugging many of the example programs used in this book, as well as device drivers, virtual device drivers, and similar "under-the-hood" programs. Surprisingly, many of those low-level techniques are also extremely useful in high-level application development.

The *debugging version* of Windows and the Windows *kernel debugger* are two of the most powerful tools included in the Software Development Kit (SDK). Unfortunately, they are also two of the most under-utilized development aids. In this chapter, we will introduce these tools so you can start taking advantage of them. Once you start using them, you'll find them indispensable additions to the development process (even for high-level applications).

The Debugging Version of Windows

We are all familiar with the *retail version* of Windows, the one end users use and love (☺). But there is another version: the *debugging version*. While functionally similar to the retail version, the debugging version contains additional code (as well as symbolic information) to assist in debugging. The symbolic information is needed as a road map when using the kernel debugger (discussed next). The additional code contained in the debugging version of Windows keeps you appraised of what's happening in the system, informing you of events ranging

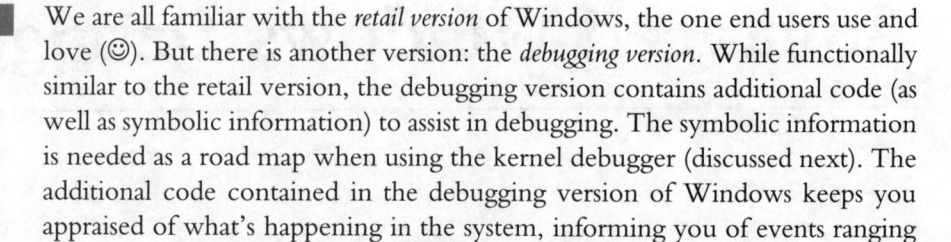

CHAPTER 3
ADVANCED WINDOWS DEBUGGING

from the loading of a module or a font, to a General Protection (GP) fault. In addition, it performs extensive validation of parameters and keeps track of overall application and system soundness. It can inform you of such common (but hard-to-detect) errors as forgetting to free resources and attempting to free resources that you do not own. Furthermore, the debugging version can be instructed to perform additional memory-management checks such as emulating a memory full condition, ensuring that buffers are writeable, and ensuring that you do not write to memory after it is freed. Considering the vulnerability of the Windows memory-management system, where all applications share the same address space, any tool that can help in this respect is a major blessing.

The debugging version of Windows consists of replacement DLLs for the various Windows components and the matching symbolic information (SYM) files. The debugging DLLs include the GDI, KRNL286, KRNL386, USER, and MMSYSTEM. Those components are part of the standard SDK. In addition, the Device Driver Kit (DDK) contains the debugging version of WIN386, which you will need if you intend to develop virtual device drivers (VxDs). Installing the debugging version is most easily performed by simply replacing the retail DLLs with the debugging ones.

While the final testing of all applications should be done with the retail version (after all, that is how your application will be run), no commercial product should be released without testing with the debugging version. You would be surprised how many well-known commercial applications have never been tested with the debugging version, and how many potential problems this tool reveals. The following is a sample listing of the output generated by the debugging version of Windows.

```
t Kernel: Loading C:\WIN31\PBRUSH.EXE
t Kernel: GrowHeap: 15000 allocated
t Kernel: Loading PBRUSH.DLL
wn Kernel: Segment 0001 of PBRUSH must be preload
t Kernel: Loading PBRUSH Nonresident name table
t Kernel:     looking for WEP
t Kernel: Loading OLESVR.DLL
t Kernel: GrowHeap: 20000 allocated
t Kernel: Loading PBRUSH Nonresident name table
t Kernel:     looking for VBITBLT
t Kernel: Loading PBRUSH Nonresident name table
t Kernel:     looking for DISCARDBAND
t Kernel: Loading PBRUSH Nonresident name table
t Kernel:     looking for DISCARDBAND
t Kernel: Loading PBRUSH Nonresident name table
```

```
t Kernel:      looking for GETVCACHEDC
t Kernel: Loading PBRUSH Nonresident name table
t Kernel:      looking for VBITBLT
t Kernel: Loading PBRUSH Nonresident name table
t Kernel:      looking for VCREATEBITMAP
t Kernel: Loading PBRUSH Nonresident name table
t Kernel:      looking for GETVCACHEDC
t Kernel: Loading PBRUSH Nonresident name table
t Kernel:      looking for VPATBLT
t Kernel: Loading PBRUSH Nonresident name table
t Kernel:      looking for VBITBLT
t Kernel: Loading PBRUSH Nonresident name table
t Kernel:      looking for VDELETEOBJECT
t Kernel: Demand load OLESVR(3) on PBRUSHX
t Kernel: PBRUSHX: reading resource String.7
t Kernel: PBRUSHX: reading resource String.13
t Kernel: PBRUSHX: reading resource GroupIcon.2CD
t Kernel: PBRUSHX: reading resource GroupCursor.2BA
t Kernel: Loading PBRUSH Nonresident name table
t Kernel:      looking for VBITBLT
t Kernel: Demand load PBRUSHX(E) on PBRUSHX
t Kernel: PBRUSHX: reading resource GroupCursor.2C3
t Kernel: Loading PBRUSH Nonresident name table
t Kernel:      looking for GETVCACHEDC
t Kernel: Loading PBRUSH Nonresident name table
t Kernel:      looking for VPATBLT
t Kernel: Loading PBRUSH Nonresident name table
t Kernel:      looking for VBITBLT
t Kernel: Loading PBRUSH Nonresident name table
t Kernel:      looking for VSTRETCHBLT
t Kernel: Demand load PBRUSHX(21) on PBRUSHX
t Kernel: Loading PBRUSH Nonresident name table
t Kernel:      looking for GETVCACHEDC
t Kernel: Loading PBRUSH Nonresident name table
t Kernel:      looking for VBITBLT
t Kernel: Demand load PBRUSHX(16) on PBRUSHX
t Kernel: PBRUSHX: reading resource String.1A
err PBRUSHX LOADSTRING+C: Invalid global handle: 0xf9f9


FatalExit code = 0x6022

Abort, Break, Exit or Ignore?
t  USER: Beginning app termination cleanup...
```

CHAPTER 3
ADVANCED WINDOWS DEBUGGING

```
wn  USER: Window not destroyed: 2a10
t   USER: End of app termination cleanup
t   Kernel: Loading PBRUSH Nonresident name table
t   Kernel:     looking for WEP
t   Kernel: Loading PBRUSH Nonresident name table
t   Kernel:     looking for WEP
```

Seeing is Believing

By default, the output from the debugging version goes to the AUX port. However, the DBWIN utility, included in the SDK, allows you to redirect the output to a monochrome card or to an on-screen window. Furthermore, you can use the `OutputTo=` variable in the `[Debug]` section of SYSTEM.INI to redirect the output to a file or disable the output by redirecting it to NUL.

In addition to displaying the debugging output, DBWIN allows you to control the behavior of the debugging version, including controlling which trace messages are displayed, which additional memory checks are performed, and when to break to the debugger (see the discussion later in this chapter). Figure 3-1 shows WBWIN's various options.

Besides using the DBWIN program, you can control the behavior of the debugging version directly with the GetWinDebugInfo and SetWinDebugInfo APIs.

Both GetWinDebugInfo and SetWinDebugInfo pass information in the WINDEBUGINFO structure, which is defined below. By studying the various options that can be set with SetDebugInfo, you can learn what the various DBWIN options actually do. Let's examine this structure in detail.

```
typedef struct tagWINDEBUGINFO
    {
    UINT flags;
    DWORD dwOptions;
    DWORD dwFilter;
    char achAllocModule[8];
    DWORD dwAllocBreak;
    DWORD dwAllocCount;
    } WINDEBUGINFO;
```

MODIFYING WINDOWS

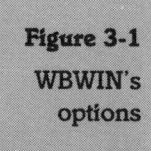

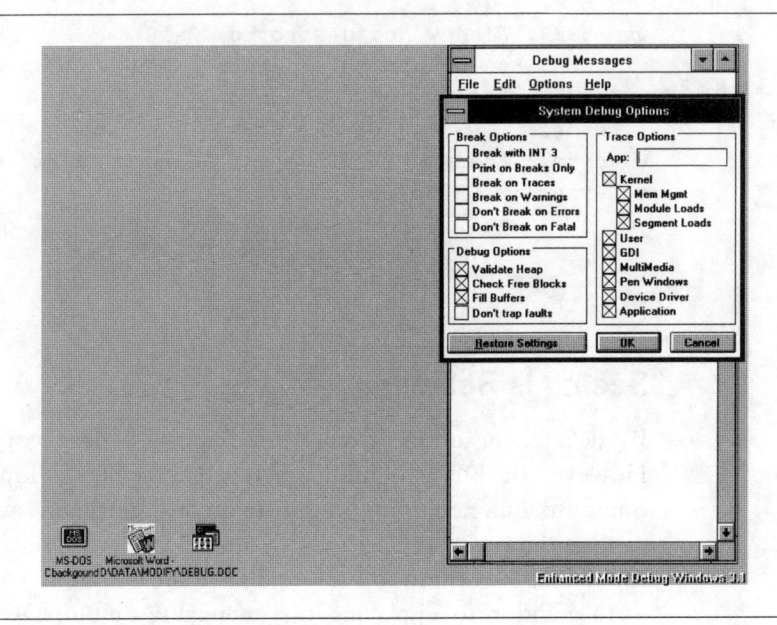

Figure 3-1
WBWIN's options

Member	Description		
flags	Specifies which members of the WINDEBUGINFO structure are valid. Possible values are one or more (ORed together) of the following:		
		WDI_OPTIONS	Specifies that dwOptions is valid
		WDI_FILTER	Specifies that dwFilter is valid
		WDI_ALLOCBREAK	Specifies that achAllocModule, dwAllocBreak, and dwAllocCount are valid
dwOptions	Specifies debugging options. Possible values are one or more (ORed together) of the following:		
		DBO_CHECKHEAP	Perform local heap checking in relevant APIs.
		DBO_BUFFERFILL	Check for buffers' writeability by writing 0xF9 to buffers passed to APIs.
		DBO_DISABLEGPTRAPPING	Disable GP fault trapping.
		DBO_CHECKFREE	Check for writes to unallocated memory by filling all free memory with 0xFB and validate it when allocating memory. DBO_CHECKFREE works only with DBO_CHECKHEAP.
		DBO_INT3BREAK	Break to the kernel debugger when encountering an INT 3.

CHAPTER 3
ADVANCED WINDOWS DEBUGGING

Member	Description	
	DBO_NOFATALBREAK	Do not break to kernel debugger on DBF_FATAL messages.
	DBO_NOERRORBREAK	Do not break to kernel debugger on DBF_ERROR messages.
	DBO_WARNINGBREAK	Break to kernel debugger on DBF_WARNING messages.
	DBO_TRACEBREAK	Break to kernel debugger on DBF_TRACE messages that match the dwFilter.
	DBO_SILENT	Does not display warning, error, or fatal messages except in cases where a break to the kernel debugger would occur.
`dwFilter`	BF_TRACE messages. Only messages that pass the filter are displayed (and cause a break to the kernel debugger if DBO_TRACEBREAK). Possible values are one or more (ORed together) of the following:	
	DBF_KRN_MEMMAN	KERNEL local and global memory management messages
	DBF_KRN_LOADMODULE	KERNEL module loading messages
	DBF_KRN_SEGMENTLOAD	KERNEL segment loading messages
	DBF_APPLICATION	Application messages
	DBF_DRIVER	Device driver messages
	DBF_PENWIN	PENWIN messages
	DBF_MMSYSTEM	MMSYSTEM messages
	DBF_GDI	GDI messages
	DBF_USER	USER messages
	DBF_KERNEL	Any KERNEL messages
`achAllocModule`	Name of application module for memory allocation monitoring.	
`dwAllocBreak`	Number of memory (global and local) allocations to allow before all subsequent allocations will fail (including memory allocated indirectly by calls to Windows APIs). A value of zero in this field does not fail allocations but still enables counting of memory allocations in `dwAllocCount`.	
`dwAllocCount`	Memory allocation count (returned value only).	

To get the current state of system debugging you can call the GetWinDe bugInfo API.

MODIFYING WINDOWS

BOOL GetWinDebugInfo

Get Windows debugging information

```
BOOL GetWinDebugInfo (pwdi, flags);

WINDEBUGINFO FAR * lpwdi;    // -> WINDEBUGINFO structure
UINT              flags;     // which WINDEBUGINFO elements
                             // to return
```

Returns:
If successful TRUE; else FALSE.

Possible values for `flags` are one or more of the following:

flags	WINDEBUGINFO Returned Members
WDI_OPTIONS	dwOptions
WDI_FILTER	dwFilter
WDI_ALLOCBREAK	achAllocModule, dwAllocBreak, and dwAllocCount

To set the system debugging state you can use the SetWinDebugInfo API.

BOOL SetWinDebugInfo

Set Windows debugging information

```
BOOL SetWinDebugInfo(lpwdi);

const WINDEBUGINFO FAR* lpwdi;    // ->WINDEBUGINFO
```

Returns:
If successful TRUE; else FALSE.

When calling SetWinDebugInfo, the `flags` of WINDEBUGINFO specifies which information should be set. Only the fields indicated by flags need be valid when calling the API.

CHAPTER 3
ADVANCED WINDOWS DEBUGGING

Changes in the system debugging information set by SetWinDebugInfo remain in effect only for the current Windows session. If you want the debugging kernel to start with different settings than the defaults, you can specify initial values via `DebugOptions` and `DebugFilter` in the `[Windows]` section of WIN.INI.

Your Own Message in Lights

The next step in utilizing the debugging version of Windows is outputting debugging information from your own application. This can be done with three APIs: OutputDebugString, OutputDebugStr, and DebugOutput.

The simplest of the three is OutputDebugString, which simply outputs a string.

OutputDebugString
Output debug message string

```
void OutputDebugString(lpszOutputString);

LPCSTR lpszOutputString;    // string to output
```

Returns:
VOID

OutputDebugString works in both the debug version and the retail version of Windows. Thus, you can tell your end user to change the `OutputTo` variable from NUL to filename and send you a copy of the file. The multimedia system (yes, MMSYSTEM) contains a cousin function, OutputDebugStr, which acts as a nop on the retail version. OutputDebugStr has added support for printing the content of the full 32-bit hardware registers! To output the value of a register, you must prefix its name with a pound sign (#). For example: `OutputDebugStr("AX = #AX, EBX = #EBX\n");`

Finally, for formatted output there is the DebugOutput API.

DebugOutput

Output formatted debugging information

```
void FAR _cdecl DebugOutput(flags, lpszFormat, ...);

UINT    flags;          // debugging output category and
                        // source, DBF_*
LPCSTR  lpszFormat;     // formatting string as in
                        // wsprintf,
                        // less than 160 characters
...                     // arguments as required by
                        // szFormat
```

Returns:
VOID

The flags specify the category and source of the message. The common values are:

flags	Meaning
DBF_TRACE	Trace information only (not an error). This output is not normally displayed.
DBF_APPLICATION	Trace information from an application program.
DBF_DRIVER	Trace information from a device driver.
DBF_WARNING	A possible error.
DBF_ERROR	An error that caused an API to fail.
DBF_FATAL	An error that causes the application to terminate.

When called from the retail version, this API acts as a nop.

Unfortunately, the LIBW.LIB import library included in the SDK does not include support for DebugOutput (whereas the DDK version does). Thus, in order to avoid an "unresolved external" error from the linker, you need to add the following statements to your DEF file:

```
IMPORTS
    KERNEL._DebugOutput
```

The following program uses DebugOutput to inform us which messages are received by the window procedure. A typical output of the program is shown in Figure 3-2.

Figure 3-2
DBGOUT's output as seen on DBWIN

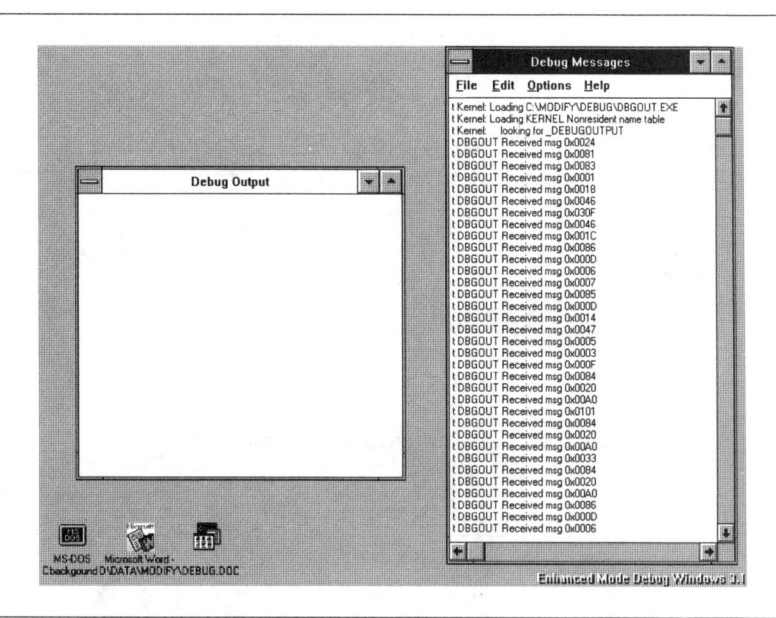

MAKEFILE

```
all: dbgout.exe

dbgout.obj: dbgout.c dbgout.h makefile
   cl -c -DSTRICT -AS -GA2 -Ox -W3 dbgout.c

dbgout.exe: dbgout.obj dbgout.def makefile
   link dbgout,,,libw slibcew, dbgout.def
   rc dbgout.exe
```

DBGOUT.C

```
// an example of displaying debug output from
// the debugging version of Windows
//
// from Modifying Windows by Asael Dror

#include <windows.h>
#include "dbgout.h"
```

MODIFYING WINDOWS

```
HINSTANCE hInst;                                        // current instance

                                                        // application E.P.
int PASCAL WinMain(HINSTANCE hInstance, HINSTANCE hPrevInstance,
             LPSTR LPCmdLine, int nCmdShow)

   {
   MSG msg;

   if (!hPrevInstance)                                  // if first instance
      if (!InitApplication(hInstance))                  // init app
         return(FALSE);

   if (!InitInstance(hInstance, nCmdShow))              // init instance
      return(FALSE);

                                                        // msg loop
   while (GetMessage(&msg, NULL, 0, 0))                 // get any msg/any wnd
      {
      TranslateMessage(&msg);                           // translate virt keys
      DispatchMessage(&msg);                            // dispatch message
      }
   return(msg.wParam);
   }

BOOL InitApplication(HINSTANCE hInstance)               // init app
   {
                                                        // reg main wnd class
   WNDCLASS wc;

                                                        // fill wnd class str
   wc.style = 0;
   wc.lpfnWndProc = MainWndProc;                        // window proc
   wc.cbClsExtra = 0;
   wc.cbWndExtra = 0;
   wc.hInstance = hInstance;                            // class owner
   wc.hIcon = LoadIcon(NULL, IDI_APPLICATION);          // def app icon
   wc.hCursor = LoadCursor(NULL, IDC_ARROW);            // standard cursor
   wc.hbrBackground = (HBRUSH)(COLOR_WINDOW + 1);       // wnd bckgnd clr
   wc.lpszMenuName = "MainMenu";
   wc.lpszClassName = "MyClass";                        // window class name

   return(RegisterClass(&wc));                          // register wnd class
   }
```

```c
                                            // instance init
BOOL InitInstance(HINSTANCE hInstance, int nCmdShow)
  {
  HWND   hWnd;                          // window handle

  hInst = hInstance;                    // save in static var

  hWnd = CreateWindow (                 // main window
          "MyClass",                    // class name
          "Debug Output",               // title bar text
          WS_OVERLAPPEDWINDOW | WS_VISIBLE,  // normal & visible
          CW_USEDEFAULT,                // default x
          nCmdShow,                     // default y,
                                        // show as requested
          CW_USEDEFAULT,                // default width
          CW_USEDEFAULT,                // default height
          HWND_DESKTOP,                 // no parent
          NULL,                         // use class menu
          hInstance,                    // inst of mod for win
          NULL);                        // not used
  if (!hWnd) return(FALSE);
  UpdateWindow(hWnd);                   // send WM_PAINT msg
  return (TRUE);                        // OK
  }


LRESULT __export CALLBACK MainWndProc(
                          HWND hWnd,        // window handle
                          UINT message,     // message
                          WPARAM wParam,    // param
                          LPARAM lParam)    // param
  {
  DebugOutput(DBF_APPLICATION, "Received msg 0x%04X", message);
// ***********************************************************

  switch (message)
     {
     case WM_DESTROY:
        PostQuitMessage(0);                 // bye bye, rc = 0
        break;

     default:                               // default proc & ret
        return (DefWindowProc(hWnd, message,
                          wParam, lParam));
     }
  return(0);
  }
```

DBGOUT.H

```
LRESULT __export CALLBACK MainWndProc(HWND, UINT, WPARAM, LPARAM);
BOOL InitApplication(HINSTANCE);
BOOL InitInstance(HINSTANCE, int);
```

DBGOUT.DEF

```
NAME            DBGOUT

DESCRIPTION     'Debug Output Example'

EXETYPE         WINDOWS

STUB            'WINSTUB.EXE'

CODE PRELOAD MOVEABLE DISCARDABLE
DATA PRELOAD MOVEABLE MULTIPLE

HEAPSIZE        1024
STACKSIZE       8192

IMPORTS
                KERNEL._DebugOutput
```

Real Windows Developers Use a Debugging Terminal

As we've seen, by using your own debugging output messages you can monitor the execution of your program in a nonintrusive way, and in real time. This is especially important when writing low-level applications, such as hooks (discussed in Chapter 5) or hardware device drivers, where the presence of a debugger may effect the execution of the program or make high-level debuggers completely unusable. Nevertheless, as long as the debugging output is going to the screen, we are still going through Windows, using the Windows hooks, GDI, device driver, etc. A bug that affects any of those components will disable the output. A better approach is to send the debugging output, via a null modem, to a serial terminal attached to a serial port, i.e., a *debugging terminal*.

The Kernel Debugger

Once you have a debugging terminal attached to your development machine, the obvious next step is to run the *kernel debugger*. This not only allows you to passively watch the debugging output, but also gives you a powerful, interactive debugging tool.

The kennel debugger is a powerful, "Microsoft internal" tool that comes with the SDK. It is composed of the debugger (WDEB386.EXE) and a virtual device driver (WINDEBUG.386), which provides services for the debugger. While originally intended for debugging Windows itself, the kernel debugger has the ability to break on debug output (as well as on DebugBreak and FatalExit and manually with ALT+CTRL+SYS RQ), has access to ring 0 (the processor's most privileged level), and allows utilization of the 386 hardware debugging support. All this makes it an excellent tool for hard-to-trace bugs as well as for general snooping around. For debugging low-level routines such as device drivers and virtual device drivers (VxDs), the kernel debugger is a must.

The kernel debugger has two types of commands: the *internal* or *generic* debugger commands, and the *external* or *dot* commands.

The internal commands are the usual set of commands one would expect in a character-based, protected-mode debugger. These include traditional commands such as dump (d), compare (c), and enter (e); and breakpoint control commands such as execute-breakpoint (bp), breakpoint disable (bd), and access-breakpoint using the 386 debug registers (br). Other commands allow access to 386 tables. These commands include dump the GDT (dg) and dump the TSS (dt). Additional commands allow external symbol management (lm, ln, etc.), and a set of commands allows you to control the "default command" (zd, zl, zs) and perform conditional command execution (j). A list of the commands can be viewed using the help (?) command.

The external commands are preceded by a dot (.) and are environment-specific commands; in our case the environment is Windows. They include commands such as: dump module list (.dm), dump the free list (.df), and the most useful command of all (.reboot).

If you are using the debugging version of WIN386.EXE (included in the DDK but not in the SDK), additional dot commands are available to help in debugging virtual device drivers. You can get a list of the available dot commands by issuing the dot help command (.?).

While working concurrently on multiple machines does require a reorganization of your desk, the benefits are well worth the investment. (Finally, here is a use for those old Z80/8080/etc. machines.)

Chapter 4

Superclassing and Subclassing

SUPERCLASSING and subclassing are extremely useful techniques that allow us to build on existing (and hopefully debugged!) window procedures. Using these techniques, we can extend and add value to existing applications and even to Windows itself.

Some of the more common uses for superclassing and subclassing include customizing predefined controls, dynamically modifying the behavior of a window at run-time, and adding features to existing applications for which we do not have the source code.

Overview

As we know, each window has a window procedure that reacts to messages sent to the window, and hence defines the behavior of that window. When we define a new window class (with RegisterClass) we specify (via the WNDCLASS structure) the address of the window procedure for the newly registered window class. Subsequently, when a new window of this class is created (using CreateWindow or CreateWindowEx), Windows copies the address of the window procedure from a data structure that describes the class, to a data structure that describes the individual window's instance. This is the address of the procedure that will be called to handle all messages for that particular window instance.

We can use an existing window procedure as a basis for creating our own window procedure. The new window procedure can process selected messages while calling the original window procedure with the CallWindowProc API to process all other messages. Thus, we use the existing window procedure as a mold to create a customized window procedure. There are two basic techniques for building on an existing window procedure: *superclassing* and *subclassing*. With superclassing we create a *new* window class based on an existing

CHAPTER 4
SUPERCLASSING AND SUBCLASSING

class. With subclassing we *modify* an existing window or window class. We'll look at superclassing first, and then, at greater detail, at subclassing.

Superclassing

Adding a new window class using superclassing is useful when you need to create many windows of the modified class—for example, when you need many instances of a modified control. By creating a new window class (superclassing), you can create many modified windows simply by using the new class, rather than using the old class and modifying each one of the windows individually (subclassing).

To create a new window class using superclassing, we register a new window class that is based on an existing window class. To achieve this, we first use GetClassInfo to fill a WNDCLASS structure with information about the existing window class.

GetClassInfo
Get information about a window class

```
BOOL GetClassInfo(hinst, lpszClassName, lpwc);

HINSTANCE hinst;              // instance that registered the
                              // class, NULL for Windows
                              // predefined classes

LPCSTR    lpszClassName;      // class name (string or
                              // MAKEINTRESOURCE)
WNDCLASS FAR *lpwc ;          // WNDCLASS structure to receive
                              // class info. lpszClassName and
                              // lpszMenuName not returned
```

Returns:
If successful TRUE; else FALSE.

We then modify the WNDCLASS structure for the new class. First we specify the new class name in the `lpszClassName` field, and then we specify the new class's `Instance`. Next we save the address of the old window procedure from the `lpfnWndProc` field and replace it with the address of our new window procedure. Finally we register the new class using RegisterClass. Whenever the new window procedure receives a message, it can either process it, or pass the message on to the original window procedure (using the CallWindowProc API) for processing. The message passed to the original procedure (if any) can be the original message, a modified version of the message, or a completely different message than the original.

CallWindowProc

Call a window procedure to process a message

```
LRESULT CallWindowProc(WndProc, hWnd, uMsg,
                       wParam, lParam)

WNDPROC  WndProc;   // address of window procedure
                    // to be called
HWND     hWnd;      // window to receive message
UINT     uMsg;      // message ID
WPARAM   wParam;    // message param
LPARAM   lParam;    // message param
```

Returns:
A message-specific value.

SUPERCLASSING EXAMPLE PROGRAM

The following example uses superclassing to create a new window class called "beeper". Beeper is identical to the predefined button control, except that it sounds a Beep when it receives a **WM_LBUTTONDOWN** message. All messages received by the beeper window procedure are passed unmodified to the button window procedure for processing. The example program's menu allows the creation of multiple button and beeper windows.

MAKEFILE

```
all: super.exe

super.res: super.rc super.h makefile
   rc -r super.rc
```

```
super.obj: super.c super.h makefile
   cl -c -DSTRICT -AS -GA2 -Ox -W3 super.c

super.exe: super.obj super.def super.res makefile
   link super,,,libw slibcew, super.def
   rc super.res
```

SUPER.C

```c
// Superclassing example
//
// from Modifying Windows by Asael Dror
//

#include <windows.h>
#include "super.h"

HINSTANCE hInst;                                        // current instance
int childID = 0;
WNDPROC OrgWndProc;                                     // button win proc

                                                        // application E.P.
int PASCAL WinMain(HINSTANCE hInstance, HINSTANCE hPrevInstance,
            LPSTR LPCmdLine, int nCmdShow)

   {
   MSG msg;
   if (!hPrevInstance)                                  // is first instance

      if (!InitApplication(hInstance))                  // than init app
         return(FALSE);

   if (!InitInstance(hInstance, nCmdShow))              // init instance
      return(FALSE);

                                                        // msg loop
   while (GetMessage(&msg, NULL, 0, 0))                 // get any msg/any wnd
      {
      TranslateMessage(&msg);                           // translate virt keys
      DispatchMessage(&msg);                            // dispatch message
      }
   return(msg.wParam);
   }

BOOL InitApplication(HINSTANCE hInstance)               // init app
```

MODIFYING WINDOWS

```
   {
                                              // reg main wnd class
   WNDCLASS wc;

                                              // fill wnd class str
   wc.style = 0;
   wc.lpfnWndProc = MainWndProc;          // window proc
   wc.cbClsExtra = 0;
   wc.cbWndExtra = 0;
   wc.hInstance = hInstance;              // class owner
   wc.hIcon = LoadIcon(NULL, IDI_APPLICATION);  // def app icon
   wc.hCursor = LoadCursor(NULL, IDC_ARROW);    // standard cursor
   wc.hbrBackground = (HBRUSH)(COLOR_WINDOW + 1); // wnd bckgnd clr
   wc.lpszMenuName = "MainMenu";
   wc.lpszClassName = "SuperClassing";        // window class name

   return(RegisterClass(&wc));            // register wnd class
   }

                                              // instance init
BOOL InitInstance(HINSTANCE hInstance, int nCmdShow)
   {
   HWND   hWnd;                           // window handle
   WNDCLASS wc;

   hInst = hInstance;                     // save in static var


                                              // superclass button
                                              // -----------------
   GetClassInfo(
             NULL,                        // predefined
             "button",                    // button class
             &wc);

   wc.lpszMenuName = NULL;                // no menu
   wc.hInstance = hInstance;              // new class owner
   wc.lpszClassName = "beeper";           // new class name
   OrgWndProc = wc.lpfnWndProc;           // save old win proc addr
   wc.lpfnWndProc = BeeperWndProc;        // new window proc addr
   RegisterClass(&wc);                    // register wnd class


   hWnd = CreateWindow (                  // main window
            "Superclassing",              // class name
            "Superclassing",                  // title bar text
            WS_OVERLAPPEDWINDOW | WS_VISIBLE, // normal & visible
            CW_USEDEFAULT,                    // default x
```

```
                    nCmdShow,                       // default y,
                                                    // show as requested
                    CW_USEDEFAULT,                  // default width
                    CW_USEDEFAULT,                  // default height
                    HWND_DESKTOP,                   // no parent
                    NULL,                           // use class menu
                    hInstance,                      // inst of mod for win
                    NULL);                          // not used
   if (!hWnd) return(FALSE);
   UpdateWindow(hWnd);                              // send WM_PAINT msg
   return (TRUE);                                   // OK
   }


LRESULT __export CALLBACK MainWndProc(
                    HWND hWnd,              // window handle
                    UINT message,           // message
                    WPARAM wParam,          // param
                    LPARAM lParam)          // param
   {

   switch (message)
       {
       case WM_DESTROY:
          PostQuitMessage(0);                       // bye bye, rc = 0
          break;

       case WM_COMMAND:
          switch (wParam)
              {
              case IDM_ORG_BUTTON:
                 CreateWindow("button", "button",
                 BS_PUSHBUTTON | WS_VISIBLE | WS_CHILD,
                 24 * childID, 24 * childID, 58, 20,
                 hWnd, (HMENU)++childID, hInst, NULL);
                 break;

              case IDM_BEEP_BUTTON:
                 CreateWindow("beeper", "beeper",
                 BS_PUSHBUTTON | WS_VISIBLE | WS_CHILD,
                 24 * childID, 24 * childID, 58, 20,
                 hWnd, (HMENU)++childID, hInst, NULL);
                 break;

              default:                       // default proc & ret
                 return (DefWindowProc(hWnd, message,
                                wParam, lParam));
              }
```

```
        break;

    default:                            // default proc & ret
        return (DefWindowProc(hWnd, message,
                         wParam, lParam));
    }
    return(0);
}


// superclassing window procedure

LRESULT __export CALLBACK BeeperWndProc(
                        HWND hWnd,          // window handle
                        UINT message,       // message
                        WPARAM wParam,      // param
                        LPARAM lParam)      // param
{
    if (message == WM_LBUTTONDOWN) MessageBeep(-1);

    return
        (CallWindowProc(OrgWndProc, hWnd, message, wParam, lParam));
}
```

SUPER.H

```
LRESULT __export CALLBACK MainWndProc(HWND, UINT, WPARAM, LPARAM);
LRESULT __export CALLBACK BeeperWndProc(HWND, UINT, WPARAM, LPARAM);
BOOL InitApplication(HINSTANCE);
BOOL InitInstance(HINSTANCE, int);

#define IDM_ORG_BUTTON  100
#define IDM_BEEP_BUTTON 101
```

SUPER.RC

```
#include <windows.h>
#include "super.h"

MainMenu    MENU    PRELOAD
            {
            MENUITEM    "&Original Button", IDM_ORG_BUTTON
            MENUITEM    "&Beeping Button", IDM_BEEP_BUTTON
            }
```

```
SUPER.DEF

NAME            SUPER

DESCRIPTION     'Superclass a button'

EXETYPE         WINDOWS

STUB            'WINSTUB.EXE'

CODE PRELOAD MOVEABLE DISCARDABLE
DATA PRELOAD MOVEABLE MULTIPLE

HEAPSIZE        1024
STACKSIZE       8192
```

Figure 4-1 shows a typical output screen for the program.

Subclassing

Perhaps even more interesting than adding a new window class is the technique for modifying an existing window. This is done by replacing the address of the

Figure 4-1
Typical output of superclassing example program

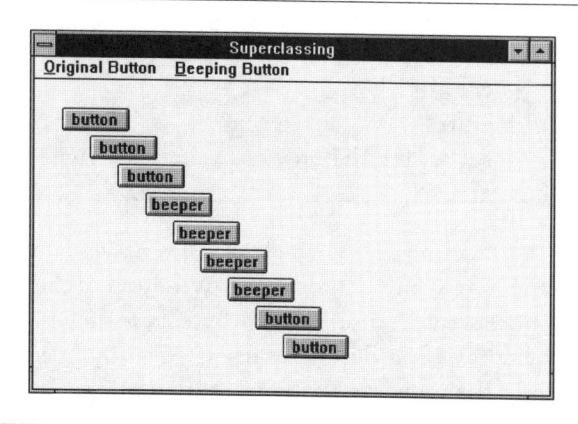

window procedure. Using this technique, we can change the behavior of an existing window or of an entire window class. Our replacement window procedure can still call the original window procedure to perform any processing we do not want to handle ourselves.

There are two approaches to subclassing. The first approach involves using the SetClassLong API to replace the window procedure address of a window class. When we replace the window procedure of a window class, it affects *all* windows of that class created *from that point onward*. (You can still change each of the created windows individually with SetWindowLong.) The second approach involves replacing the address of an instance window's window procedure. This is done with the SetWindowLong API and affects only one specific window instance.

Subclassing a Class

Before we discuss the various issues and pitfalls of subclassing, let's look at how to subclass an entire window class. Subclassing a window class is done with the SetClassLong API.

SetClassLong

Set a long value into a window class's extra memory

```
LONG SetClassLong(hwnd, nOffset, nVal);

HWND hwnd;       // identifies the class
                 // via a window of the class
int nOffset;     // offset of value to be set,
                 // or a GCW_ value
LONG nVal;       // new value
```

Returns:
If successful, the previous value; otherwise, zero.

Once the class is subclassed, *any* newly created window of the class will use the new window procedure. Windows of the class created before the class was subclassed are not affected by subclassing the class (since the address of the window procedure they use has already been copied from the class structure into the individual window structure).

AN EXAMPLE OF SUBCLASSING A CLASS

As an example of subclassing a class, we can modify the button class so that all buttons (created after the subclassing takes place) will beep on receiving WM_LBUTTONDOWN messages. The example is composed of two programs: SUBCLS.EXE and NBUTTON.DLL. SUBCLS.EXE creates a button (so we can have an hWnd for SetClassLong) and subclasses its class before destroying the button window. The new window procedure for the button class (BeeperWndProc) resides in NBUTTON.DLL, and SUBCLS.EXE uses GetModuleHandle and GetProcAddress to retrieve this address when subclassing the button class. The address of the old button window procedure is stored by SUBCLS.EXE in an exported variable (OrgWndProc) located in NBUTTON.DLL's data segment. Note that SUBCLS.EXE does not terminate. This is essential (at least until Chapter 6), since SUBCLS.EXE is the program that loaded NBUTTON.DLL. If SUBCLS.EXE terminates, NBUTTON.DLL's use-count will be zero and Windows will discard it from memory, even though every button in the system is actually using NBUTTON.DLL's code! Windows is only aware that SUBCLS.EXE uses NBUTTON.DLL.

NBUTTON.DLL is a short DLL that contains only the new window procedure for the button class. This procedure beeps on receiving a WM_LBUTTONDOWN message and passes all messages to the original window procedure (via CallWindowProc) for processing. Since this code is called by different tasks in the system, it resides in a DLL rather than an EXE (as we discussed in Chapter 2).

MAKEFILE

```
all: nbutton.dll subcls.exe


nbutton.obj: nbutton.c makefile
    cl -c -DSTRICT -AS -GD2 -Ox -W3 nbutton.c

nbutton.dll: nbutton.obj nbutton.def makefile
    link nbutton, nbutton.dll, ,libw sdllcew, nbutton.def
    rc nbutton.dll

subcls.obj: subcls.c makefile
    cl -c -DSTRICT -AS -GA2 -Ox -W3 subcls.c
```

```
subcls.exe: subcls.obj subcls.def makefile
    link subcls,,,libw slibcew, subcls.def
    rc subcls.exe
```

SUBCLS.C

```c
// Subclassing a class example program
//
// This program subclasses the button class
// and loads the DLL containing the new window procedure
//
// from Modifying Windows by Asael Dror
//

#include <windows.h>
extern WNDPROC __far OrgWndProc;                    // in NBUTTON.DLL

                                                    // application E.P.
int PASCAL WinMain(HINSTANCE hInstance, HINSTANCE hPrevInstance,
                LPSTR LPCmdLine, int nCmdShow)

    {
    MSG msg;
    HWND hWndButton;


                                                    // get an hWnd
    hWndButton = CreateWindow("button", "",
            BS_PUSHBUTTON | WS_DISABLED,
            0, 0, 0, 0,
            HWND_DESKTOP, NULL, hInstance, NULL);

                            // subclass the class
                            // new win proc in NBUTTON.DLL
    OrgWndProc = (WNDPROC)
        SetClassLong(hWndButton, GCL_WNDPROC, (LONG)
            GetProcAddress(GetModuleHandle("NBUTTON.DLL"),
                    "BeeperWndProc"));

    DestroyWindow(hWndButton);                      // done with it

                                                    // msg loop
    while (GetMessage(&msg, NULL, 0, 0))  // get any msg/any wnd
        {
        TranslateMessage(&msg);                     // translate virt keys
        DispatchMessage(&msg);                      // dispatch message
```

```
        }
    return(msg.wParam);
    }
```

SUBCLS.DEF

```
NAME            SUBCLASS

DESCRIPTION     'Loader for class subclassing DLL'

EXETYPE         WINDOWS

STUB            'WINSTUB.EXE'

CODE PRELOAD MOVEABLE DISCARDABLE
DATA PRELOAD MOVEABLE MULTIPLE

HEAPSIZE        1024
STACKSIZE       8192

IMPORTS
                NBUTTON._OrgWndProc
```

NBUTTON.C

```c
// Subclassing a class example program
//
// This is the DLL containing the new window procedure for the
// (modified) button class
//
// from Modifying Windows by Asael Dror
//

#include <windows.h>

WNDPROC OrgWndProc;        // address of original window procedure
                           // an exported variable
                           // (filled in by subcls.exe)


                           // new window procedure
```

MODIFYING WINDOWS

```c
LRESULT __export CALLBACK BeeperWndProc(
                            HWND hWnd,            // window handle
                            UINT message,         // message
                            WPARAM wParam,        // param
                            LPARAM lParam)        // param
{
if (message == WM_LBUTTONDOWN) MessageBeep(-1);

return      // pass all messages to original wnd proc
   (CallWindowProc(OrgWndProc, hWnd, message, wParam, lParam));
}
```

NBUTTON.DEF

```
LIBRARY          NBUTTON

DESCRIPTION      'Subclassing the button class DLL'

EXETYPE          WINDOWS

STUB             'WINSTUB.EXE'

CODE PRELOAD MOVEABLE DISCARDABLE
DATA PRELOAD MOVEABLE SINGLE

HEAPSIZE         1024

EXPORTS
                 BeeperWndProc    @1
                 _OrgWndProc      @2
```

UNSUBCLASSING A CLASS

In our example program, the subclassing remains in effect for the entire Windows session. There is no mechanism for *unsubclassing,* i.e. removing our subclassing window procedure and restoring the original one. While it may seem that unsubclassing can simply be done by replacing the address of the original window procedure in the class structure (using SetClassLong), it's not quite that simple. Let's assume that another program subclassed the button class after we subclassed it. In such a case, the second subclassing program will call our window procedure for its default message processing, as is illustrated in Figure 4-2.

If we unsubclassed our subclassing by replacing the original window procedure address into the class structure, we would also unsubclass any other subclasses that occurred after our subclassing. Furthermore, every existing button in the system will continue to call our window procedure, even if we restore the class information. The easiest way to overcome this problem is by simply never unsubclassing a class! Instead, we can disable the subclassing by adding a switch that will cause our subclassing window procedure to simply call CallWindowProc for all messages.

Subclassing a Window

Subclassing a *single* window is done with the SetWindowLong API. This form of subclassing is generally more useful than subclassing an entire class, because it affects only the specific window we want to subclass, rather than every window of the class in the entire system.

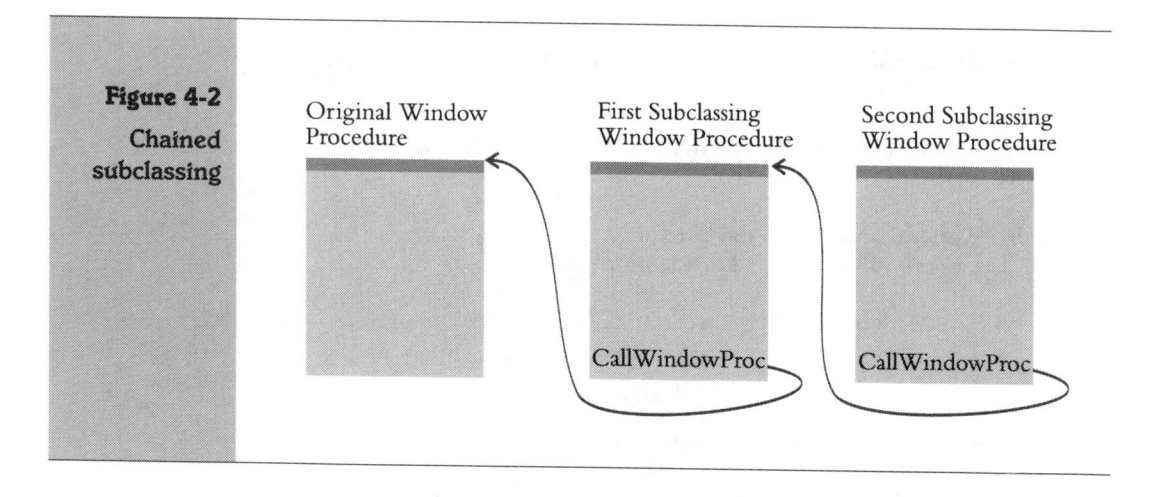

Figure 4-2
Chained subclassing

Original Window Procedure   First Subclassing Window Procedure   Second Subclassing Window Procedure

CallWindowProc   CallWindowProc

MODIFYING WINDOWS

> ### SetWindowLong
>
> **Set a long value into a window's extra memory**
>
> ```
> LONG SetWindowLong(hwnd, nOffset, nVal);
>
> HWND hwnd;      // identifies the window
> int nOffset;    // offset of value to be set,
>                 // or a GWL_ value
>                 //(or DWL_ for a dialog box)
> LONG nVal;      // new value
> ```
>
> Returns:
> If successful, the previous value; otherwise zero.

SUBCLASSING EXAMPLE PROGRAM

The following program uses subclassing to add a "Boss" option to Solitaire. In this new and improved Solitaire, there is an additional menu item: "Boss". Whenever the "Boss" option is selected (by using the mouse or pressing ALT-B), the Solitaire window becomes invisible. Thus, this program not only demonstrates subclassing, but also dramatically decreases your chance of being caught while brushing up on your Solitaire skills.

MAKEFILE

```
all: boss.dll newsol.exe


boss.obj: boss.c boss.h makefile
    cl -c -DSTRICT -AS -GD2 -Ox -W3 boss.c

boss.dll: boss.obj boss.def makefile
    link boss, boss.dll, , libw sdllcew, boss.def
    rc boss.dll

boss.lib: boss.dll boss.def
    implib boss.lib boss.def
```

CHAPTER 4
SUPERCLASSING AND SUBCLASSING

```
newsol.obj: newsol.c boss.h makefile
   cl -c -DSTRICT -AS -GA2 -Ox -W3 newsol.c

newsol.exe: newsol.obj newsol.def makefile boss.lib
   link newsol,,, libw slibcew boss, newsol.def
   rc newsol.exe
```

NEWSOL.C

```
// Subclassing an application example
//
// This program starts solitaire and calls the BOSS.DLL BossIt API
// to subclass it and add a "Boss" menu selection
//
// from Modifying Windows by Asael Dror
//

#include <windows.h>
#include "boss.h"

int PASCAL WinMain(HINSTANCE hInstance, HINSTANCE hPrevInstance,
                LPSTR LPCmdLine, int nCmdShow)
   {
   HWND hWndSol;                            // hwnd of solitaire window
   MSG msg;

   WinExec("sol.exe", nCmdShow);            // start solitaire
                                            // get its window
   if (hWndSol = FindWindow("Solitaire", "Solitaire"))
      {
      BossIt(hWndSol);         // subclass it, adding "Boss"

      while (GetMessage(&msg, NULL, NULL, NULL))   // message loop
         DispatchMessage(&msg);                    // spin forever

      return ((int) msg.wParam);
      }

   return (NULL);
   }
```

NEWSOL.DEF

```
NAME            NEWSOL

DESCRIPTION     'Solitaire game with a Boss menu item'

EXETYPE         WINDOWS

STUB            'WINSTUB.EXE'

CODE PRELOAD MOVEABLE DISCARDABLE
DATA PRELOAD MOVEABLE MULTIPLE

HEAPSIZE        1024
STACKSIZE       5120
```

BOSS.C

```c
// Subclassing an application example
//
// This is the DLL that subclasses and
// adds a "Boss" menu selection
//
// from Modifying Windows by Asael Dror
//

#include <windows.h>
#include "boss.h"

WNDPROC OrgWndProc;

                    // add "Boss" to window's menu and subclass
BOOL __export WINAPI BossIt(HWND hWndOrg)
   {
                    // add "Boss" to window's menu
   AppendMenu(GetMenu(hWndOrg), MF_STRING, MID_BOSS ,"&Boss");
   DrawMenuBar(hWndOrg);              // redraw menu

                                      // subclass window
   OrgWndProc = (WNDPROC) SetWindowLong(hWndOrg, GWL_WNDPROC,
   (LONG) GetProcAddress(GetModuleHandle("BOSS.DLL"), "NewWinProc"));

   return (TRUE);
```

CHAPTER 4
SUPERCLASSING AND SUBCLASSING

```
    }
                                    // new (subclassing) WinProc
LRESULT __export CALLBACK NewWinProc(
    HWND hWnd,                      // window handle
    UINT message,                   // message
    WPARAM wParam,                  // param
    LPARAM lParam)                  // param

{
  switch (message)
    {
    case WM_COMMAND:
      if (wParam == MID_BOSS)       // if "Boss" selected
        {                           // then hide window
          SetWindowPos(hWnd, HWND_BOTTOM,
                  0, 0, 0, 0,
                  SWP_HIDEWINDOW | SWP_NOMOVE |
                  SWP_NOSIZE | SWP_NOZORDER);

          return(0);
        }                           // else call org WinProc
                                    //   and return
        else return (CallWindowProc(OrgWndProc, hWnd, message,
                            wParam, lParam));

    default:                        // call org. WinProc & ret
       return (CallWindowProc(OrgWndProc, hWnd, message,
                       wParam, lParam));
    }
  return(NULL);
}
```

BOSS.H

```
BOOL __export WINAPI BossIt(HWND);

#define MID_BOSS 2797
```

BOSS.DEF

```
LIBRARY         BOSS
```

```
DESCRIPTION        'A DLL to a add Boss menu item and subclass'

EXETYPE            WINDOWS

STUB               'WINSTUB.EXE'

CODE PRELOAD MOVEABLE DISCARDABLE
DATA PRELOAD MOVEABLE SINGLE

HEAPSIZE           1024

EXPORTS
                   NewWinProc      @2
                   BossIt          @3
```

The output of the new solitaire game is shown in Figure 4-3.

The program is composed of two parts: an executable (EXE) called NEWSOL and a DLL called BOSS.

When NEWSOL is run, it activates the original Solitaire program (SOL.EXE) with a WinExec call. Then NEWSOL gets a handle to SOL's window (via FindWindow) and calls the BossIt routine in the BOSS DLL, passing Solitaire's window handle as a parameter. After the call to BossIt, the program simply goes into a message loop.

BOSS is a DLL for adding a "Boss" menu item to any application. It has two exported functions: BossIt and NewWinProc.

The BossIt routine receives as an argument the handle of the window to be

Figure 4-3
The improved solitaire game

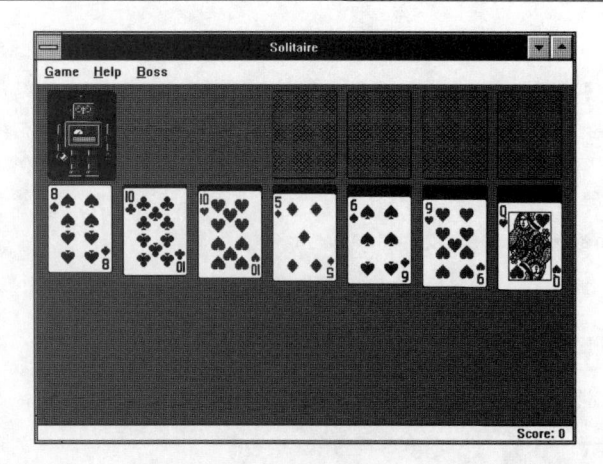

subclassed. It adds a "Boss" item to that window's menu, and then subclasses that window. The actual subclassing is done with the SetWindowLong API using the GWL_WNDPROC parameter. This replaces the address of the window procedure with a new address, while returning the address of the old window procedure. We save the old address in the OrgWndProc variable. The new window procedure address is the address of the NewWinProc routine in the BOSS DLL. This is found by calling the GetProcAddress API with the handle of the BOSS DLL (retrieved by the GetModuleHandle API) and the routine's name (which is "NewWinProc").

Once we have changed the window procedure address, all subsequent messages to the window are handled by the NewWinProc window procedure in the BOSS DLL.

NewWinProc is the new window procedure. Once the window is subclassed, this routine is called for all messages for the window. The NewWinProc window procedure calls the old window procedure (with CallWindowProc) to process all messages except a WM_COMMAND with a `wParam` of MID_BOSS (i.e., when the "Boss" menu entry is selected).

When the "Boss" menu entry is selected, the window is hidden with the SetWindowPos API.

Figure 4-4 shows the message flow for the subclassed Solitaire game.

RESTORING THE SOLITAIRE WINDOW

This leaves us with only one problem (or so it may seem): how do we make the window visible again so we can continue our game? The answer is to run a new copy of the original Solitaire (SOL, not NEWSOL—at least not for now). When Solitaire starts, it will see that another instance is running and will make

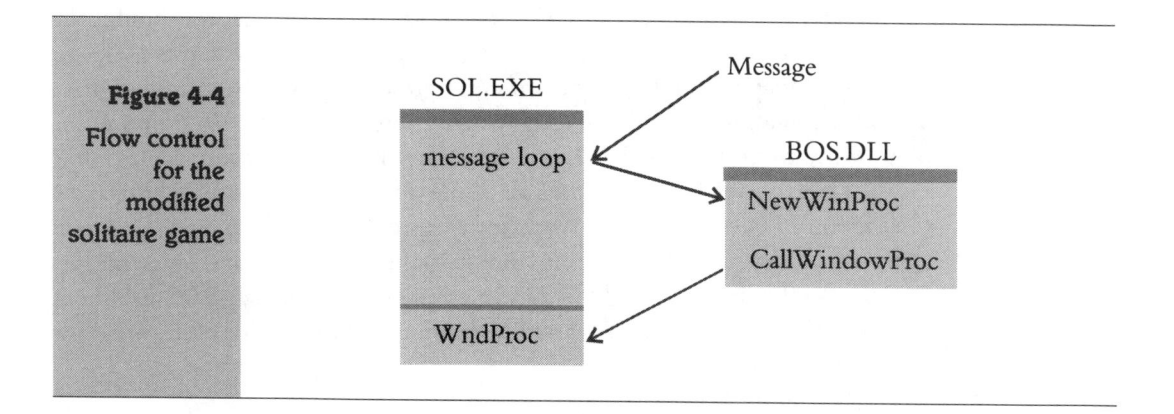

Figure 4-4
Flow control for the modified solitaire game

that instance active and visible.

All that's left to do is to use the Program Manager to "borrow" the Solitaire icon for our new application so that we can start playing. There are, however, a few additional issues and pitfalls associated with subclassing. Let's look at some of them, and then modify the example program accordingly.

Getting a Window Handle

To use the SetWindowLong API, we need a handle to the window we want to subclass. There are a several ways to get this handle. One is to use the GetActiveWindow API immediately after starting the program containing the window to be subclassed. While this approach will *usually* work, it may not be compatible with a true multitasking version of Windows (in which another window may become active between the time the WinExec and the GetActiveWindow APIs execute). Yes, it's time to start thinking about multitasking! Even under Windows 3.1, using GetActiveWindow may lead to problems—for example, if the SOL.EXE program was not executed (you are a serious programmer who deleted all the game programs from your machine, right?). In such a case, we could mistakenly subclass the wrong window (the Program Manager, for example).

The best approach for finding the handle of the window to be subclassed is the direct one: just ask for it explicitly using the FindWindow API. To use FindWindow, however, you need to know the window's name and its class name. The window's name is easy; it's in the title bar. The class name can be found using the SPY utility.

Staying Out of the Way

An important requirement of subclassing is that the added features should not break the old features, something that can easily happen by way of side effects. In our example program, we add a menu item to the application's menu bar. The new menu item should be assigned an unused menu ID. We can use the SPY utility to find out which IDs are used by the original window. In some cases, this may not be trivial, because some applications dynamically change their menus. I guess you could overcome the problem by writing a super-smart application that would constantly monitor the menu bar and dynamically allocate the IDs, but that might be carrying things a little too far. We can almost always avoid such problems by carefully examining the behavior of the window we want to subclass.

Another example of avoiding side effects to the original window procedure is making sure we do not send it any information about objects it does not know exist. For example, we should not pass on to the original window procedure any WM_MENUSELECT messages that refer to an item we added to the menu.

This is a good place to mention that Microsoft's *Windows 3.1 Programmer's Reference* states that "An application should not attempt to create a window subclass for standard Windows controls such as combo boxes and buttons" (*Volume 2: Functions, page 887*). Notice that our class subclassing example violated this rule, and rightfully so! I feel that this rule should not be taken at its face value. Subclassing standard controls is a powerful and very useful technique. We should, however, remember that when we subclass a predefined control class, we will affect all other applications, and some of those applications may be very dependent on the control's behavior (maybe even on undocumented features of the control). So we need to carefully examine the behavior of the window we intend to subclass, and—needless to say—debug our code to perfection.

EXE or DLL

A subclassing window procedure can reside in either an EXE or a DLL. When we subclass a window that belongs to our own application, there is no reason not to have the new window procedure be part of our EXE file. However, if we subclass a window that belongs to another application (which is usually the case when we subclass an entire class), then it is highly recommended that we place the new window procedure in a DLL.

There are a few compelling reasons for this, one of which is to ensure compatibility with future versions of Windows. Furthermore, if we think about it, when we subclass another application's window, that window procedure really belongs to the other application. It's not part of our program anymore, and logically should not be included in our EXE. For this reason, both the button class and the NEWSOL example programs use DLLs for the window procedures.

From a practical point of view, when we subclass a window of another task, the window procedure will run with that task's SS. Consequently, the window procedure may run with DS != SS. Although there are ways around such problems, it is easier to simply put the window procedure in a DLL.

When Can We Terminate?

If the new window procedure resides in our program, it is clear that we cannot terminate our program until all users of the new window procedure terminate. On the other hand, it may seem that we can terminate our program if the new window procedure is in a DLL. However, this is not the case.

As we discussed in Chapter 2, a DLL is not a unit of execution, but rather a piece of code that is executed by other tasks. When the first program that uses a specific DLL is loaded (or explicitly loads the DLL), Windows loads the DLL into memory. Windows maintains a use-count for each DLL, counting how many programs are currently using that DLL. Upon loading, the use-count is set to one. Whenever another program that calls the DLL is loaded, Windows increments the use-count of the DLL (Windows does not need to reload the DLL from the disk; it only has to increment the counter). When a program that uses the DLL terminates, Windows decrements the DLL's use-count. When the use-count reaches zero, the DLL is freed from memory.

In our example program, NEWSOL calls the DLL (by calling BossIt) and thus increments the use-count. The Solitaire program does not call the DLL, at least not as far as Windows is concerned. SOL.EXE does not have any external references to the BOSS DLL, nor does it use dynamic run-time linking to access the DLL. We artificially transplanted the address of a procedure within the DLL (NewWinProc) into its window's description structure. Thus, if NEWSOL terminates, Windows will decrease the use-count and free the DLL, even though SOL is still calling it. This is the reason that NEWSOL should not terminate.

Leaving around a program that does not terminate, however, is bad programming practice. Furthermore, the BOSS DLL will never be freed from memory because its use-count will never reach zero. To solve this problem, we have modified NewWinProc so that at termination (when it receives a WM_DESTROY message) it will kill NEWSOL by posting—not sending—it a WM_QUIT message (using the PostAppMessage API). This, in turn, will cause NEWSOL to terminate and so decrease the use-count of BOSS. For NewWinProc to be able to post this termination message to NEWSOL, NEWSOL passes its task ID (retrieved via GetCurrentTask) to the BOSS DLL when it calls BossIt.

The final change to the program is the inclusion of a check to see if another instance of NEWSOL is running (now that NEWSOL actually does terminate). If another instance is running, the program makes SOL's window visible. Consequently, we can now use either SOL or NEWSOL to continue a game interrupted by the "Boss."

CHAPTER 4
SUPERCLASSING AND SUBCLASSING

MAKEFILE

```
all: boss.dll newsol.exe

boss.obj: boss.c boss.h makefile
    cl -c -DSTRICT -AS -GD2 -Ox -W3 boss.c

boss.dll: boss.obj boss.def makefile
    link boss, boss.dll, , libw sdllcew, boss.def
    rc boss.dll

boss.lib: boss.dll boss.def
    implib boss.lib boss.def


newsol.obj: newsol.c boss.h makefile
    cl -c -DSTRICT -AS -GA2 -Ox -W3 newsol.c

newsol.exe: newsol.obj newsol.def makefile boss.lib
    link newsol,,, libw slibcew boss, newsol.def
    rc newsol.exe
```

NEWSOL.C

```
// Subclassing an application example
//
// This program starts solitaire and calls the BOSS.DLL BossIt API
// to subclass it and add a "Boss" menu selection
//
// from Modifying Windows by Asael Dror
//

#include <windows.h>
#include "boss.h"

int PASCAL WinMain(HINSTANCE hInstance, HINSTANCE hPrevInstance,
                LPSTR LPCmdLine, int nCmdShow)
    {
    HWND hWndSol;                           // hwnd of solitaire window
    MSG msg;

    if (hPrevInstance)                      // if running - show it
```

```
    {
    SetWindowPos(FindWindow("Solitaire", "solitaire"),
            HWND_TOP, 0, 0, 0, 0, SWP_SHOWWINDOW |
            SWP_NOMOVE | SWP_NOSIZE | SWP_NOZORDER);
    return (NULL);
    }

    else
    {
    WinExec("sol.exe", nCmdShow);         // start solitaire
                                          // get its window
    if (hWndSol = FindWindow("Solitaire", "Solitaire"))
       {
       BossIt(hWndSol, GetCurrentTask());    // subclass it,
                                             //  adding "Boss"

       while (GetMessage(&msg, NULL, NULL, NULL))   // msg loop
          DispatchMessage(&msg);

       return ((int) msg.wParam);
       }

    return (NULL);
    }
}
```

NEWSOL.DEF

```
NAME            NEWSOL

DESCRIPTION     'Solitaire game with a Boss menu item'

EXETYPE         WINDOWS

STUB            'WINSTUB.EXE'

CODE PRELOAD MOVEABLE DISCARDABLE
DATA PRELOAD MOVEABLE MULTIPLE

HEAPSIZE        1024
STACKSIZE       5120
```

BOSS.C

```c
// Subclassing an application example
//
// This is the DLL that subclasses and
// adds a "Boss" menu selection
//
// from Modifying Windows by Asael Dror
//

#include <windows.h>
#include "boss.h"

WNDPROC OrgWndProc;
HTASK hOwnerTask;                          // hTask of DLL's owner

                    // add "Boss" to window's menu and subclass
BOOL __export WINAPI BossIt(HWND hWndOrg, HTASK hTask)
  {
  hOwnerTask = hTask;                      // save DLL owner's task

                    // add "Boss" to window's menu
  AppendMenu(GetMenu(hWndOrg), MF_STRING, MID_BOSS ,"&Boss");
  DrawMenuBar(hWndOrg);                    // redraw menu

                                           // subclass window
  OrgWndProc = (WNDPROC) SetWindowLong(hWndOrg, GWL_WNDPROC,
    (LONG) GetProcAddress(GetModuleHandle("BOSS.DLL"), "NewWinProc"));

  return (TRUE);
  }

                                   // new (subclassing) WinProc
LRESULT __export CALLBACK NewWinProc(
    HWND hWnd,                             // window handle
    UINT message,                          // message
    WPARAM wParam,                         // param
    LPARAM lParam)                         // param

  {
  switch (message)
     {
     case WM_COMMAND:
```

```c
        if (wParam == MID_BOSS)         // if "Boss" selected
        {                               // then hide window
    SetWindowPos(hWnd, HWND_BOTTOM,
                 0, 0, 0, 0,
                 SWP_HIDEWINDOW | SWP_NOMOVE |
                 SWP_NOSIZE | SWP_NOZORDER);

    return(0);
        }                               // else call org WinProc
                                        //   and return
        else return (CallWindowProc(OrgWndProc, hWnd, message,
                                    wParam, lParam));
    case WM_MENUSELECT:
       if (wParam == MID_BOSS)          // do not pass WM_MENUSELECT
                                        // for "Boss"
    return(0);

        else return (CallWindowProc(OrgWndProc, hWnd, message,
                                    wParam, lParam));

    case WM_DESTROY:
                                        // post WM_QUIT to DLL's owner
       PostAppMessage(hOwnerTask, WM_QUIT, 0, NULL);
       return (CallWindowProc(OrgWndProc, hWnd, message,
                              wParam, lParam));

    default:                            // call org WinProc & ret
       return (CallWindowProc(OrgWndProc, hWnd, message,
                              wParam, lParam));
    }
 return(NULL);
 }
```

BOSS.DEF

```
LIBRARY         BOSS

DESCRIPTION     'A DLL to add a Boss menu item and subclass'

EXETYPE         WINDOWS

STUB            'WINSTUB.EXE'

CODE PRELOAD MOVEABLE DISCARDABLE
DATA PRELOAD MOVEABLE SINGLE
```

```
HEAPSIZE         1024

EXPORTS
                 NewWinProc      @2
                 BossIt          @3
```

A Better Mousetrap?

There seems to be a more elegant solution to the issue of freeing the DLL. Unfortunately, this solution does not actually work in Windows 3.1. So feel free to skip the following academic discussion.

The real user of the BOSS DLL is SOL. If there was a way for us to let Windows know that SOL is using BOSS, our problem would be solved. Windows would increase the use-count to reflect the additional user of the DLL, and we could simply terminate NEWSOL after performing the subclassing. Eventually, when SOL terminates, Windows would decrease the use-count and free the DLL.

As we mentioned before, SOL does not have an external reference to the DLL. However, there is another way to load a DLL (or increase its use-count if it's already loaded). This is by using explicit dynamic linking via the LoadLibrary API, as discussed in Chapter 2.

The task that executes the LoadLibrary call for the BOSS DLL should be SOL, not NEWSOL. Thus, we cannot perform the LoadLibrary call in the BossIt procedure, since this procedure is executed by the NEWSOL task. We need to somehow get the SOL task to perform the LoadLibrary call. This can be achieved by sending a user-defined message to the SOL window after it is subclassed. This will cause SOL's new window procedure (NewWinProc) to be called, this time running under the SOL task. When we get the user-defined message, we can perform the LoadLibrary call and so force SOL to own the DLL, and this almost solves the problem of freeing the DLL.

The question then becomes: When will SOL free the DLL via a call to FreeLibrary? The answer is that we should *not* call FreeLibrary for the BOSS DLL from NewWinProc. Doing so is like committing programming suicide, because it is telling Windows that it can free the code that is currently running! So what do we do? We can simply terminate without freeing the DLL and let Windows decrease the use-count as part of its cleanup work. Unfortunately, this does not work. While Windows frees implicitly loaded libraries, it does not free explicitly loaded ones. This probably accounts for some of the wasted system resources when running Windows. Interestingly enough, if the task aborts—for example, due to a GP fault—Windows does perform the correct cleanup and decreases the use-count. This behavior may not be a bug, but rather a restriction imposed on Windows by some (ill-behaved) applications that load a DLL in one task and use it in another task. When this "feature" is corrected, we will be able to improve the subclassing program.

Chapter 5

Hooks

THE behavior of a window is determined by its window procedure and the messages it receives. In the previous chapter, we saw how to modify a window procedure of a particular window or window class with superclassing and subclassing. In this chapter, we will look at hooks, a mechanism for intercepting and modifying messages.

Here are some situations where hooks are useful: Macro recorders can use a *journal record* hook to record keyboard and mouse events, which can later be played back via a *journal playback* hook. Computer-based training (CBT) programs can use the *CBT* hook to monitor and control the user's actions. Utilities (such as the SDK's SPY) can use hooks to monitor the messages received by any window in the system. A HELP program that explains to the user what's under the cursor at any given moment will find hooks useful. Hooks are also essential for debuggers and shells.

The hooks API has been overhauled in Windows 3.1, making hooks faster and easier to use. Unfortunately, the SDK documentation has not kept up. Much of the information is undocumented, and whatever is documented is a muddled mix-up of Windows 3.0 and Windows 3.1. Hooks are probably the worst-documented feature in Windows. In fact, they are so badly documented that I recommend *not* reading the official documentation at all—it's more confusing than helpful.

Rather than discussing the way hooks *used* to work in earlier versions of Windows, and looking at obsolete APIs such as SetWindowsHook and DefHookProc, this chapter will discuss the way hooks work *today,* focusing on Windows 3.1 *only*.

CHAPTER 5
HOOKS

Overview

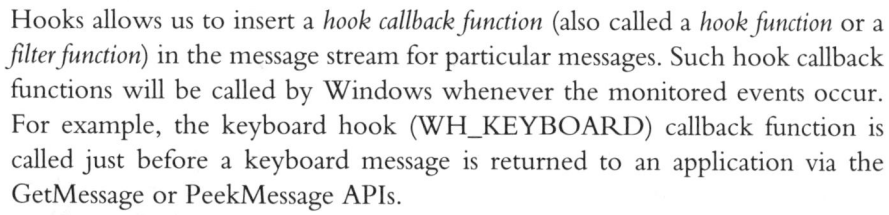

Hooks allows us to insert a *hook callback function* (also called a *hook function* or a *filter function*) in the message stream for particular messages. Such hook callback functions will be called by Windows whenever the monitored events occur. For example, the keyboard hook (WH_KEYBOARD) callback function is called just before a keyboard message is returned to an application via the GetMessage or PeekMessage APIs.

Some hooks allow intercepting messages for an individual task only; others allow intercepting messages on a system basis only (all tasks in the system); and still other hooks allow intercepting messages both for a particular task or on a system basis. Some hooks allow modifying messages, while others only allow filtering the messages (i.e., continue processing or disregard the message). While the details differ from one hook type (such as the keyboard hook or the CBT hook) to another, the overall mechanism is basically the same for all hook types. Let's first look at the overall mechanism, and later at the details of each particular hook type.

Using Hooks

Windows maintains a collection of chained lists to keep track of the active hook callback functions in the system. For each hook type, Windows maintains several chains of active hook callback functions. One chain is used for all callback functions (of the same hook type) that have a system scope. Additional chains are maintained for task-specific callback functions (one chain for each hook type for each monitored task).

The SetWindowsHookEx API installs a hook callback function in the appropriate chain (determined by the hook type and its scope: the particular task or system). The newly installed hook is added to the top (beginning) of the appropriate hook chain.

SetWindowsHookEx

Install a Windows hook callback function

```
HHOOK SetWindowsHookEx(idHook, lpfn, hInstance, hTask);

int idHook;              // hook type
HOOKPROC lpfn;           // address of hook callback function
HINSTANCE hInstance;     // instance of hook callback function
                         // (another case where hModule will do)
HTASK hTask;             // task to be hooked,
                         // NULL == system hooking (all tasks)
```

Returns:
If the hook was successfully installed, hook handle; otherwise NULL.

The possible `idHook` values are

idHook Value	Used for
WH_CALLWNDPROC	Sent (not posted) messages
WH_CBT	Computer-based training
WH_DEBUG	Debugging
WH_GETMESSAGE	Posted (not sent) messages
WH_HARDWARE	Hardware event messages
WH_JOURNALPLAYBACK	Playback input messages
WH_JOURNALRECORD	Record input messages
WH_KEYBOARD	Keyboard messages
WH_MOUSE	Mouse messages
WH_MSGFILTER	Filter messages—task
WH_SHELL	Shell
WH_SYSMSGFILTER	Filter messages—system

If the hook monitors the same task as the application installing it, the callback function may be part of your application (EXE). However, if an application is monitoring a different task, as is always the case for hooks with a system scope, the callback routine must reside in a DLL, because it will run in the context of another task. (The discussion in the EXE or DLL section of Chapter 2 holds true in the case of hooks as well; see it for more details.)

CHAPTER 5
HOOKS

Once our hook is installed, it will be called whenever a message-event monitored by that particular hook occurs. Windows calls the first hook in the chain for the occurring message-event (i.e., the last hook added to the chain).

A hook callback function is defined as follows:

Hook callback function

```
LRESULT CALLBACK hookcallbackfunctionname
                (nCode, wParam, lParam);

int nCode;        // hook action code
                  // (nCode < 0 are obsolete
                  // in Windows 3.1)
WPARAM wParam;    // parameter: hook type and
                  // nCode dependent
LPARAM lParam;    // parameter: hook type and
                  // nCode dependent
```

Returns:
hook type and `nCode` dependent value.

When a hook callback function is called by Windows, it is passed a code—`nCode`—that tells the callback function what action is requested of it. This is similar in concept to the message ID passed to a window procedure. In addition, the callback function receives two parameters, whose meaning depends on the hook type and the `nCode`. When the callback function finishes its processing, it returns to Windows a result code—`lResult`—the meaning of which depends on the hook type and `nCode`.

As part of its processing, the hook callback function may call the next hook callback function in the current chain by using the CallNextHookEx API. This allows multiple hook callback functions to act on the same notification. CallNextHookEx may be called at any stage of the processing (beginning, middle, end) or not called at all. If there are no more callback functions in the current chain, CallNextHookEx returns 0; otherwise the return value is determined by the called function.

CallNextHookEx

Call next hook callback function in the current chain

```
LRESULT CallNextHookEx(hHook, nCode, wParam, lParam);

HHOOK hHook;       // handle of current hook (the caller)
int nCode;         // hook action code
WPARAM wParam;     // parameter: hook type
                   // and nCode dependent
LPARAM lParam;     // parameter: hook type
                   // and nCode dependent
```

Returns:
If there are more hooks in the chain, this function returns the value returned by the called function; otherwise it returns 0 (the "default" value).

note: *If there is both a task hook chain and a system hook chain for the occurring event, Windows calls the first hook callback function in the task chain. The system hook chain is not called by Windows directly. Calling CallNextHookEx, by the last callback function in the task chain, would call the first callback function in the system chain, as we'll see later.*

When a hook function is no longer needed, it should be removed from the hook chain by calling the UnhookWindowsHookEx API. Hooks can be removed in any order.

UnhookWindowsHookEx

Remove a hook callback function from the chain

```
BOOL UnhookWindowsHookEx(hHook);

HHOOK hHook;    // hook handle
```

Returns:
If successful, TRUE; otherwise FALSE.

Order, Please!

As we mentioned, some hook types may have both a task chain and a system chain. In such cases, if the monitored event is for a task that has a hook chain, the first hook callback function in the task chain will be called. The hook callback function in the system chain will only be called when the last callback function in the task hook chain calls the CallNextHookEx API. This is shown in Figure 5-1.

Performance Issues

Hook callback functions are in the middle of the message processing flow, a critical path for Windows performance. This is especially true for hooks with system scope, which affect all Windows applications. Thus, when writing hooks, special attention must be given to system performance.

The first step to minimize adverse performance effects is to use task hooks rather than system hooks whenever possible. Second, install the hook only when it's needed, and uninstall it as soon as possible. Third, unless it's essential to your application, avoid using hooks that will be called often, especially the WH_CALLWNDPROC hook, which is called whenever a message is sent. Futhermore, write your code to be as fast as possible, especially for events that

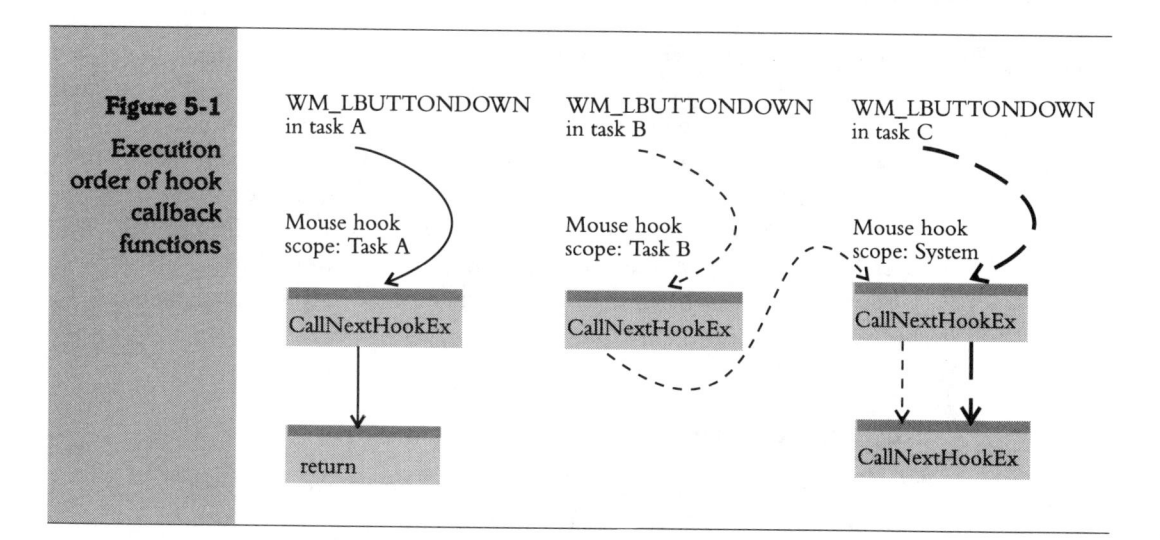

Figure 5-1 Execution order of hook callback functions

occur often and for events on which your hook takes no action. You might also consider (dare I mention it?) writing your hook callback function in assembly language. Finally, remember that while programs that degrade overall system performance may be acceptable in development and analysis tools, they will not be acceptable in end-user applications.

Hook Types

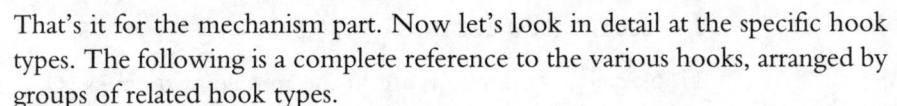

That's it for the mechanism part. Now let's look in detail at the specific hook types. The following is a complete reference to the various hooks, arranged by groups of related hook types.

As you read though the various hook types, you will notice that there is some overlap among different hook types, and that in some cases different hook types can be used to perform the same chore. Which hook type you use in your particular application may depend on what seems more "natural" to you, and on which hook will have the least impact on the system's performance. Also, while certain hooks were designed with a specific use in mind, you are of course free to find new and innovative uses for them.

System Queue Hooks

As you may recall, Windows maintains two types of message queues: an application message queue for each task in the system, and a global system message queue. All messages from input devices (a mouse, a keyboard, and other input hardware such as a pen) are kept in the system queue. Windows supplies three hooks that can be used to monitor when a message is about to be retrieved from the system message queue by a GetMessage or a PeekMessage API. The three hooks are the *keyboard hook,* the *mouse hook,* and the *hardware event hook.* All three hooks can be installed with either a task or a system scope and can discard, but cannot modify, messages.

Keyboard Hook

The keyboard hook is called whenever a keyboard event message is about to be returned by GetMessage or PeekMessage.

Keyboard Hook

idHook == WH_KEYBOARD

nCode	Description

HC_ACTION	The message is being removed from the system queue.
	    wParam Virtual key code
	    lParam Same as for a WM_KEYDOWN message
	    lResult 0 == process message; 1 == discard message

HC_NOREMOVE	The message is not being removed from the queue; this is due to a call to PeekMessage with PM_NOREMOVED.
	    wParam Virtual key code
	    lParam Same as for a WM_KEYDOWN message
	    lResult 0 == process message; 1 == discard message

The `lParam` for both `nCode`s is as follows:

Bits	Description
0-15	Repeat count
16-23	Scan code
24	1 for extended key, otherwise 0
25-26	Not used
27-28	Used internally by Windows
29	Context code: ON if ALT key was down when key pressed
30	Previous key state: 0 if key was down before this message was generated, 1 if up
31	Key-transition state: 0 if key is being pressed, 1 if key is being released

Mouse Hook

The mouse hook is called whenever a mouse event message is about to be returned by GetMessage or PeekMessage.

Mouse Hook

idHook == WH_MOUSE

nCode	Description
HC_ACTION	The message is being removed from the system queue. 　　wParam　Message ID 　　lParam　LPMOUSEHOOKSTRUCT 　　lResult　0 == process message; 1 == discard message
HC_NOREMOVE	The message is not being removed from the queue; this is due to a call to PeekMessage with PM_NOREMOVED. 　　wParam　Message ID 　　lParam　LPMOUSEHOOKSTRUCT 　　lResult　0 == process message; 1 == discard message

MOUSEHOOKSTRUCT is defined as:

```
POINT     pt              // mouse x, y coordinates
WHND      hwnd            // window to receive msg
UINT      wHitTestCode    // HT* value
DWORD     dwExtraInfo     // for GetMessageExtraInfo
```

Hardware Event Hook

The hardware hook is called whenever a hardware event message is about to be returned by GetMessage or PeekMessage. A hardware event is an input message for a device other than the keyboard or mouse, such as a pen.

CHAPTER 5
HOOKS
139

Hardware Event Hook

idHook = **WH_HARDWARE**

nCode	Description

HC_ACTION	The message event is being removed from the system queue.
	    wParam NULL
	    lParam LPHARDWAREHOOKSTRUCT
	    lResult 0 == process message; 1 == discard message

HC_NOREMOVE	The message is not being removed from the queue; this is due to a call to PeekMessage with PM_NOREMOVED.
	    wParam NULL
	    lParam LPHARDWAREHOOKSTRUCT
	    lResult 0 == process message; 1 == discard message

HARDWAREHOOKSTRUCT is defined as:

```
HWND      hWnd
UINT      wMessage
WPARAM    wParam
LPARAM    lParam
```

MOUSE HOOK EXAMPLE

Our mouse hook example is a real "killer application." It uses a system mouse hook to monitor the mouse, waiting for a "right button down" message. When this message is received, the hook callback function posts a WM_QUIT message to the window under the mouse pointer. This literally kills the underlying application by terminating its message loop (no confirmation, nothing saved, just a quick death). This application will kill any Windows application or even a DOS box, the Program Manager, or the Desktop itself.

Since the hook callback function is in a DLL (it must be, because we are using a hook with system scope), we need a stub application to load the DLL. In this example program, for the sake of simplicity, the DLL and the stub program are not terminated. See Chapter 4 for a detailed discussion about loading a DLL with a stub program, and for a discussion about termination issues.

The stub program is (appropriately) named KILLERAP. This program does nothing except give a warning beep and load the MOUHOOK1 DLL. After loading the DLL with a LoadLibrary call, it simply goes into a message loop. The DLL is never explicitly called by the stub program. (Don't you just love DLLs?!) When KILLERAP is terminated, it gives another warning beep and frees the DLL with a call to FreeLibrary. (Since this example does not provide a way to terminate the stub application that loaded the DLL, the DLL will be unloaded, and this code executed, only when Windows terminates.)

The MOUHOOK1 DLL is where the real work is done. When the DLL is loaded, it is automatically initialized. In the initialization routine (LibMain), a mouse hook is installed. The mouse hook is unhooked when the DLL is terminated (WEB entry).

The mouse hook callback function (RButtonKill) is called just before an application retrieves a mouse message via GetMessage or PeekMessage. When RButtonKill is called, it checks to determine if the message event is a "right button down" (either an WM_RBUTTONDOWN or an WM_NCRBUTTONDOWN). If it is, the underlying window is posted a WM_QUIT message. By returning a 1 from the callback function, Windows is told to discard the "right button down" message. For all other messages, the next hook in the chain is called and its return code is returned by RButtonKill.

caution: *This program is a real killer. It's dangerous (but also lots of fun and very addictive). Applications killed by KILLERAP might not release, close, or free system resources and files. Be especially careful about killing the Program Manager or the Desktop!*

MAKEFILE

```
all: mouhook.dll killerap.exe

mouhook.obj: mouhook.c mouhook.h makefile
    cl -c -DSTRICT -AS -GD2 -Ox -W3 mouhook.c
```

```
mouhook.dll: mouhook.obj mouhook.def makefile
    link mouhook, mouhook.dll, , libw sdllcew, mouhook.def
    rc mouhook.dll


killerap.obj: killerap.c mouhook.h makefile
    cl -c -DSTRICT -AS -GA2 -Ox -W3 killerap.c

killerap.exe: killerap.obj killerap.def makefile
    link killerap,,, libw slibcew, killerap.def
    rc killerap.exe
```

KILLERAP.C

```
// Mouse hook example
//
// This program is a stub whose only purpose
// is to load MOUHOOK.DLL
//
// from Modifying Windows by Asael Dror
//

#include <windows.h>

HINSTANCE hMouHookLib;

int PASCAL WinMain(HINSTANCE hInstance, HINSTANCE hPrevInstance,
              LPSTR LPCmdLine, int nCmdShow)
    {
    MSG msg;

    MessageBeep(-1);                              // at birth
    hMouHookLib = LoadLibrary("MOUHOOK.DLL");     // load & init DLL

    while (GetMessage(&msg, NULL, NULL, NULL))    // message loop
       DispatchMessage(&msg);

    MessageBeep(-1);                              // at death
    FreeLibrary(hMouHookLib);                     // WEP & free DLL
    return ((int) msg.wParam);
    }
```

KILLERAP.DEF

```
NAME            KILLERAP

DESCRIPTION     'A stub program for the mouse hook DLL'

EXETYPE         WINDOWS

STUB            'WINSTUB.EXE'

CODE PRELOAD MOVEABLE DISCARDABLE
DATA PRELOAD MOVEABLE MULTIPLE

HEAPSIZE        1024
STACKSIZE       8192
```

MOUHOOK.C

```c
// Mouse hook example
//
// Mouse hook DLL that posts a WM_QUIT message to the application
// under the cursor when the right mouse button is pressed
//
// from Modifying Windows by Asael Dror
//
// Warning: see text for the possible side effects of this program!
//

#include <windows.h>
#include "mouhook.h"

HHOOK hHook;

                                            // DLL init
int __export WINAPI LibMain(HINSTANCE hInstance, WORD wDataSeg,
                    WORD cbHeapSize, LPSTR lpszCmdLine)

   {                                        // hook mouse messages
   hHook = SetWindowsHookEx(WH_MOUSE, (HOOKPROC)
           GetProcAddress(hInstance, "RButtonKill"),
                        hInstance, NULL);

   return (1);
```

CHAPTER 5
HOOKS

```c
  }
                                        // DLL termination
int __export WINAPI _WEP (int bSystemExit)
  {
  UnhookWindowsHookEx(hHook);           // unhook mouse msg

  return (1);
  }


                                        // kill app on right button down
LRESULT __export CALLBACK RButtonKill(
  int code,                             // action code
  WPARAM wParam,                        // message ID
  LPARAM lParam)                        // LPMOUSEHOOKSTRUCT
  {
  LPMOUSEHOOKSTRUCT ms;

                                        // if right mouse down
  if ((wParam == WM_RBUTTONDOWN) || (wParam == WM_NCRBUTTONDOWN))
    {
    MessageBeep(-1);                    // beep
    ms = (LPMOUSEHOOKSTRUCT) lParam;
    PostMessage(ms->hwnd, WM_QUIT, 0, 0);  // kill that window
    return (1);                         // discard message
    }

                                        // call next hook & return
  return (CallNextHookEx(hHook, code, wParam, lParam));
  }
```

MOUHOOK.H

```c
int __export WINAPI LibMain(HINSTANCE, WORD, WORD, LPSTR);
int __export WINAPI _WEP (int);
LRESULT __export CALLBACK RButtonKill(int, WPARAM, LPARAM);
```

MOUHOOK.DEF

```
LIBRARY         MOUHOOK

DESCRIPTION     'A mouse hook DLL'
```

```
EXETYPE             WINDOWS

STUB                'WINSTUB.EXE'

CODE PRELOAD MOVEABLE DISCARDABLE
DATA PRELOAD MOVEABLE SINGLE

HEAPSIZE            1024

EXPORTS
                    WEP @1 RESIDENTNAME
```

Message Transfer Hooks

As we know, messages can be transferred in two ways: they can be sent, or they can be posted. The *call window procedure hook* (WH_CALLWNDPROC) monitors sent messages, and the *get message hook* (WH_GETMESSAGE) monitors posted messages. Both hooks can have a task or system scope, and both can modify, but cannot discard, the received message.

Call Window Procedure Hook

This hook callback function is called whenever a window is about to receive a message sent to it via the SendMessage API. Since there are so many time-critical messages sent under Windows, this hook degrades overall system performance and is usually used in development and analysis tools rather than end user applications.

Call Window Procedure Hook

idHook == **WH_CALLWNDPROC**

nCode	Description
HC_ACTION	Process sent message
	wParam TRUE for an intra-task message (message sent from a task to itself); FALSE for inter-task message
	lParam LPCALLWNDPROCHOOKSTRUCT
	lResult 0

The definition of CALLWNDPROCHOOKSTRUCT does not exist in WINDOWS.H, but it should have been defined as:

```
WORDHI  lParam    // HIGH word of lParam
WORDLO  lParam    // LOW word of lParam
WPARAM  wParam
UINT    message
HWND    hWnd
```

Get Message Hook

This hook callback function is called when GetMessage or PeekMessage is about to return a message.

\[Get Message Hook — idHook == **WH_GETMESSAGE**\]	
nCode	**Description**

HC_ACTION	Process posted message
	    wParam NULL
	    lParam LPMSG
	    lResult 0

MSG, of course, is defined as:

```
HWND    hwnd
UINT    message
WPARAM  wParam
LPARAM  lParam
DWORD   time
POINT   pt
```

Message Filter Hooks

The message filter hook callback functions are called when a dialog box, message box, scroll bar, or menu retrieves a message or when the user presses ALT-TAB or ALT-ESC. There are two message filter hook types: *task message filter hook* (`idHook == WH_MSGFILTER`), which can have a task scope only; and *system message filter hook* (idHook == WH_SYSMSGFILTER), which can have a system scope only. If an event occurs that triggers both hook types, the WH_SYSMSGFILTER hook chain is called first, and only if it returns 0 is the WH_MSGFILTER hook chain called (it is called directly by Windows, not by the CallNextHookEx API, because this is a different hook type). Both hook types can modify as well as discard the message.

An application can also use the message filter hook mechanism for any message by calling the CallMsgFilter API. This is similar to what Windows does internally for dialog boxes, message boxes, scroll bars, menus, ALT-TAB, and ALT-ESC. If CallMsgFilter returns 0, your application should discard the message. To avoid conflicts with Windows nCodes, use an nCode of MSGF_USER or higher. (This, however, does not solve the problem of conflicting nCodes between applications that call CallMsgFilter and use the system message filter hook.)

CallMsgFilter

Call message filter hook

```
BOOL CallMsgFilter(lpmsg, nCode);

LPMSG lpmsg;     // far pointer to MSG structure
int nCode;       // action code >= MSGF_USER
```

Returns:
0 == process message, 1 == discard message

Task Message Filter Hook

This hook is called when a dialog box, message box, scroll bar, or menu retrieves a message or when the user presses ALT-TAB or ALT-ESC while the task being monitored is active. This hook has a task scope only!

> ### Task Message Filter Hook
>
> idHook ==**WH_MSGFILTER**
>
> ```
> wParam  NULL
> lParam  LPMSG
> lResult 0==process message, 1==discard message
> ```
>
> The `nCode` specifies who the message is for. Possible values are
>
> > MSGF_DIALOGBOX
> > MSGF_SCROLLBAR
> > MSGF_MENU
> > MSGF_NEXTWINDOW
>
> or any `nCode` an application specifies while calling CallMsgFilter

Note that message boxes are called with the MSGF_DIALOGBOX `nCode`.

System Message Filter Hook

This hook is called when a dialog box, message box, scroll bar, or menu retrieves a message or when the user presses ALT-TAB or ALT-ESC. This hook has a system scope only!

> ### System Message Filter Hook
>
> idHook==**WH_SYSMSGFILTER**
>
>   wParam   NULL
>   lParam   LPMSG
>   lResult 0==process message, 1==discard message
>
> The nCode specifies who the message is for. Possible values are
>
>   MSGF_DIALOGBOX
>   MSGF_SCROLLBAR
>   MSGFF_MENU
>   MSGF_NEXTWINDOW
>
> or any nCode an application specifies while calling CallMsgFilter.

Note that message boxes are called with the MSGF_DIALOGBOX nCode.

Journal Hooks

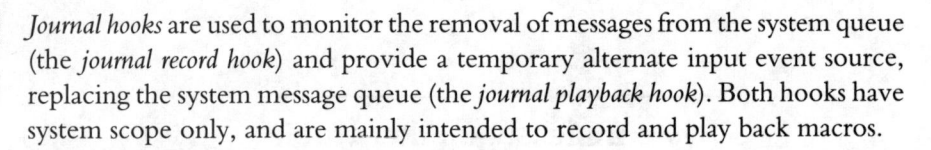

Journal hooks are used to monitor the removal of messages from the system queue (the *journal record hook*) and provide a temporary alternate input event source, replacing the system message queue (the *journal playback hook*). Both hooks have system scope only, and are mainly intended to record and play back macros.

Journal Record Hook

This hook callback function is called when an event is removed from the system queue. It is also informed when a system modal dialog box appears and when it is removed. While a system modal dialog box is up, the journal record hook is not called. When the system modal dialog box is removed, journal recording will continue. However, you may want to abort a record operation if a system modal dialog box appears while recording. The journal record hook cannot modify or discard the messages.

Journal Record Hook

idHook == WH_JOURNALRECORD

nCodes	Description

HC_ACTION	Record message event pointed to by lParam
	    wParam NULL
	    lParam LPEVENTMSG // *not* MSG
	    lResult 0

HC_SYSMODALON	Received when a system modal dialog box appears
	    wParam NULL
	    lParam NULL
	    lResult 0

HC_SYSMODALOFF	Received when a system modal dialog box is removed
	    wParam NULL
	    lParam NULL
	    lResult 0

EVENTMSG is defined as:

```
UINT   message
UINT   paramL
UINT   paramH
DWORD  time
```

Journal Playback Hook

When a journal playback hook is installed, Windows calls it to receive a message whenever a request is made to receive a message from the system message queue. This hook is used to simulate the insertion of a keyboard, mouse, or other input hardware message into the message stream. It is commonly used to play back events previously recorded by a journal record hook, but it can be used to simulate any user input messages.

When a journal playback hook is installed, user input from the input devices (keyboard, mouse, and other hardware via the hardware-event) is queued in the system queue. However, mouse move events are discarded.

If a system modal dialog box appears while a journal playback hook is installed, Windows temporarily disables the hook and receives input from the user. When the system modal dialog box is removed, the playback hook may continue. However, you may want to abort the playback, because a system modal dialog box usually indicates a serious error that probably makes the continuation of playback inappropriate.

Journal Playback Hook
idHook == WH_JOURNALPLAYBACK

nCode	Description

HC_GETNEXT	Return an event message into the structure pointed to by lParam
	    wParam NULL
	    lParam LPEVENTMSG (You may wish to update the time element of this structure.)
	    lResult Number of clock ticks Windows should wait before processing the event message

HC_SKIP	Advance to next event message
	    wParam NULL
	    lParam NULL
	    lResult 0

HC_SYSMODALON	Received when a system modal dialog box appears
	    wParam NULL
	    lParam NULL
	    lResult 0

Windows may call the hook callback function with a HC_GETNEXT nCode multiple times, and the callback function should continue to return the same event, until Windows instructs it to advance to the next event by a HC_SKIP nCode. Remember that if the callback function specifies a delay (lResult > 0), it should update the delay value on each subsequent call, or an infinite loop may result. Do not unhook the journal playback function as a result of this nCode; Windows may ask for the same message multiple times.

In contrast to HC_GETNEXT, the HC_SKIP nCode does not return an event. However, the HC_SKIP nCode may cause the callback function to reach the end of the playback, so you may unhook the journal playback hook in response to an HC_SKIP nCode.

JOURNAL HOOKS EXAMPLE

The following example uses the journal hooks to create a simple (and surprisingly useful) macro recorder controlled by the right mouse button. The first time you click the right mouse button, the recording process starts; the next right button click stops the recording; and a third right button click starts the playback. At the end of the playback, the cycle is restarted.

As in the previous example, a stub program—MOUMACRO.EXE—is used to load and initialize the DLL containing the hooks—JRNLHOOK.DLL. When the DLL is initialized, a journal record hook is installed.

The JRNLHOOK.DLL has a state machine with four possible states: three in the journal record callback function, and the fourth in the playback callback function.

The four states are:

- **M** Monitor state. Monitors events, looking for the "right mouse button up" message. When the right mouse button is released, the `RecIndex` is reset to zero and the state is switched to R.

- **R** Record state. Records input event messages with the exception of "right button down" messages. A "right button up" message indicates the end of recording and switches the state to L. If during recording the end of the tape is reached, the recording terminates, a beep is sounded, and the state is reset to M.

- **L** Loaded state. Waits for a "right mouse up" message, which indicates that playback should begin. When playback begins, the program resets the `PlayIndex` variable and installs the journal playback hook (the P state).

- **P** Playback state. Events are played back from the tape array. An HC_GETNEXT `nCode` causes an event message to be returned, while an HC_SKIP advances to the next element in the tape array. When the tape reaches the end of the recording, the journal playback hook is uninstalled and we go back to state M.

A few points to observe are that playback is performed at maximum speed, i.e., the program returns a delay of zero. The event messages time field is also modified to the current system tick count (even though this time does not seem to affect the way Windows processes the message).

If during recording or playback a WH_SYSMODALON `nCode` is received, the recording or playback is aborted with a beep, and the state is reset to M.

MODIFYING WINDOWS

Notice that, unlike the mouse hook example, this program only checks for the WM_LBUTTON* messages and not the WM_NCLBUTTON* messages. This is because the journal record hook is called with the generic mouse message, not with a message intended for a specific window.

Finally, note that since this simple macro recorder does not use a mouse hook, the right mouse button messages are passed to the application, and some applications may react to those messages.

MAKEFILE

```
all: jrnlhook.dll moumacro.exe

jrnlhook.obj: jrnlhook.c jrnlhook.h makefile
    cl -c -DSTRICT -AS -GD2 -Ox -W3 jrnlhook.c

jrnlhook.dll: jrnlhook.obj jrnlhook.def makefile
    link jrnlhook, jrnlhook.dll,, libw sdllcew, jrnlhook.def
    rc jrnlhook.dll

moumacro.obj: moumacro.c jrnlhook.h makefile
    cl -c -DSTRICT -AS -GA2 -Ox -W3 moumacro.c

moumacro.exe: moumacro.obj moumacro.def makefile
    link moumacro,,, libw slibcew, moumacro.def
    rc moumacro.exe
```

MOUMACRO.C

```c
// Journal hooks example
//
// This program is a stub whose only purpose
// is to load JRNLHOOK.DLL
//
// from Modifying Windows by Asael Dror
//

#include <windows.h>

HINSTANCE hMouHookLib;

int PASCAL WinMain(HINSTANCE hInstance, HINSTANCE hPrevInstance,
```

CHAPTER 5
HOOKS

```
                    LPSTR LPCmdLine, int nCmdShow)
{
MSG msg;

MessageBeep(-1);                                    // at birth
hMouHookLib = LoadLibrary("JRNLHOOK.DLL");          // load & init DLL

while (GetMessage(&msg, NULL, NULL, NULL))          // message loop
   DispatchMessage(&msg);

MessageBeep(-1);                                    // at death
FreeLibrary(hMouHookLib);                           // WEP & free DLL
return ((int) msg.wParam);
}
```

MOUMACRO.DEF

```
NAME            MOUMACRO

DESCRIPTION     'A stub program for the journal hook DLL'

EXETYPE         WINDOWS

STUB            'WINSTUB.EXE'

CODE PRELOAD MOVEABLE DISCARDABLE
DATA PRELOAD MOVEABLE MULTIPLE

HEAPSIZE        1024
STACKSIZE       8196
```

JRNLHOOK.C

```
// Journal hooks example
//
// A simple macro recorder operated by the right mouse button
//
// from Modifying Windows by Asael Dror
//

#include <windows.h>
#include "jrnlhook.h"
```

MODIFYING WINDOWS

```c
HINSTANCE hInst;
HHOOK hJrnlRecHook;
HHOOK hJrnlPlayHook;
char state = 'M';                          // init state is Monitor
EVENTMSG Tape[TapeSize];
int RecIndex;
int PlayIndex;

                                           // DLL init
int __export WINAPI LibMain(HINSTANCE hInstance, WORD wDataSeg,
                       WORD cbHeapSize, LPSTR lpszCmdLine)

  {                          // install journal record hook
  hJrnlRecHook = SetWindowsHookEx(WH_JOURNALRECORD, (HOOKPROC)
         GetProcAddress(hInstance, "JrnlRec"), hInstance, NULL);
  hInst = hInstance;
  return (1);
  }
                                           // DLL termination
int __export WINAPI _WEP (int bSystemExit)
  {
  UnhookWindowsHookEx(hJrnlRecHook);   // unhook journal rec

  return (1);
  }


                          // journal record callback hook
LRESULT __export CALLBACK JrnlRec(
  int code,                              // action code
  WPARAM wParam,                         // message ID
  LPARAM lParam)                         // LPEVENTMSG
  {
  LPEVENTMSG lpem;

  if ((code == HC_SYSMODALON) && (state == 'R'))     // abort rec
    {
    MessageBeep(-1);
    state = 'M';
    return (CallNextHookEx(hJrnlRecHook, code, wParam, lParam));
    }

  if (code != HC_ACTION)                 // no point to look at msg
     return (CallNextHookEx(hJrnlRecHook, code, wParam, lParam));

  lpem = (LPEVENTMSG) lParam;
  switch (state)
```

```
   {
   case ('M'):                                // monitor messages
      if (lpem->message == WM_RBUTTONUP)      // if RButton up
         {
         state = 'R';                                 // start recording
         RecIndex = 0;                        // rec from start of tape
         }
      break;

   case ('R'):                                // recording
      if (lpem->message == WM_RBUTTONDOWN) break;
      if (lpem->message == WM_RBUTTONUP)      // if RButton up
         {
         state = 'L';                                 // stop recording
         }
      else
         {
         Tape[RecIndex] = *lpem;              // record event msg
         if (++RecIndex >= TapeSize)          // if end of tape
            {
            state = 'M';                              // reset to M state
            }
         }
      break;

   case ('L'):                                // monitor messages
      if (lpem->message == WM_RBUTTONUP)      // if RButton up
         {
         state = 'P';                                 // start playback
         hJrnlPlayHook = SetWindowsHookEx(WH_JOURNALPLAYBACK,
            (HOOKPROC) GetProcAddress(hInst, "JrnlPlay"), hInst, NULL);
         PlayIndex = 0;                       // play from start of tape
         }
      break;

   }

   return (CallNextHookEx(hJrnlRecHook, code, wParam, lParam));
   }

LRESULT __export CALLBACK JrnlPlay(          // hook playback function
   int code,                                 // action code
   WPARAM wParam,                            // NULL
   LPARAM lParam)                            // LPEVENTMSG
   {
   LPEVENTMSG lpem;

   switch (code)
```

MODIFYING WINDOWS

```
    {
    case HC_SKIP:                            // advance to next event
      if (++PlayIndex >= RecIndex)           // if end of recording
         {
         state = 'M';
         UnhookWindowsHookEx(hJrnlPlayHook);            // unhook
         }
      break;

    case HC_GETNEXT:                         // get event
    lpem = (LPEVENTMSG) lParam;
      *lpem = Tape[PlayIndex];
      lpem->time = GetTickCount();           // update event time to now
      break;

    case HC_SYSMODALON:                      // if sys modal - abort
      MessageBeep(-1);
      state = 'M';
      UnhookWindowsHookEx(hJrnlPlayHook);            // unhook
      break;

    }
  return (0);                                // playback at max speed
  }
```

JRNLHOOK.H

```
int __export WINAPI LibMain(HINSTANCE, WORD, WORD, LPSTR);
int __export WINAPI _WEP (int);
LRESULT __export CALLBACK JrnlRec(int, WPARAM, LPARAM);
LRESULT __export CALLBACK JrnlPlay(int, WPARAM, LPARAM);


#define TapeSize 500
```

JRNLHOOK.DEF

```
LIBRARY          JRNLHOOK
```

```
DESCRIPTION        'A journal hook DLL'

EXETYPE            WINDOWS

STUB               'WINSTUB.EXE'

CODE PRELOAD MOVEABLE DISCARDABLE
DATA PRELOAD MOVEABLE SINGLE

HEAPSIZE           1024

EXPORT
                   WEP @1 RESIDENTNAME
```

Computer-Based Training (CBT)

Computer-based training is an application that teaches the user how to use another application. Thus, there are two applications running concurrently, and the teaching application needs to monitor and have control over how the user interacts with the target application. For this reason, the *CBT hook* gives extensive control over the running environment. The CBT hook is so versatile that it can be used to create utilities that have nothing to do with computer-based training. It can have a task or system scope and can modify as well as prevent events from occurring.

Since a CBT application may use journal playback hooks to emulate user input, a mechanism is needed for the CBT hook to differentiate between real user input and journal playback emulated input. One way to do this is by posting a WM_QUERYSYNC message. The WM_QUERYSYNC message is unique in that it is a non-input event message that goes into the *system* message queue and so can be used as an indicator that input is coming from the queue rather than the journal playback hook. When Windows removes the WM_QUERYSYNC message from the system queue, it will call the CBT hook with a HCBT_QS nCode.

Computer-Based Training Hook

idHook == **WH_CBT**

nCode	Description

HCBT_ACTIVATE	A window is about to become active.
	    wParam hWindow of window to be activated
	    lParam LPCBTACTIVATESTRUCT
	    lResult
	    0 == window will be activated,
	    1 == window will not be activated

HCBT_CREATEWND	A window is about to be created.
	    wParam hWindow of window being created
	    lParam LPCBT_CREATEWND
	    lResult
	    0 == window will be created,
	    1 == window will not be created

HCBT_DESTROYWND	A window is about to be destroyed.
	    wParam hWindow of window to be destroyed
	    lParam 0
	    lResult
	    0 == window will be destroyed,
	    1 == window will not be destroyed

HCBT_MINMAX	A window is about to be minimized or maximized.
	    wParam
	     hWindow of window being minimized or maximized
	    lParam
	    HIWORD == 0,
	    LOWORD == SW_*
	    indicating operation
	    lResult
	    0 == window will be minimized or maximized,
	    1 == window will not be minimized or maximized

HCBT_MOVESIZE	A window is about to be moved or sized.
	    wParam hWindow being moved or sized
	    lParam
	    LPRECT of new window's position and size
	    lResult
	    0 == window will be moved or sized,
	    1 == window will not be moved or sized

CHAPTER 5
HOOKS

HCBT_SYSCOMMAND	A window received a system command. wParam System command ID, i.e., SC_* lParam If wParam == SC_HOTKEY, then LOWORD of lParam is the hWindow of the window that will be made active. Or, if the system command was selected with the mouse, then lParam is the x,y of the cursor coordinates when the command was selected. In any other case, lParam is undefined. lResult 0 == system command is processed, 1 == system command discarded
HCBT_CLICKSKIPPED	A mouse message is removed from the system queue and there is an active mouse hook. wParam Message ID lParam LPMOUSEHOOKSTRUCT lResult 0
HCBT_KEYSKIPPED	A keyboard message is removed from the system queue and there is an active keyboard hook. wParam Virtual key code lParam Same as for a WM_KEYDOWN message lResult 0
HCBT_QS	A WM_QUERYSYNC message is removed from the system queue. wParam NULL lParam NULL lResult 0
HCBT_SETFOCUS	Windows is about to set the focus. wParam hWindow to receive the focus lParam LOWORD == hWindow that loses focus, HIWORD == NULL lResult 0 == set focus, 1 == do not set focus

CBTACTIVATESTRUCT is defined as:

```
BOOLfMouse        // TRUE if window activated due to a mouse
                  // click,otherwise FALSE
HWND hWndActive   // current active window
```

MODIFYING WINDOWS

LPCBT_CREATEWND is defined as:

```
CREATESTRUCT FAR* lpcs    // initialization parameters that
                          // will be passed to window procedure
                          // via WM_CREATE and WM_NCCREATE messages
// HWND hwndInsertAfter   // z order, 0 == top-most,
                          // 1 == bottom-most
```

RECT is the old familiar:

```
int left
int top
int right
int bottom
```

See the mouse hook section for the definition of MOUHOOKSTRUCT. See the keyboard hook for the possible lParam values for the HCBT_KEYSKIPPED nCode.

The CBT callback function is called with the HCBT_CREATEWND nCode, after the window is created but before it receives a WM_NCCREATE or a WM_CREATE message. Thus, while the callback function can send messages to the window, you must remember that the window's initialization process might not have completed. Similarly, the CBT callback function is called with the HCBT_DESTROYWND nCode before the window receives the WM_DESTROY message. Thus, the callback function can send messages to the window, but you need to remember that termination might have begun.

Note that the CBT callback function is called with HCBT_CLICKSKIPPED and HCBT_KEYSKIPPED nCodes regardless of whether the mouse/keyboard hook callback function discarded the message or not. The nCode names are misleading.

Shell Hook

The *shell hook* allows a shell (or any program) to be notified when a top-level unowned window is being created or destroyed. The shell hook has a system scope only and cannot modify or discard events.

CHAPTER 5
HOOKS

Shell Hook

`idHook == WH_SHELL`

nCode	Description

HSHELL_WINDOWCREATED	A top-level unowned window was created.
	    `wParam` `hWindow` of created top-level unowned window
	    `lParam` NULL
	    `lResult` 0

HSHELL_WINDOWDESTROYED	A top-level unowned window is about to be destroyed.
	    `wParam`
	    `hWindow` of top-level unowned window to be destroyed
	    `lParam` NULL
	    `lResult` 0

HSHELL_ACTIVATESHELLWINDOW	A top-level unowned window that was the active window was destroyed—the shell program should make its window active.
	    `wParam` NULL
	    `lParam` NULL
	    `lResult` 0

Debug Hook

Since hook callback functions are called asynchronously, debugging them can be great fun. Also, a debugger, even if not used to debug the actual hook callback function, must be able to intercept any hook callback function installed by the debuggee. To this end, the *debug hook* exists. The debug hook callback function is called before any hook callback function (except WH_DEBUG) is called and can modify the parameters passed to the callback function or prevent the callback function from being called. The debug hook can have a system scope only!

MODIFYING WINDOWS

Debug Hook
idHook == WH_DEBUG

nCode	Description

HC_ACTION	A hook callback function is about to be called.
	    wParam hTask of hook callback function installer
	    lParam LPDEBUGHOOKINFO
	    lResult 0 == call the hook, 1 == do not call it

DEBUGHOOKINFO is defined as:

```
HMODULE   hModuleHook
LPARAM    reserved
LPARAM    lParam
WPARAM    wParam
int       code                    // nCode
```

Chapter 6

Installable Device Drivers:
Conventional and
Unconventional Uses

WHEN we modify Windows itself, using techniques such as subclassing or hooks, we usually have to use DLLs rather than EXEs for the modifications. This is because the modified code is used by multiple tasks, as we discussed in Chapter 2. How do we load such DLLs? Until now we have used stub EXE programs for this purpose. The stub simply loads the DLL and then spins forever in its message loop. To have the DLL load when Windows starts, we used the WIN.INI `load` command to cause the stub to be executed when Windows is started (or we simply put the stub program in the Windows startup program group).

Although this solution works, it is neither elegant nor efficient. Creating a task that performs no useful function (except to keep the DLL's use-count at one) is a waste of system resources. In this chapter, we'll introduce a better way to load such a DLL. This technique is based on an unconventional use of *Installable Device Drivers*. Before we can discuss the technique, we need to discuss the conventional uses of installable device drivers, and before we do that, let's take a quick look at Device Drivers in general.

Device Drivers: An Overview

Device drivers are the lowest level of software interface to the hardware. Device drivers translate device-independent I/O requests, such as "draw a pixel on the screen," to a physical action on the specific hardware. Thus, device drivers shield the application (and even the operating system) from the details of the underlying hardware, making the software device independent and portable across multiple hardware platforms.

Since device drivers interact with the hardware at the lowest level (i.e., physical memory, I/O, DMAs, and interrupts), it is common for device drivers to be considered an extension of the operating system and to run at the most privileged protection level. This low-level capability makes device drivers of interest to anyone interested in serious system-level work, whether there is hardware involved or not.

In Windows 3.x, there are two very different types of device drivers. One type is simply called a *device driver,* and the other type is called a *virtual device driver* (or a *VxD*).

Device Drivers

Under Windows 3.x, only two protection rings (of the four supported by the 80386 hardware) are utilized. All applications, DLLs, and even Windows itself run in the least privileged protection ring possible: ring 3 (ring 1 in Windows 3.0). Only the enhanced-mode layer of Windows (including the virtual device drivers) runs in ring 0 most privileged.

Windows device drivers also run in ring 3; thus, they have no special privileges (they are not running at CPL<=IOPL). If you are unfamiliar with the 80x86 protection mechanism and would like to know all about it, I strongly recommend the book *80x86 Architecture & Programming* by Rakesh Agarwal (Prentice Hall, 1991). Contrary to popular belief, any Windows application *can* perform I/O instructions just like a device driver.

Windows device drivers are implemented as dynamic link libraries so that they can provide services to multiple application programs (as well as to Windows itself). Moreover, using a DLL rather than accessing the hardware directly from within the application helps keep the application device independent. For more on the reasons to use DLLs rather than an EXE for manipulating the hardware, see Chapter 2.

In order to communicate with the hardware, a device driver may access physical memory, I/O ports, and hook interrupts. Interrupt handling code must be reentrant (i.e., it may be called a subsequent time with another interrupt before it is finished handling the previous interrupt) and fixed in memory (page-locked in enhanced mode) along with any data accessed at interrupt time. Furthermore, since Windows is non-reentrant, an interrupt routine may not call any Windows application or issue any non-reentrant Windows APIs. This is because the interrupt routine may have been called while the API was executing. Calling the API again from the interrupt requires that the API be reentrant, and that's not the case. Fortunately, there are a few reentrant APIs in Windows 3.x (mostly newer APIs written as part of the multimedia support). The reentrant API are PostMessage, PostAppMessage, OutputDebugStr, DriverCallback, timeGetSystemTime, timeGetTime, timeSetEvent, timeKillEvent, midiOutShortMsg, and midiOutLongMsg.

Windows 3.*x* device drivers can be subdivided into two groups: *standard device drivers* and *installable device drivers*.

STANDARD DEVICE DRIVERS

Windows includes a collection of required drivers for such hardware as the display, keyboard, mouse, serial port, etc. Most of these drivers contain tenths of thousands lines of code written mainly in assembly language.

INSTALLABLE DEVICE DRIVERS

Windows 3.1 has added support for a new kind of device driver, known as an *installable device driver*. Installable device drivers are drivers for handling non-standard hardware devices (i.e., not the display, keyboard, mouse, etc.).

If you develop a new hardware device, you need to create a device driver to support it. While it is possible to simply write a DLL that will act as a device driver, Windows 3.1 supports a standard mechanism for adding your own device driver to the system: an installable device driver. Furthermore, Windows 3.1 defines a protocol for communications between Windows, the installable device driver, and the applications that request services from the device. While most existing installable device drivers are used for multimedia devices, such a driver can be used for any device. In this chapter, we will first examine installable device drivers in detail. Later, we'll return to the question of how to use installable device drivers to install DLLs.

Virtual Device Drivers

When running in 386 Enhanced mode, Windows runs multiple virtual machines (VMs) concurrently (the Windows VM and any DOS VMs). What happens if multiple VMs try to write to a device, such as the printer, at the same time? Virtual device drivers were originally designed to solve such problems. Using the 386 features that allow I/O and memory accesses to be trapped, virtual device drivers can *virtualize* devices. By virtualizing the devices, the device driver gives the software (mainly device drivers) the illusion that it has the device all to itself, while in reality it is communicating with a virtual device driver. The virtual device driver emulates the hardware on one hand, and communicates with the actual hardware on the other hand.

VxDs are 32-bit programs that run in protection ring 0 on a flat address space. Consequently, they are very powerful and can do much more than simply virtualize devices.

CHAPTER 6
INSTALLABLE DEVICE DRIVERS: CONVENTIONAL AND UNCONVENTIONAL USES

Because Windows device drivers are not IOPL, there is a large overhead associated with performing I/O and receiving interrupts via a device driver. Consequently, device drivers can use a companion VxD to perform I/O and handle interrupts on their behalf. This is especially important for devices that require lots of I/O or a short interrupt latency.

The Device Driver Kit

While it is possible to write a device driver for your own custom hardware without the Device Driver Kit (DDK), I would not attempt it for a standard device driver (such as the display, keyboard, mouse, etc.) or for a VxD. Among other goodies, included in the DDK are tools needed to create VxDs (such as a special version of MASM and LINK, as well as the debugging version of WIN386—see Chapter 3 for a discussion of the kernel debugger, an essential tool for debugging device drivers and VxDs), tools for creating printer device drivers, and test software for verifying that a display or printer device driver works correctly. But the real treasure is the collection of drivers, both device drivers and virtual device drivers, for which the DDK contains the source code. This source code is essential if you want to tweak an existing driver, and even more important, it's the best documentation on how to write (and how not to write) a device driver. The only warning you should bear in mind is that, although it may be easy to tweak an existing driver to support new hardware, many of the DDK drivers are not well written (they were written many years ago and have gone through endless hacking). So if you want a really good driver, it might be better to start from scratch (after you carefully examine the existing driver to figure out what should be done, but not necessarily how it should be done).

Installable Device Drivers

Being new, the documentation for installable device drivers is scattered, incomplete, and often just wrong. For this reason, we will not only present the structural overview, but also provide a complete reference to all the fine details required to develop installable device drivers.

An installable device driver is a DLL that (usually) controls a hardware device. Every installable device driver must contain an exported callback routine named DriverProc. The DriverProc routine receives notification messages from Windows and applications that utilize the driver, in a manner somewhat similar to the way a window procedure receives messages.

DriverProc

Installable device driver callback procedure

```
LRESULT CALLBACK DriverProc(dwDrvID, hDrv, msg,
                            lParam1, lParam2);

DWORD   dwDrvID;    // driver ID
HDRVR   hDrv;       // driver handle
UINT    msg;        // message ID
LPARAM  lParam1;    // parameter 1 - msg specific
LPARAM  lParam2;    // parameter 2 - msg specific
```

Returns:
Message-specific value, but generally TRUE (or a non-zero message-specific value) if successful and FALSE if failed.

The installable device driver should call the DefDriverProc API to perform default processing of messages it does not handle itself. (This is similar to the way a window procedure can call the DefWindowProc API.)

DefDriverProc

Perform default message processing for an installable device driver

```
LRESULT WINAPI DefDriverProc(dwDrvID, hDrv, msg,
                             lParam1, lParam2);

DWORD   dwDrvID;    // driver ID
HDRVR   hDrv;       // driver handle
UINT    msg;        // message ID
LPARAM  lParam1;    // parameter 1 - msg specific
LPARAM  lParam2;    // parameter 2 - msg specific
```

Returns:
Message-specific value, but it usually returns TRUE. See specific messages later in this chapter for details.

Let's first examine how an application communicates with an installable device driver. Later we'll take a detailed look at the messages the driver can receive.

APIs for Communicating with an Installable Device Driver

Before an application can utilize an installable device driver, it must open the driver with the OpenDriver API.

OpenDriver

Open an installable device driver

```
HDRVR WINAPI OpenDriver(szDriverName, szSectionName,
                        lParam2);

LPCSTR szDriverName;     // driver filename, or entry in
                         // SYSTEM.INI
LPCSTR szSectionName;    // section name in SYSTEM.INI
                         // where DriverName appears,
                         // or NULL for [drivers]
LPARAM lParam2;          // driver-specific parameter
                         // (passed to the driver as
                         // lParam2 in the DRV_OPEN
                         // message)
```

Returns:
If successful, hDrv; otherwise FALSE.

The OpenDriver API opens a new instance of the specified installable device driver. The driver is either specified by its filename or by a section and entry name in SYSTEM.INI. The first time a driver is opened, Windows loads the driver's DLL and sends it the DRV_LOAD, DRV_ENABLE, and DRV_OPEN messages (in that order). The driver's use-count is set to one. Subsequent OpenDriver calls to the same driver increase the driver's use-count, and Windows sends the driver only the DRV_OPEN message.

When an application has no further need for the driver, it should close it by calling the CloseDriver API.

CloseDriver

Close an installable device driver

```
LRESULT WINAPI CloseDriver (hDrv, lParam1, lParam2);

HDRVR  hDrv;        // driver handle
LPARAM lParam1;     // driver-specific parameter,
                    // passed in DRV_CLOSE message
LPARAM lParam2;     // driver-specific parameter,
                    // passed in DRV_CLOSE message
```

Returns:
If successful, TRUE; otherwise FALSE.

CloseDriver closes an instance of the specified driver by sending it a DRV_CLOSE message and decreasing its use-count. When the use-count reaches zero, the driver is sent DRV_DISABLE and DRV_FREE messages and is then freed from memory.

Once a driver is open, an application can communicate with it by sending messages using the SendDriverMessage API.

SendDriverMessage

Send a message to an installable device driver

```
LRESULT WINAPI SendDriverMessage(hDrv, msg, lParam1,
                                 lParam2);

HDRVR  hDrv;        // driver handle
UINT   msg;         // message ID
LPARAM lParam1;     // message-specific parameter
LPARAM lParam2;     // message-specific parameter
```

Returns:
The convention is to return a non-zero message-specific value for success and FALSE for failure.

Installable Device-Driver Messages

Let's look at the messages an installable device driver may receive. There are three ranges of `msg` values:

- `msg < DRV_RESERVED`   Globally defined messages used by all installable device drivers
- `msg >= DRV_RESERVED` to `msg <= DRV_USER`   Defined driver protocols, such as the media-control interface (MCI) driver protocol
- `msg > DRV_USER`   Driver-specific messages

We'll examine only the globally defined messages, and not get into specific protocols and drivers. Some of these globally defined messages are sent by the Windows installable device driver interface, while others are sent by a driver installation program such as the Control Panel Drivers application.

Messages Sent by Windows to Installable Device Drivers

The first message sent to the driver after it is being loaded is the DRV_LOAD message. (Actually, there is an undocumented message (`msg` ID = 0) that is sent before the DRV_LOAD message.)

When receiving DRV_LOAD, a driver will typically read its configuration settings from SYSTEM.INI and perform any needed one-time initialization of its data structures.

Load driver
msg: DRV_LOAD

```
lParam1  0

lParam2  0
```

Returns:
If successful, TRUE; otherwise FALSE. (If DRV_LOAD fails, Windows will unload the driver without sending it a DRV_FREE message.)

DefDriverProc returns TRUE.

MODIFYING WINDOWS

Windows sends the driver a DRV_ENABLE message after the driver's initial loading (and the sending of DRV_LOAD), and whenever returning to Windows from a DOS session in standard mode (see the DRV_DISABLE message for more details). When a driver receives this message, it normally sets up the hardware and hooks interrupts.

Enable driver

msg: DRV_ENABLE

lParam1   0

lParam2   0

Returns:
Value ignored.

The DRV_OPEN message is sent by Windows when a new instance of the driver is being opened due to an OpenDriver call. This may be either for the initial instance or for subsequent instances of the same driver. When receiving this message, the driver can allocate and initialize any required instance data.

Open driver instance

msg: DRV_OPEN

lParam1   Points to an ASCII string containing parameters found after the device driver's filename in SYSTEM.INI (NULL if none)

lParam2   lParam2 from OpenDriver API

Returns:
If successful, dwDrvID; otherwise FALSE.

DefDriverProc returns FALSE (DRV_OPEN failed!).

If DRV_OPEN is successful, it should return a value that the driver can use to identify the new instance — dwDrvID. This value is determined by the driver and may or may not be unique for the particular instance. The Windows installable driver interface stores this number internally and returns a unique hDrv to the application. Whenever an application sends a message to the driver, Windows supplies the driver with the dwDrvID (in addition to the hDrv). Thus, at the application level, each driver instance has a unique handle, but the driver has another mechanism (the dwDrvID) to identify itself. This ID is determined by the driver itself and need not be unique for each instance.

The following messages do not pass a dwDrvID to the DriverProc (dwDrvID is set to zero, except for the DRV_OPEN message, where it is set to the hDrv): DRV_LOAD, DRV_ENABLE, DRV_OPEN, DRV_DISABLE and DRV_FREE.

Note that DefDriverProc returns FALSE. Consequently, an installable device driver must handle the DRV_OPEN message or the OpenDriver call will fail.

When an instance of the driver is being closed as a result of a CloseDriver call, Windows sends the driver a DRV_CLOSE message. Closing the driver also decreases its use-count. When the use-count reaches zero, Windows frees the driver (after sending it DRV_DISABLE and DRV_FREE messages).

Drivers commonly use the DRV_CLOSE notification to free any instance-specific data structures.

Close driver instance

msg: DRV_CLOSE

lParam1   lParam1 from CloseDriver

lParam2   lParam2 from CloseDriver

Returns:
If successful, TRUE else FALSE.

DefDriverProc returns FALSE (DRV_CLOSE failed!)

As with DRV_OPEN, an installable device driver must handle the DRV_CLOSE message or the CloseDriver call will fail (in which case the driver instance will remain active, and the use-count will not be decreased).

A DRV_DISABLE message is sent by Windows when the driver is about to be freed, or when entering a DOS session in Windows Standard mode. In Standard mode (unlike in 386 Enhanced mode), Windows does not run the DOS session in parallel with the Windows session, but rather swaps between

MODIFYING WINDOWS

the two sessions. Consequently, when the Windows session is about to be swapped out, the device driver must unhook any interrupts and reset the hardware. When a DOS session exits, Windows will send the driver a DRV_ENABLE message, which allows the driver to set the hardware and re-hook interrupts. Note that in the interval between receiving the DRV_DISABLE message and the DRV_ENABLE message, the driver cannot assume that any part of itself resides in memory.

In some cases, the driver may receive a DRV_DISABLE message while driving the hardware, for example while playing a tune on a sound card. In such a case, the driver should pause the action, and continue it after receiving a DRV_ENABLE message.

Disable driver

msg DRV_DISABLE

```
lParam1   0

lParam2   0
```

Returns:
Value ignored.

The last message Windows sends to a driver before the driver is discarded is DRV_FREE. The driver can use this message to perform any final clean-up required.

Free driver

msg: DRV_FREE

```
lParam1   0

lParam2   0
```

Returns:
Value ignored.

Whenever an application exits, Windows sends a DRV_EXITAPPLICATION to all open installable device drivers.

Application exit

msg: DRV_EXITAPPLICATION

lParam1   Type of exit; possible values are

- DRVEA_NORMALEXIT
- DRVEA_ABNORMALEXIT

lParam2   0

Returns:
Value ignored.

When Windows is about to terminate, it sends a DRV_EXITSESSION to all open installable device drivers. The message is received before the installable device drivers are disabled, and while the Windows environment is still active.

Windows session terminates

msg: DRV_EXITSESSION

lParam1   0

lParam2   0

Returns:
Value ignored.

In systems that conform to the Advance Power Management (APM) specifications, device drivers receive a DRV_POWER message when the system is about to enter or exit suspended mode.

> ### Power management notification
> #### msg: DRV_POWER
>
> `lParam1` Event description; possible values are
>
> - PWR_SUSPENDREQUEST   The system is about to enter suspended mode.
>
> - PWR_SUSPENDRESUME   The system is about to resume operation after being in suspended mode.
>
> - PWR_CRITICALRESUME   The system is about to resume operation after being in suspended mode. Suspended mode was entered without first sending a PWR_SUSPENDREQUEST message to the driver.
>
> `lParam2` 0
>
> Returns:
> For PWR_SUSPENDRESUME and PWR_CRITICALRESUME, the return value is ignored. For PWR_SUSPENDREQUEST, possible return values are
>
> - PWR_OK   OK to enter suspended mode
>
> - PWR_FAIL   Do not enter suspended mode

Driver Installation Messages

The following messages are typically sent to a driver by a driver installation program, such as the Windows Control Panel Drivers application. Since these messages are not sent by Windows itself, but rather by an application, the parameters and return values may vary somewhat from one installation program

CHAPTER 6
INSTALLABLE DEVICE DRIVERS: CONVENTIONAL AND UNCONVENTIONAL USES

to another. Consequently, your program should verify the parameters (making sure a pointer is valid, for example) before using them.

When the driver is being installed (added to the list of installed drivers—in the case of the Control Panel that would be in the [drivers] section of SYSTEM.INI), it is sent the DRV_INSTALL message. Typically, a driver would configure itself and update SYSTEM.INI when receiving this message.

Install device driver

msg: DRV_INSTALL

lParam1   0

lParam2   Optional configuration information. The Control Panel Drivers program passes a pointer to a DRVCONFIGINGO structure.

Returns:
Possible values are

- DRVCNF_OK   Installation OK.
- DRVCNF_CANCEL   Installation failed. The Control Panel Drivers installation program seems to treat this the same as a DRVCNF_OK.
- DRVCNF_RESTART   Installation will take effect after Windows is restarted.

The driver configuration information structure DRVCONFIGINGO is defined as:

```
typedef struct tagDRVCONFIGINFO
{
    DWORD   dwDCISize;              // size of structure
    LPCSTR  lpszDCISectionName;     // section name
    LPCSTR  lpszDCIAliasName;       // entry name
} DRVCONFIGINFO;
```

The DRV_QUERYCONFIGURE message is used by a driver installation program to determine if a driver is user-configurable. The driver installation program will typically enable the "configure" or "setup" button for drivers that return TRUE for this message.

Query if driver is user-configurable

msg: DRV_QUERYCONFIGURE

`lParam1`   Not used by Control Panel

`lParam2`   Not used by Control Panel

Returns:
TRUE if the driver supports user configuration, FALSE if the driver does not.

DefDriverProc returns FALSE

Some drivers support user configuration of the driver. Such configuration is controlled by a dialog box that the driver displays when it receives the DRV_CONFIGURE message. The DRV_QUERYCONFIGURE message should be used to check whether a driver supports user configuration. Only drivers that support user configuration should be sent the DRV_CONFIGURE message.

Typically, a driver installation program will send the DRV_CONFIGURE message to the driver after its initial installation, and whenever the user requests to reconfigure the driver.

A driver may use the configuration dialog box to set such options as port addresses and interrupt levels. Such information should be stored in SYSTEM.INI under a section that has the driver's name. Non-user-controlled configuration, which the driver performs automatically, should be performed in response to the DRV_INSTALL message rather than DRV_CONFIGURE.

CHAPTER 6
INSTALLABLE DEVICE DRIVERS: CONVENTIONAL AND UNCONVENTIONAL USES

Manually configure a driver

msg: DRV_CONFIG

lParam1   LOWORD(lParam1) == hWindows of parent for the configuration dialog box.

lParam2   Optional configuration information. The Control Panel Drivers program passes a pointer to a DRVCONFIGINFO structure.

Returns:
Possible values are

- ◆ DRVCNF_OK   Configuration OK.
- ◆ DRVCNF_CANCEL   Configuration failed. The Control Panel Drivers configuration program seems to treat this the same as a DRVCNF_OK.
- ◆ DRVCNF_RESTART   Configuration will take effect after Windows is restarted.

Finally, when a driver is being removed from the list of installed drivers, it is sent the DRV_REMOVE message. When receiving this message, the driver should remove any information it stored in SYSTEM.INI.

Remove (uninstall) a driver

msg: DRV_REMOVE

lParam1   0

lParam2   0

Returns:
Possible values are DRVCNF_OK, DRVCNF_CANCEL, and DRVCNF_RESTART. The Control Panel seems to treat all return values as DRVCNF_RESTART.

MODIFYING WINDOWS

INSTALLABLE DEVICE DRIVER SKELETON

The following listing is for a skeleton installable device driver and a sample program that uses the driver. Note that unlike most DLLs, an installable device driver must have an exported WEP or Windows will refuse to load it. Finally, giving the driver a DRV suffix (rather than DLL) is for convention only, and is not a requirement.

MAKEFILE

```
all: instdrv.drv usedrv.exe

instdrv.obj: instdrv.c instdrv.h makefile
    cl -c -DSTRICT -AS -GD2 -Ox -W3 instdrv.c

instdrv.drv: instdrv.obj instdrv.def makefile
    link instdrv, instdrv.drv, , libw sdllcew, instdrv.def
    rc instdrv.drv

usedrv.res: usedrv.rc usedrv.h instdrv.h makefile
    rc -r usedrv.rc

usedrv.obj: usedrv.c usedrv.h instdrv.h makefile
    cl -c -DSTRICT -AS -GA2 -Ox -W3 usedrv.c

usedrv.exe: usedrv.obj usedrv.def usedrv.res makefile
    link usedrv,,, libw slibcew, usedrv.def
    rc usedrv.res
```

USEDRV.C

```
//
// Use an installable device driver example
//
// from Modifying Windows by Asael Dror
//

#include <windows.h>
#include "usedrv.h"
#include "instdrv.h"
```

CHAPTER 6
INSTALLABLE DEVICE DRIVERS: CONVENTIONAL AND UNCONVENTIONAL USES

```c
HINSTANCE hInst;                                // current instance
HDRVR hDrv = NULL;                              // indicate drv closed

                                                // application E.P.
int PASCAL WinMain(HINSTANCE hInstance, HINSTANCE hPrevInstance,
            LPSTR LPCmdLine, int nCmdShow)

  {
  MSG msg;

  if (!hPrevInstance)                           // if first inst
    if (!InitApplication(hInstance))            // then init app
      return(FALSE);

  if (!InitInstance(hInstance, nCmdShow))       // init instance
    return(FALSE);

                                                // msg loop
  while (GetMessage(&msg, NULL, 0, 0))          // get any msg/any wnd
    {
    TranslateMessage(&msg);                     // xlate virt keys
    DispatchMessage(&msg);                      // dispatch message
    }
  return(msg.wParam);
  }

BOOL InitApplication(HINSTANCE hInstance)       // init application
  {
                                                // reg main wnd class
  WNDCLASS wc;

                                                // fill wnd class str
  wc.style = NULL;
  wc.lpfnWndProc = MainWndProc;                 // window proc
  wc.cbClsExtra = 0;
  wc.cbWndExtra = 0;
  wc.hInstance = hInstance;                     // class owner
  wc.hIcon = LoadIcon(NULL, IDI_APPLICATION);   // def app icon
  wc.hCursor = LoadCursor(NULL, IDC_ARROW);     // standard cursor
  wc.hbrBackground = (HBRUSH)(COLOR_WINDOW + 1); // window bkg clr
  wc.lpszMenuName = "MainMenu";
  wc.lpszClassName = "UseDrvClass";             // wnd class name

  return(RegisterClass(&wc));                   // reg wnd class
  }

                                                // instance init
BOOL InitInstance(HINSTANCE hInstance, int nCmdShow)
```

```
{
HWND   hWnd;                                          // main wnd handle

hInst = hInstance;                                    // save it

hWnd = CreateWindow (                                 // main window
        "UseDrvClass",                                // class name
        "Use InstDrv",                                // title bar text
        WS_OVERLAPPEDWINDOW | WS_VISIBLE,             // "normal" & vsbl
        CW_USEDEFAULT,                                // default x
        nCmdShow,                                     // default y,
                                                      // show as req
        CW_USEDEFAULT,                                // default width
        CW_USEDEFAULT,                                // default height
        HWND_DESKTOP,                                 // no parent
        NULL,                                         // use class menu
        hInstance,                                    // inst of mod win
        NULL);                                        // not used
if (!hWnd) return(FALSE);
UpdateWindow(hWnd);                                   // snd WM_PAINT
return (TRUE);                                        // OK
}

LRESULT __export CALLBACK MainWndProc(
                         HWND hWnd,                   // window handle
                         UINT message,                // message
                         WPARAM wParam,               // param
                         LPARAM lParam)               // param
{
switch (message)
    {
    case WM_DESTROY:
        if (hDrv)                                     // if drv open
            {
            CloseDriver(hDrv, 0, 0);                  // close drv
            hDrv = NULL;                              // indc drv closed
            }

        PostQuitMessage(0);                           // bye bye, rc = 0
        return(0);
        break;

    case WM_COMMAND:
        switch (wParam)
            {
            case IDM_OPEN:                            // open inst drv
                if (!hDrv) hDrv=OpenDriver(InstDrvName, NULL, NULL);
                break;
```

```c
            case IDM_CLOSE:                          // close inst drv
               if (hDrv)
                  {
                  CloseDriver(hDrv, 0, 0);
                  hDrv = NULL;                       // ind drv closed
                  }
               break;

            case IDM_BEEP:                           // sound a beep
               if (hDrv)
                  SendDriverMessage(hDrv, DRV_WDL_BEEP,
                                    DURATION_CNT, FREQ_CNT);
               break;

            default:
              return(DefWindowProc(hWnd, message, wParam, lParam));
            }
         return(0);
         break;

      default:
         break;
      }
                                                     // def proc & ret
   return (DefWindowProc(hWnd, message, wParam, lParam));
   }
```

USEDRV.H

```c
LRESULT __export CALLBACK MainWndProc(HWND, UINT, WPARAM, LPARAM);
BOOL InitApplication(HINSTANCE);
BOOL InitInstance(HINSTANCE, int);

#define IDM_OPEN  101
#define IDM_CLOSE 102
#define IDM_BEEP  103

#define DURATION_CNT 100L
#define FREQ_CNT     2500L

#define InstDrvName "instdrv.drv"
```

USEDRV.RC

```
#include <windows.h>
#include "usedrv.h"

MainMenu    MENU    PRELOAD
            {
                MENUITEM    "&Open",  IDM_OPEN
                MENUITEM    "&Beep",  IDM_BEEP
                MENUITEM    "&Close", IDM_CLOSE
            }
```

USEDRV.DEF

```
NAME            USEDRV

DESCRIPTION     'Use an installable device driver'

EXETYPE         WINDOWS

STUB            'WINSTUB.EXE'

CODE PRELOAD MOVEABLE DISCARDABLE

DATA PRELOAD MOVEABLE MULTIPLE

HEAPSIZE        1024
STACKSIZE       5120
```

INSTDRV.C

```
//
// Installable device driver example
//
// from Modifying Windows by Asael Dror
//

#include <windows.h>
#include "instdrv.h"
```

CHAPTER 6
INSTALLABLE DEVICE DRIVERS: CONVENTIONAL AND UNCONVENTIONAL USES

```c
LRESULT CALLBACK DriverProc(DWORD dwDrvID, HDRVR hDrv, UINT msg,
                  LPARAM lParam1, LPARAM lParam2)
{
switch (msg)
    {
    case DRV_LOAD:                           // load OK
        return(TRUE);
        break;

    case DRV_ENABLE:
        break;

    case DRV_OPEN:
        return(TRUE);                        // open OK
        break;

    case DRV_WDL_BEEP:       // beep on internal speaker
                             // LOWORD(lParam1): duration counter
                             // LOWORD(lParam2): frequency counter
        __asm
          {
          in ax, SpeakerPort          // read port
          mov bx, word ptr lParam1    // bx = duration counter
keep_beeping:
          xor ax, SpeakerBit          // toggle speaker
          mov cx, word ptr lParam2    // cx = frequency counter
kill_time_loop:
          loop kill_time_loop         // decay frequency counter
          out SpeakerPort, ax         // write port
          dec bx                      // decay duration counter
          jnz keep_beeping
          }
        return(TRUE);
        break;

    case DRV_CLOSE:
        return(TRUE);                        // close OK
        break;

    case DRV_DISABLE:
        break;

    case DRV_FREE:
        break;

    case DRV_QUERYCONFIGURE:
        return(FALSE);                       // non user configurable
```

```
            break;

        default:
            break;
    }
    return(DefDriverProc(dwDrvID, hDrv, msg, lParam1, lParam2));
}
```

INSTDRV.H

```
#define DRV_WDL_BEEP DRV_USER + 100

#define SpeakerPort 0x61
#define SpeakerBit  0x02
```

INSTDRV.DEF

```
LIBRARY         INSTDRV

DESCRIPTION     'beeper: Installable Drive Driver'

EXETYPE         WINDOWS

STUB            'WINSTUB.EXE'

CODE            MOVABLE DISCARDABLE PRELOAD
DATA            MOVABLE PRELOAD SINGLE

HEAPSIZE        1024

EXPORTS
                WEP             @1 RESIDENTNAME
                DriverProc      @2 RESIDENTNAME
```

Figure 6-1 shows output of the program that uses the installable device driver.

Installing an Installable Device Driver

In the example, the driver is opened explicitly by specifying its filename. (Make sure the driver is on the path.) More commonly, an application would use the

CHAPTER 6
INSTALLABLE DEVICE DRIVERS: CONVENTIONAL AND UNCONVENTIONAL USES   189

Figure 6-1
USEDRV's output

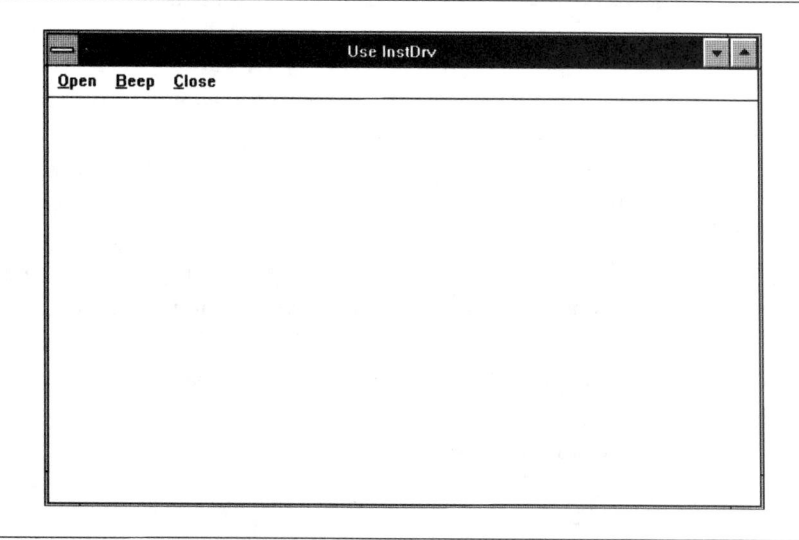

driver's entry name from SYSTEM.INI to access the file. By using an entry name rather than a filename, the application is independent of the actual driver being used. For example, it can use the audio wave-form driver whose entry name is "wave," regardless of the actual hardware-specific driver being used.

The quick-and-dirty way to install a device driver so that it can be accessed via its entry is to manually add an entry to the SYSTEM.INI file. The entry's format should be:

entry_name = installable_driver_filename

For example:

```
instdrv = c:\modify\chapter6\instdrv\instdrv.dll
```

The entry can either be in the [drivers] section (in which case the third parameter of OpenDriver can be NULL) or in another section (in which case the section name must be specified by OpenDriver). Such a section might look like this:

```
[MODIFY]
InstDrv = c:\modify\chapter6\instdrv\instdrv.drv
```

A more user-friendly way to install a driver is with an installation program. You can either write your own, or use the Control Panel's Drivers installation program.

Control Panel's Drivers Program

The Control Panel Drivers application allows users to install, configure (set up), and remove installable device drivers. When installing a driver, the application copies the driver's DLL to the WINDOWS\SYSTEM directory, adds an entry in the [drivers] section of SYSTEM.INI, and saves the driver's description in the [drivers.desc] section of CONTROL.INI.

To use the Control Panel to install your driver, you must first use the correct convention to describe your driver in the module-definition file:

DESCRIPTION *'entry_name[,entry_name...]:description'*

For example:

```
DESCRIPTION
'beeper, Modifying Windows sample inst drv'
```

Next you must supply an OEMSETUP.INF file that contains two sections. First, the [disks] section indicates the file's location and describes the distribution disks. For example:

```
[disks]
1=\instdrv, "Modifying Windows diskette"
```

Next, the [installable.drivers] section specifies the location of the installable driver and its description in the following format:

driver_name=disk_number:filename,
entry_name[,entry_name...],description [,vxd_disk_number:filename][,parameters]

For example:

```
sample=1:instdrv.dll,beeper,
"Modifying Windows sample inst drv"
```

The installation program uses the entry_name(s) to create an entry (or multiple entries) in the [drivers] section of SYSTEM.INI. In our example, the entry would be:

```
beeper=instdrv.drv
```

The description is used by the Control Panel to describe the driver and is stored in the [drivers.desc] section of CONTROL.INI. (If the Control Panel cannot find the description in CONTROL.INI, it will look for it in MMSETUP.INF, and finally in the driver's header where the description from the DEF file is placed.)

The parameters will be placed after the filename in SYSTEM.INI (so lParam1 will point at them when the driver receives a DRV_OPEN message).

APIs for Getting Information about Installable Device Drivers

Finally, let's look at the APIs that allow an application to retrieve information about the installable device driver currently loaded in the system.

GetDriverInfo

Get information about an installable device driver

```
BOOL GetDriverInfo (hdrv, lpDIS);

HDRVR               hrv;           // driver handle
DRIVERINFOSTRUCT FAR* lpDIS;       // -> structure for
                                   // returned information
```

Returns:
If successful, TRUE; otherwise FALSE.

Where DRIVERINFOSTRUCT is defined as:

```
typedef struct tagDRIVERINFOSTRUCT {   // drvinfst
    UINT      length;                  // sizeof(DRIVERINFOSTRUCT)
                                       // filled before calling API
    HDRVR     hDriver;                 // driver handle
    HINSTANCE hModule;                 // driver's hModule
    char      szAliasName[128];        // name or entry under which
                                       // driver was loaded
} DRIVERINFOSTRUCT;
```

GetNextDriver

Enumerate installable device drivers

```
HDRVR GetNextDriver(hDrv, fdwFlags);

HDRVR hDrv;       // hDrv of last returned driver, or
                  // NULL for first driver
DWORD fdwFlags;   // search flags
```

`fdwFlags` can have the following values:

- ◆ GND_FIRSTINSTANCEONLY   Return information only about the first instance of each driver
- ◆ GND_FORWARD   Enumerate the drivers in forward order (the order in which they were loaded)
- ◆ GND_REVERSE   Enumerate the drivers in reverse order

Returns:
If successful, hDrv; otherwise FALSE.

GetDriverModuleHandle

Get driver module handle

```
HINSTANCE GetDriverModuleHandle(hdrvr);

HDRVR hDrv;   // driver handle
```

Returns:
If successful, hModule; otherwise FALSE.

AN EXAMPLE THAT LISTS INSTALLABLE DEVICE DRIVERS

The following program uses the above APIs to list the currently loaded installable device drivers in the system. A typical output of the program is shown in Figure 6-2.

CHAPTER 6
INSTALLABLE DEVICE DRIVERS: CONVENTIONAL AND UNCONVENTIONAL USES

MAKEFILE

```
all: listdrv.exe

listdrv.res: listdrv.rc listdrv.h makefile
   rc -r listdrv.rc

listdrv.obj: listdrv.c listdrv.h makefile
   cl -c -DSTRICT -AS -GA2 -Ox -W3 listdrv.c

listdrv.exe: listdrv.obj listdrv.def listdrv.res makefile
   link listdrv,,, libw slibcew, listdrv.def
   rc listdrv.res
```

LISTDRV.C

```c
//
// List installable device drivers loaded
//
// from Modifying Windows by Asael Dror
//

#include <windows.h>
#include "listdrv.h"

HINSTANCE hInst;                                    // current instance

                                                    // application E.P.
int PASCAL WinMain(HINSTANCE hInstance, HINSTANCE hPrevInstance,
              LPSTR LPCmdLine, int nCmdShow)

   {
   MSG msg;

   if (!hPrevInstance)                              // if first inst
      if (!InitApplication(hInstance))              // then init app
         return(FALSE);

   if (!InitInstance(hInstance, nCmdShow))          // init instance
      return(FALSE);

                                                    // msg loop
   while (GetMessage(&msg, NULL, 0, 0))             // get any msg/wnd
```

MODIFYING WINDOWS

```c
      {
      TranslateMessage(&msg);                    // xlate virt keys
      DispatchMessage(&msg);                     // dispatch message
      }
   return(msg.wParam);
   }

BOOL InitApplication(HINSTANCE hInstance)        // init application
   {
                                                 // reg main wnd class
   WNDCLASS wc;

                                                 // fill wnd class str
   wc.style = NULL;
   wc.lpfnWndProc = MainWndProc;                 // window proc
   wc.cbClsExtra = 0;
   wc.cbWndExtra = 0;
   wc.hInstance = hInstance;                     // class owner
   wc.hIcon = LoadIcon(NULL, IDI_APPLICATION);   // def app icon
   wc.hCursor = LoadCursor(NULL, IDC_ARROW);     // standard cursor
   wc.hbrBackground = (HBRUSH)(COLOR_WINDOW + 1); // window bkg clr
   wc.lpszMenuName = "MainMenu";
   wc.lpszClassName = "ListDrv";                 // window class name

   return(RegisterClass(&wc));                   // reg wnd class
   }

                                                 // instance init
BOOL InitInstance(HINSTANCE hInstance, int nCmdShow)
   {
   HWND hWnd;                                    // main wnd handle

   hInst = hInstance;                            // save it

   hWnd = CreateWindow (                         // main window
           "ListDrv",                            // class name
           "List loaded installable drivers",    // title bar text
           WS_OVERLAPPEDWINDOW | WS_VISIBLE,     // "normal" & vsbl
           CW_USEDEFAULT,                        // default x
           nCmdShow,                             // default y,
                                                 // show as req
           CW_USEDEFAULT,                        // default width
           CW_USEDEFAULT,                        // default height
           HWND_DESKTOP,                         // no parent
           NULL,                                 // use class menu
           hInstance,                            // inst for win
           NULL);                                // not used
   if (!hWnd) return(FALSE);
```

CHAPTER 6
INSTALLABLE DEVICE DRIVERS: CONVENTIONAL AND UNCONVENTIONAL USES

```
      UpdateWindow(hWnd);                        // snd WM_PAINT msg
      return (TRUE);                             // OK
   }


LRESULT __export CALLBACK MainWndProc(
                       HWND hWnd,             // window handle
                       UINT message,          // message
                       WPARAM wParam,         // param
                       LPARAM lParam)         // param
{
HDC hDC;
HDRVR hDrv;
DRIVERINFOSTRUCT DrvInfo;
WORD x,y;
PAINTSTRUCT ps;
TEXTMETRIC tm;

DrvInfo.length=sizeof(DrvInfo);
x = y = 5;

switch (message)
   {
   case WM_DESTROY:
      PostQuitMessage(0);                       // bye bye, rc = 0
      break;

   case WM_COMMAND:
      if (wParam == IDM_UPDATELIST)
         {
         InvalidateRect(hWnd, NULL, TRUE);
         return(0);
         }
      break;

   case WM_PAINT:
      hDC = BeginPaint(hWnd, &ps);
      GetTextMetrics(hDC, &tm);
      hDrv = NULL;             // traverse from beginning
                               // loading order, all instances
      while (hDrv = GetNextDriver(hDrv, GND_REVERSE)
            {
            if (GetDriverInfo(hDrv, &DrvInfo))
               {
               TextOut(hDC, x, y , DrvInfo.szAliasName,
                    strlen(DrvInfo.szAliasName));
               y += tm.tmHeight + tm.tmExternalLeading;
               }
```

```
            }
        EndPaint(hWnd, &ps);
        return(0);
        break;

    default:                        // default proc & ret
        return (DefWindowProc(hWnd, message, wParam, lParam));
    }
    return(NULL);
}
```

LISTDRV.H

```
LRESULT __export CALLBACK MainWndProc(HWND, UINT, WPARAM, LPARAM);
BOOL InitApplication(HINSTANCE);
BOOL InitInstance(HINSTANCE, int);

#define IDM_UPDATELIST 100
```

LISTDRV.RC

```
#include <windows.h>
#include "listdrv.h"

MainMenu    MENU    PRELOAD
            {
                MENUITEM    "&Update", IDM_UPDATELIST
            }
```

LISTDRV.DEF

```
NAME            LISTDRV

DESCRIPTION     'List loaded installable drivers'

EXETYPE         WINDOWS

STUB            'WINSTUB.EXE'
```

CHAPTER 6
INSTALLABLE DEVICE DRIVERS: CONVENTIONAL AND UNCONVENTIONAL USES

```
CODE PRELOAD MOVEABLE DISCARDABLE
DATA PRELOAD MOVEABLE MULTIPLE

HEAPSIZE        1024
STACKSIZE       5120
```

Now that we know all about the conventional uses of installable device drivers, the next section introduces a very useful unconventional use.

Resident Dynamic Link Libraries

Windows, as we know, is mainly a collection of dynamic link libraries (DLLs) such as GDI, USER, etc. When we extend or modify Windows, we often do so with our own DLLs. For example, when we use hooks (see Chapter 5), we often need to do so with a DLL. Such a DLL is an extension of Windows itself, and not part of any particular application. This raises the problem of who will load the DLL and how we can keep the DLL resident (i.e., prevent Windows from freeing it). We addressed this issue at length in the chapter on subclassing (Chapter 4) and again in the chapter on hooks (Chapter 5). The (unsatisfactory) solution we came up with was to use a stub program that never terminates in order to load the DLL and keep it resident.

Figure 6-2
Output of the LISTDRV program showing a typical list of installed drivers

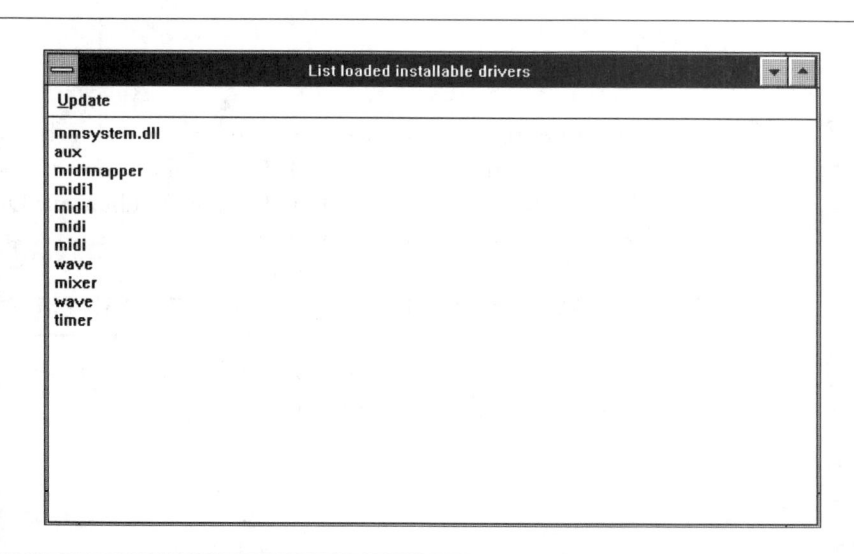

As an example of this not-too-satisfactory approach, look back at the KILLERAP example in Chapter 5. The example uses a simple mouse hook to send a WM_QUIT message to the application under the mouse cursor when the mouse's right button is clicked. It employs a stub program that loads the hook's DLL (see the relevant text in Chapter 5 for more on this example).

What we would really like, is to eliminate the stub program, and instead force Windows itself to load the DLL. We can achieve this by converting the DLL into an installable device driver.

Because device drivers were designed to be an extension of the Windows system, a mechanism is in place (installable device drivers) for making them an integral part of Windows. We can piggyback on this mechanism to make any DLL (even if it has nothing to do with any hardware) a part of the Windows system.

The simplest way to convert the DLL into an installable device driver is to add a DriverProc callback function. When the callback function receives a message, it simply passes it on to the DefDriverProc API for default processing.

If you remember the details of our discussion of installable device drivers above, you know that the DefDriverProc API returns a FALSE to the DRV_OPEN messages, so the driver must handle that message. However, in our case, the driver (i.e., the DLL) should be loaded, but it should never be open. Any attempt by an application to actually open the DLL *should* fail.

Once our DLL looks like an installable device driver, we need only add its filename (or entry name from the [drivers] section of SYSTEM.INI) to the drivers= line in the [boot] section of SYSTEM.INI. For example:

```
[boot]
drivers=c:\mouhook.dll
```

This line tells Windows that the driver must be loaded (and sent DRV_LOAD and DRV_ENABLE messages) but not opened (i.e., no DRV_OPEN message) at Windows boot time. Thus, our DLL has become an integrated extension of Windows itself.

RESIDENT DYNAMIC LINK LIBRARY EXAMPLE

The following listings show the hooks DLL after it is converted into an installable device driver (no stub required).

CHAPTER 6
INSTALLABLE DEVICE DRIVERS: CONVENTIONAL AND UNCONVENTIONAL USES

MAKEFILE

```
all: mouhook.drv

mouhook.obj: mouhook.c mouhook.h makefile
    cl -c -DSTRICT -AS -GD2 -Ox -W3 mouhook.c

mouhook.drv: mouhook.obj mouhook.def makefile
    link mouhook, mouhook.drv, , libw sdllcew, mouhook.def
    rc mouhook.drv
```

MOUHOOK.C

```c
// Resident Dynamic Link Library example
//
// Mouse hook DLL that posts a WM_QUIT message to the application
// under the cursor when the right mouse button is pressed
//
// from Modifying Windows by Asael Dror
//
// Warning: see text for the possible side effects of this program!
//

#include <windows.h>
#include "mouhook.h"

HHOOK hHook;

                                      // DLL init
int __export WINAPI LibMain(HINSTANCE hInstance, WORD wDataSeg,
                    WORD cbHeapSize, LPSTR lpszCmdLine)

    {                                 // hook mouse messages
    hHook = SetWindowsHookEx(WH_MOUSE, (HOOKPROC)
            GetProcAddress(hInstance, "RButtonKill"),
                        hInstance, NULL);

    return (1);
    }
```

MODIFYING WINDOWS

```c
                                            // DLL termination
int __export WINAP _WEP (int bSystemExit)
   {
   UnhookWindowsHookEx(hHook);          // unhook mouse msg

   return (1);
   }


                                            // kill app on right button down
LRESULT __export CALLBACK RButtonKill(
   int code,                            // action code
   WPARAM wParam,                       // message ID
   LPARAM lParam)                       // LPMOUSEHOOKSTRUCT
   {
   LPMOUSEHOOKSTRUCT ms;

                                            // if right mouse down
   if ((wParam == WM_RBUTTONDOWN) || (wParam == WM_NCRBUTTONDOWN))
      {
      MessageBeep(-1);                                  // beep
      ms = (LPMOUSEHOOKSTRUCT) lParam;
      PostMessage(ms->hwnd, WM_QUIT, 0, 0);    // kill that window
      return (1);                              // discard message
      }

                                            // call next hook & return
   return (CallNextHookEx(hHook, code, wParam, lParam));
   }

// Presto - now it's an installable device driver!

LRESULT __export CALLBACK DriverProc (DWORD dwDrvID, HDRVR hDrv,
                                      UINT msg, LPARAM lParam1
                                      LPARAM lParam2)

   {
                                    // default processing for all msgs
   return DefDriverProc(dwDrvID, hDrv, msg, lParam1, lParam2);
   }
```

MOUHOOK.H

```c
int __export WINAPI LibMain(HMODULE, WORD, WORD, LPSTR);
int __export WINAPI _WEP (int);
LRESULT __export CALLBACK RButtonKill(int, WPARAM, LPARAM);
```

CHAPTER 6
INSTALLABLE DEVICE DRIVERS: CONVENTIONAL AND UNCONVENTIONAL USES

MOUHOOK.DEF

```
LIBRARY          MOUHOOK

DESCRIPTION      'A mouse hook DLL'

EXETYPE          WINDOWS

STUB             'WINSTUB.EXE'

CODE PRELOAD MOVEABLE DISCARDABLE
DATA PRELOAD MOVEABLE SINGLE

HEAPSIZE         1024

EXPORTS
                 WEP @1 RESIDENTNAME
```

Finally, let's move the initialization and termination code from the LibMain and WEP to the DRV_LOAD and DRV_FREE message handling routines. The modified RESDLL.C looks as follows:

MOUHOOK.C

```
// Resident Dynamic Link Library example
//
// Mouse hook DLL that posts a WM_QUIT message to the application
// under the cursor when the right mouse button is pressed
//
// from Modifying Windows by Asael Dror
//
// Warning: see text for the possible side effects of this program!
//

#include <windows.h>
#include "mouhook.h"

HHOOK hHook;


                              // kill app on right button down
LRESULT __export CALLBACK RButtonKill(
```

```
   int code,                                    // action code
   WPARAM wParam,                               // message ID
   LPARAM lParam)                               // LPMOUSEHOOKSTRUCT
   {
   LPMOUSEHOOKSTRUCT ms;

                                                // if right mouse down
   if ((wParam == WM_RBUTTONDOWN) || (wParam == WM_NCRBUTTONDOWN))
      {
      MessageBeep(-1);                          // beep
      ms = (LPMOUSEHOOKSTRUCT) lParam;
      PostMessage(ms->hwnd, WM_QUIT, 0, 0);     // kill that window
      return (1);                               // discard message
      }

                                                // call next hook & return
   return (CallNextHookEx(hHook, code, wParam, lParam));
   }


// An installable device driver!

LRESULT __export CALLBACK DriverProc (DWORD dwDrvID, HDRVR hDrv,
                                      UINT msg, LPARAM lParam1,
                                      LPARAM lParam2)
   {
   HMODULE hModule;

   switch(msg)
      {
      case DRV_LOAD:
                                                // hook mouse messages
      hModule = GetModuleHandle("MOUHOOK");
      hHook = SetWindowsHookEx(WH_MOUSE, (HOOKPROC)
                           GetProcAddress(hModule,"RButtonKill"),
                           hModule, NULL);

      break;

      case DRV_FREE:
         UnhookWindowsHookEx(hHook);            // unhook mouse msg
         break;

      default:                                  // default processing
         return DefDriverProc(dwDrvID, hDrv, msg, lParam1, lParam2);
      }
   return TRUE;
   }
```

Chapter 7

Toolhelp

TOOLHELP is one of those extremely useful and greatly underutilized "tools of the trade" supported by Windows. Though not designed for "general use" (whatever that means), Toolhelp can solve in easy and elegant ways some difficult real-life problems—the kind of problems that would otherwise require disassembling Windows and relying on undocumented features. For example, in Chapter 2 we mentioned that a DLL can manage per-task data in the DLL's data segment. It sounds easy, but in order to actually implement this in a DLL, we need a mechanism to notify the DLL when a task terminates. The best way to be notified of task termination is with Toolhelp.

Background

In 1990, Microsoft tried to formalize the information required to develop programming tools such as debuggers. This effort, known as *open tools,* publicized (at least to selected tool developers) information about file formats and allowed the licensing of Microsoft tools for redistribution. It also provided an API to support tool development. This API is known as *Toolhelp*. Although Toolhelp eventually made its way into the SDK for Windows 3.1, many developers are still unaware of its existence, or at least don't make use of it.

Toolhelp's Purpose

The idea behind Toolhelp is to provide tool developers with the APIs they need so that they will not need to access internal Windows data structures or use internal undocumented APIs. Using Toolhelp shields the application from version-specific internal structures. From Microsoft's point of view, this satisfies (at least some of) the tool developers' information requests, but allows Microsoft to change its internal structures in future versions of Windows (at least that's the theory!).

In general, Toolhelp APIs provide information, but do not give you access to the actual internal Windows data structures. Thus, they do little to help you modify that information directly. If, however, you *must* have access to the internal data structures of Windows, disassembling Toolhelp is a good place to start.

Using Toolhelp

Toolhelp consists of TOOLHELP.DLL, TOOLHELP.H, and TOOLHELP.LIB. TOOLHELP.DLL is included in the retail version of Windows 3.1 and redistributed with your applications to support users of Windows 3.0. TOOLHELP.H and TOOLHELP.LIB are part of the Windows 3.1 SDK.

The Toolhelp APIs serve many purposes. They allow you to retrieve information from Windows lists such as classes, tasks, and modules. They can obtain memory and heap information. They support debuggers by controlling the execution and accessing the memory of other programs. They can obtain accurate timing information, which is useful for profilers. They can perform stack tracing. Finally, they register callback functions for interrupts and notifications.

Instead of looking at exactly what the APIs do (which is documented), this chapter will look at the mechanism of using the APIs (which is not at all clear from the documentation).

From a mechanism point of view, the Toolhelp APIs can be divided into three categories:

◆ Standard APIs

◆ List-walking APIs

◆ Callback support APIs

We'll examine these three categories in turn.

Standard APIs

The Toolhelp standard APIs are similar to other Windows APIs; you call them with parameters and they return a result. However, all Toolhelp APIs have a distinctive calling convention.

As we mentioned, Toolhelp APIs pass information back rather than giving you access to Windows' internal tables. Thus, when calling a Toolhelp API, you must pass it a pointer to a structure in which the requested information will be returned. The first element of such structures, `dwSize`, contains the size of the structure and must be initialized by your application before calling the API. The API uses this parameter to find out how much information the application expects. This parameter allows newer versions of Toolhelp to supply more information, while not breaking applications designed for older versions.

All Toolhelp APIs return a BOOL value: TRUE if they succeed, FALSE if they fail.

As an example of using a standard Toolhelp API, let us examine the TimerCount API.

TimerCount

Get accurate timer count

```
BOOL TimerCount(lpTimerInfo);

TIMERINFO FAR * TimerInfo;
```

Returns:
If successful, TRUE; else FALSE.

The meanings of the fields within the TIMERINFO structure are incorrectly documented in the SDK, a situation we'll correct here. TIMERINFO is defined as follows:

```
typedef struct tagTIMERINFO
{
    DWORD dwSize;
    DWORD dwmsSinceStart;
    DWORD dwmsThisVM;
} TIMERINFO;
```

In this structure,

- ◆ `dwSize` is the size of the TIMERINFO structure. This parameter must be initialized by the application before calling the TimerCount API.

- `dwmsSinceStart` is the time, in milliseconds, since the current Virtual Machine (i.e., Windows) was started.
- `dwmsThisVM` is the total number of milliseconds that the current Virtual Machine (i.e., Windows) has been active.

Timer interrupts (ticks) are received roughly every 55 milliseconds (ms). This isn't accurate enough for many situations, so TimerCount returns timing information accurate to roughly 1ms. TimerCount uses the services of the Virtual Timer Device (VTD) when in Enhanced mode, and it reads the 8253 counters in Standard mode. In Standard mode, `dwmsSinceStart` returns the same value as `dwmsThisVM`, i.e., the total number of milliseconds that the Windows VM has been active, not counting the time when the DOS VM was running.

TimerCount is especially useful for profilers, because it gives accurate timing information and the `dwmsThisVM` information does not count time the CPU spends executing any DOS boxes that may be running in parallel with the Windows VM.

TIMERCOUNT EXAMPLE PROGRAM

The following program uses TimerCount to measure how long it takes to perform screen-to-screen bitblts on your machine, a graphics performance mini-benchmark. Notice that since the program uses `dwmsThisVM`, the timing measurements obtained with this program will not be affected by any DOS boxes that may be active. The output of the program is shown in Figure 7-1.

MAKEFILE

```
all: blttime.exe

blttime.res: blttime.rc blttime.h makefile
    rc -r blttime.rc

blttime.obj: blttime.c blttime.h makefile
    cl -c -DSTRICT -AS -GA2 -Ox -W3 blttime.c

blttime.exe: blttime.obj blttime.def blttime.res makefile
    link blttime,,,libw toolhelp slibcew, blttime.def
    rc blttime.res
```

BLTTIME.C

```c
// timing screen-to-screen bitblt - using Toolhelp
//
// from Modifying Windows by Asael Dror
//

#include <windows.h>
#include <commdlg.h>
#include <toolhelp.h>

#include "blttime.h"

HINSTANCE hInst;                                      // current instance

                                                      // application E.P.
int PASCAL WinMain(HINSTANCE hInstance, HINSTANCE hPrevInstance,
                LPSTR LPCmdLine, int nCmdShow)

  {
  MSG msg;
  if (hPrevInstance)                      // one inst only!
     return(FALSE);

  if (!InitApplication(hInstance))        // init app
     return(FALSE);

  if (!InitInstance(hInstance, nCmdShow))      // init instance
     return(FALSE);

                                               // msg loop
  while (GetMessage(&msg, NULL, 0, 0))   // get any msg/any wnd
     {
     TranslateMessage(&msg);                   // translate virt keys
     DispatchMessage(&msg);                    // dispatch message
     }
  return(msg.wParam);
  }

BOOL InitApplication(HINSTANCE hInstance)         // init app
  {
                                                  // reg main wnd class
  WNDCLASS wc;

                                                  // fill wnd class str
  wc.style = CS_BYTEALIGNCLIENT;                  // for faster bitblts
  wc.lpfnWndProc = MainWndProc;                   // window proc
```

```c
    wc.cbClsExtra = 0;
    wc.cbWndExtra = 0;
    wc.hInstance = hInstance;                   // class owner
    wc.hIcon = LoadIcon(NULL, IDI_APPLICATION); // def app icon
    wc.hCursor = LoadCursor(NULL, IDC_ARROW);   // standard cursor
    wc.hbrBackground = (HBRUSH)(COLOR_WINDOW + 1); // wnd bckgnd clr
    wc.lpszMenuName = "MainMenu";
    wc.lpszClassName = "BTClass";               // window class name

    return(RegisterClass(&wc));                 // register wnd class
    }

                                                // instance init
BOOL InitInstance(HINSTANCE hInstance, int nCmdShow)
    {
    HWND   hWnd;                                // window handle

    hInst = hInstance;                          // save in static var

    hWnd = CreateWindow (                       // main window
            "BTClass",                          // class name
            "BitBlt Timing",                    // title bar text
            WS_OVERLAPPEDWINDOW |               // normal &
            WS_VISIBLE |                        // visible &
            WS_MAXIMIZE,                        // maximized
            0, 0,                               // x,y = top left
            0, 0,                               // it's maximized anyway
            HWND_DESKTOP,                       // no parent
            NULL,                               // use class menu
            hInstance,                          // inst of mod for win
            NULL);                              // not used
    if (!hWnd) return(FALSE);
    UpdateWindow(hWnd);                         // send WM_PAINT msg
    return (TRUE);                              // OK
    }


LRESULT __export CALLBACK MainWndProc(
                            HWND hWnd,          // window handle
                            UINT message,       // message
                            WPARAM wParam,      // param
                            LPARAM lParam)      // param
    {
    HDC hDC;
    HMENU hMenu;
    int i;

    TIMERINFO TimerInfo;
```

MODIFYING WINDOWS

```
DWORD T0;
RECT rcWin;
char Str[20];

switch (message)
   {
   case WM_DESTROY:
      PostQuitMessage(0);                        // bye bye, rc = 0
      break;

   case WM_COMMAND:
      switch (wParam)
         {
         case IDM_START:
                                                 // disable menu
            hMenu = GetMenu(hWnd);
            EnableMenuItem(hMenu, IDM_START,
                        MF_BYCOMMAND | MF_GRAYED);
            DrawMenuBar(hWnd);

            TimerInfo.dwSize = sizeof(TimerInfo);

            hDC = GetDC(hWnd);                   // get window's DC

                                                 // get start time
            TimerCount(&TimerInfo);
            T0 = TimerInfo.dwmsThisVM;
                                                 // do a few blts
            for (i = 0; i < NBLT; i++)
            BitBlt (hDC, BLT_WIDTH, BLT_HIGHT,
                    BLT_WIDTH, BLT_HIGHT,
                    hDC, 0, 0,
                    SRCINVERT);

                                                 // get end time
            TimerCount(&TimerInfo);
                                                 // display results
            GetClientRect(hWnd, &rcWin);
            ExtTextOut(hDC, 5, BLT_HIGHT, ETO_OPAQUE, &rcWin, Str,
                    wsprintf(Str, "Time = %ldms",
                           TimerInfo.dwmsThisVM - T0),
                    NULL);

            ReleaseDC(hWnd, hDC);                // free DC

                                                 // enable menu
            EnableMenuItem(hMenu, IDM_START,
                        MF_BYCOMMAND | MF_ENABLED);
```

```
                DrawMenuBar(hWnd);

            break;

        default:                        // default proc & ret
            return (DefWindowProc(hWnd, message,
                                  wParam, lParam));
        }
    break;

    default:                            // default proc & ret
        return (DefWindowProc(hWnd, message,
                              wParam, lParam));
    }
    return(0);
}
```

BLTTIME.H

```
LRESULT __export CALLBACK MainWndProc(HWND, UINT, WPARAM, LPARAM);
BOOL InitApplication(HINSTANCE);
BOOL InitInstance(HINSTANCE, int);

#define IDM_START 100

#define BLT_WIDTH 250
#define BLT_HIGHT 150
#define NBLT 1000
```

BLTTIME.RC

```
#include <windows.h>
#include "blttime.h"

MainMenu    MENU    PRELOAD
            {
            MENUITEM    "&Start", IDM_START
            }
```

MODIFYING WINDOWS

```
BLTTIME.DEF

NAME            BLTTIME

DESCRIPTION     'Bitblt timing program'

EXETYPE         WINDOWS

STUB            'WINSTUB.EXE'

CODE PRELOAD MOVEABLE DISCARDABLE
DATA PRELOAD MOVEABLE MULTIPLE

HEAPSIZE        1024
STACKSIZE       8192
```

A QUICK WORD ABOUT BENCHMARKS

Most benchmarks, and especially Windows benchmarks, are not representative of real-world situations. This is especially true with benchmarks used by large and influential magazines, where doing well on the benchmark is so important that graphics card manufacturers tend to optimize their hardware and

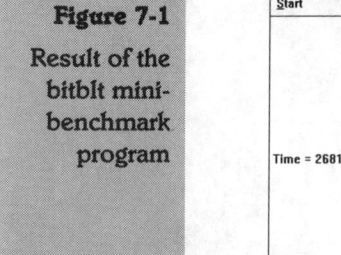

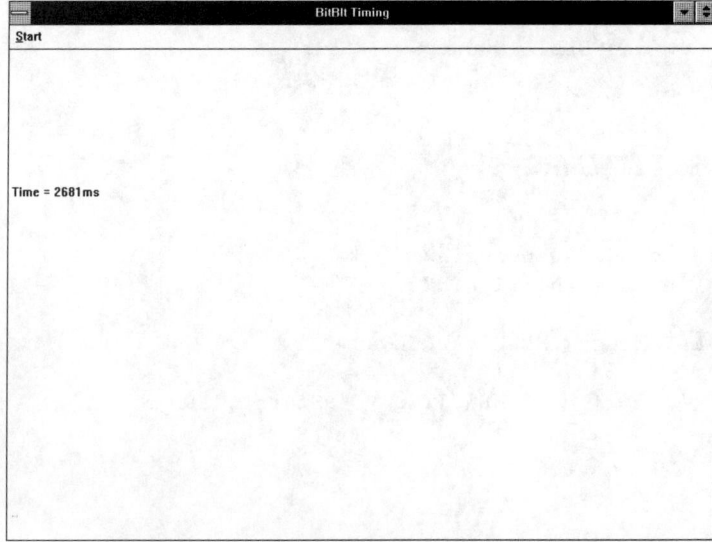

Figure 7-1
Result of the bitblt mini-benchmark program

software drivers to do well on the benchmark, rather than speed up applications. Thus, doing well on a benchmark only means that the hardware does well on the benchmark.

The BLTTIME example has two main problems. One is the lack of a check for timer overflow (unlikely to happen just when you run the benchmark, but still a case to be handled). The other problem is typical of many graphics benchmarks: the cursor is not disabled while the program is running (a trivial task to perform). To see the significance of not disabling the cursor, try running the above program once without moving the cursor while the program is running, and then again while constantly moving the cursor within the blt area. Now try this at home with a your favorite "real" benchmark!

List-Walking APIs

Our next example traverses the internal class list and displays the names of all registered Windows classes. For walking a list (of memory objects, tasks, modules, and so on), Toolhelp commonly provides a set of two APIs. One API gets information about the first element in the list (in our example, the first class in the list), and a second API gets information about the next element in the list. For the class list, those APIs are ClassFirst and ClassNext, which fill a structure of type CLASSENTRY. Once ClassFirst or ClassNext returns the CLASSENTRY information, you can use the GetClassInfo API to obtain additional information about the class.

ClassFirst

Get first class

```
BOOL ClassFirst(lpClassEntry);

CLASSENTRY FAR* lpClassEntry;
```

Returns:
If successful, TRUE; else FALSE.

CLASSENTRY is defined as:

```
typedef struct tagCLASSENTRY
{
    DWORD       dwSize;
```

MODIFYING WINDOWS

```
        HMODULE    hInst;
        char       szClassName[MAX_CLASSNAME + 1];
        WORD       wNext;
} CLASSENTRY;
```

In this structure,

- `dwSize` is the size of CLASSENTRY. This parameter must be filled in by the application before calling the ClassFirst API.
- `hInst` is the Module handle of the *module* that registered the class. (It's called `hInst` to confuse the enemy.)
- `szClassName` is the class name.
- `wNext` is a Windows internal value used to access the next class in the list when ClassNext is called.

ClassNext

Get next class

`BOOL ClassNext(lpClassEntry);`

`CLASSENTRY FAR* lpClassEntry`

Returns:
If successful, TRUE; else FALSE.

CLASS LIST EXAMPLE

The following program uses ClassFirst and ClassNext to display the names of all registered Windows classes. Figure 7-2 shows the program's output.

MAKEFILE

```
all: classlst.exe

classlst.res: classlst.rc classlst.h makefile
    rc -r classlst.rc
```

```
classlst.obj: classlst.c classlst.h makefile
   cl -c -DSTRICT -AS -GA2 -Ox -W3 classlst.c

classlst.exe: classlst.obj classlst.def classlst.res makefile
   link classlst,,,libw toolhelp slibcew, classlst.def
   rc classlst.res
```

CLASSLST.C

```c
// list of registered classes - using Toolhelp
//
// from Modifying Windows by Asael Dror
//

#include <windows.h>
#include <commdlg.h>
#include <toolhelp.h>

#include "classlst.h"

HINSTANCE hInst;                                    // current instance

                                                    // application E.P.
int PASCAL WinMain(HINSTANCE hInstance, HINSTANCE hPrevInstance,
                LPSTR LPCmdLine, int nCmdShow)

  {
  MSG msg;
  if (hPrevInstance)                      // one inst only!
     return(FALSE);

  if (!InitApplication(hInstance))        // init app
     return(FALSE);

  if (!InitInstance(hInstance, nCmdShow)) // init instance
     return(FALSE);

                                          // msg loop
  while (GetMessage(&msg, NULL, 0, 0))    // get any msg/any wnd
     {
     TranslateMessage(&msg);              // translate virt keys
     DispatchMessage(&msg);               // dispatch message
     }
  return(msg.wParam);
  }
```

MODIFYING WINDOWS

```
BOOL InitApplication(HINSTANCE hInstance)        // init app
  {
                                                 // reg main wnd class
  WNDCLASS wc;

                                                 // fill wnd class str
  wc.style = 0;
  wc.lpfnWndProc = MainWndProc;                  // window proc
  wc.cbClsExtra = 0;
  wc.cbWndExtra = 0;
  wc.hInstance = hInstance;                      // class owner
  wc.hIcon = LoadIcon(NULL, IDI_APPLICATION);    // def app icon
  wc.hCursor = LoadCursor(NULL, IDC_ARROW);      // standard cursor
  wc.hbrBackground = (HBRUSH)(COLOR_WINDOW + 1); // wnd bckgnd clr
  wc.lpszMenuName = "MainMenu";
  wc.lpszClassName = "LstClass";                 // window class name

  return(RegisterClass(&wc));                    // register wnd class
  }

                                                 // instance init
BOOL InitInstance(HINSTANCE hInstance, int nCmdShow)
  {
  HWND   hWnd;                                   // window handle

  hInst = hInstance;                             // save in static var

  hWnd = CreateWindow (                          // main window
        "LstClass",                              // class name
        "Class List",                            // title bar text
        WS_OVERLAPPEDWINDOW |                    // normal &
        WS_VISIBLE,                              // visible
        CW_USEDEFAULT,                                  // default x
        nCmdShow,                                       // default y,
                                                        // show as req
        CW_USEDEFAULT,                                  // default width
        CW_USEDEFAULT,                                  // default height
        HWND_DESKTOP,                            // no parent
        NULL,                                    // use class menu
        hInstance,                               // inst of mod for win
        NULL);                                   // not used
  if (!hWnd) return(FALSE);
  UpdateWindow(hWnd);                            // send WM_PAINT msg
  return (TRUE);                                 // OK
  }
```

```
LRESULT __export CALLBACK MainWndProc(
                            HWND hWnd,          // window handle
                            UINT message,       // message
                            WPARAM wParam,      // param
                            LPARAM lParam)      // param

{
HDC hDC;
TEXTMETRIC tm;
CLASSENTRY ce;
PAINTSTRUCT ps;
POINT pt;

switch (message)
   {
   case WM_DESTROY:
      PostQuitMessage(0);                       // bye bye, rc = 0
      break;

   case WM_COMMAND:
      if (wParam == IDM_UPDATE_NOW)
          InvalidateRect(hWnd, NULL, TRUE);
      break;

   case WM_PAINT:
      {
      pt.x = 2;
      pt.y = 2;
      ce.dwSize = sizeof(ce);

      hDC=BeginPaint(hWnd, &ps);
      if (ClassFirst(&ce))                      // get first class
         {
         GetTextMetrics(hDC, &tm);              // for text height
         TextOut(hDC, pt.x , pt.y , ce.szClassName ,
                 _fstrlen(ce.szClassName));
         while (ClassNext(&ce))                 // get next class
            {
            pt.y += tm.tmHeight + tm.tmExternalLeading;
            TextOut(hDC, pt.x , pt.y , ce.szClassName ,
                    _fstrlen(ce.szClassName) );
            }
         }
       EndPaint(hWnd, &ps);
      }
      break;

    default:                                    // def proc & ret
```

```
            return (DefWindowProc(hWnd, message, wParam, lParam));
    }
    return(NULL);
}
```

CLASSLST.H

```
LRESULT __export CALLBACK MainWndProc(HWND, UINT, WPARAM, LPARAM);
BOOL InitApplication(HINSTANCE);
BOOL InitInstance(HINSTANCE, int);

#define IDM_UPDATE_NOW 100
```

CLASSLST.RC

```
#include <windows.h>
#include "classlst.h"

MainMenu    MENU    PRELOAD
            {
                MENUITEM    "&Update now", IDM_UPDATE_NOW
            }
```

CLASSLST.DEF

```
NAME            CLASSLST

DESCRIPTION     'Registered class list'

EXETYPE         WINDOWS

STUB            'WINSTUB.EXE'

CODE PRELOAD MOVEABLE DISCARDABLE
DATA PRELOAD MOVEABLE MULTIPLE

HEAPSIZE        1024
STACKSIZE       8192
```

Figure 7-2

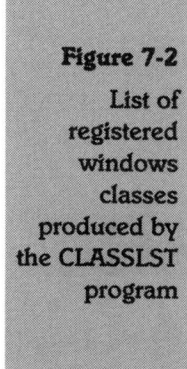

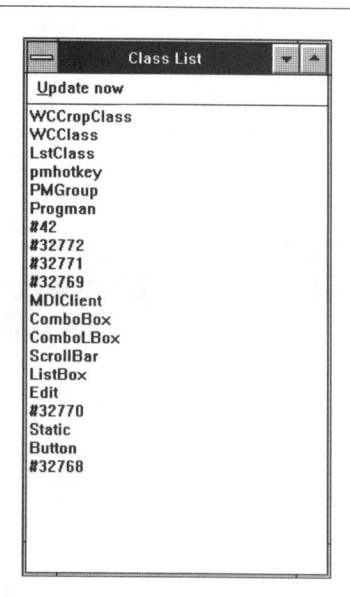

List of registered windows classes produced by the CLASSLST program

```
Class List
Update now
WCCropClass
WCClass
LstClass
pmhotkey
PMGroup
Progman
#42
#32772
#32771
#32769
MDIClient
ComboBox
ComboLBox
ScrollBar
ListBox
Edit
#32770
Static
Button
#32768
```

Callback Support APIs

Callbacks (as we discussed in Chapter 2) are routines that Windows calls when certain events occur. Hooks (see Chapter 5), for example, are implemented as callback routines. Toolhelp supports two kinds of callbacks, one for handling interrupts and faults, and the other for notifications.

MULTITASKING IN WINDOWS 3.1

As we all know, Windows 3.1 does not support true (preemptive) multitasking between Windows applications. However, 386 Enhanced mode does execute DOS boxes (which are actually additional Virtual Machines or VMs for short) concurrently (in a truly preemptive multitasking fashion) with the Windows VM. We can use this mechanism to achieve true multitasking with Windows applications. (A full discussion of this very powerful technique is beyond the scope of this book; for more information, refer to the articles in Volume II of the *Windows Developer Letter*—see this book's preface.)

The WinExec API can be used to launch a new process (i.e., start a non-Windows application in a new VM) and pass parameters to it via the command line. By using a PIF file, we can specify that the non-Windows application will run as a windowed application in the background, control its priority, and specify that the window will be closed when the application terminates. (For the sake of simplicity, the non-Windows processes in the following examples are real-mode DOS applications; however, by using DPMI, a non-Windows application can easily run in protected mode. Again, refer to the *Windows Developer Letter*.)

WinExec

Start a new program

```
UINT WINAPI WinExec(lpszCmdLine, fnCmdShow);

LPCSTR lpszCmdLine;    // command line
UINT fnCmdShow;        // initial window's show state
```

Returns:
If successful, hModule; else error code (<32).

One of the issues involved in using a non-Windows process to achieve true multitasking is knowing when it terminates. One solution is to use some kind of inter-process communication (IPC) between the non-Windows application and Windows. However, this might not work if the non-Windows process terminates abnormally. A second approach is to check whether the main window of the process can be found (and verify that the hTask and the hInstance match). We could use the WM_TIMER message to periodically check whether the process is still running by looking for its main window, but this wastes too much of the system resources (and sounds too much like "manual multitasking"). A better way is to use the Toolhelp notification services.

NOTIFICATIONS

Notifications are among Windows' most powerful features. Notifications allow us to register a callback routine that Windows will call to inform us of the occurrence of important system events, such as the starting or terminating of a task, the loading of a DLL, the loading of a segment, and similar events. (The DBWIN utility, for example, discussed in Chapter 3, uses notifications to display debugging messages from the debugging version of Windows.) Among the events for which we can get notification is the termination of any task in the system, including our WinOldAp. Registering a callback routine for notifications is done with the NotifyRegister API.

NotifyRegister

Register a notification callback routine

```
BOOL NotifyRegister(hTask, lpfn, wFlags);

HTASK hTask;       // task associated with callback rtn
                   // NULL == current task
LPFNNOTIFYCALLBACK lpfn;
                   // notification callback routine
WORD wFlags;       // type of notifications to receive,
                   // possible values are:
                   // NF_NORMAL ==  normal notifications
                   // NF_TASKSWITCH == task-switching
                   // notifications
                   // NF_RIP == abort notifications
```

Returns:
If successful, TRUE; else FALSE.

After registration, our callback routine will be called to notify us of the occurrence of system events.

The callback routine is defined as follows:

Notification Callback Routine

Notification callback routine

```
BOOL notifycallback(wID, dwData);

WORD wID;          // notification ID
DWORD dwData;      // addition info, notification specific
```

Returns:
TRUE indicates that the notification was handled by our routine. FALSE indicates that the notification should be passed to another callback routine.

MODIFYING WINDOWS

The possible `wID` values are

```
NFY_UNKNOWN
NFY_LOADSEG
NFY_FREESEG
NFY_STARTDLL
NFY_STARTTASK
NFY_EXITTASK
NFY_DELMODULE
NFY_RIP
NFY_TASKIN
NFY_TASKOUT
NFY_INCHAR
NFY_OUTSTR
NFY_LOGERROR
NFY_LOGPARAMERROR
```

When we have no future need for notifications, we should unregister the callback routine with the NotifyUnRegister API.

NotifyUnRegister

Unregister a notification callback routine

```
BOOL NotifyUnRegister(hTask);

HTASK hTask;    // task associated with callback routine
                // NULL == current task
```

Returns:
If successful, TRUE; else FALSE.

CALLBACK SAFETY

The notification callback routine is called from deep in the unknown internals of Windows, and runs in the context of the task that caused the notification to occur. Thus, the callback routine is executing with the caller's stack, and SS != DS. Furthermore, the callback routine is really part of another task, the caller. Consequently, it is a good idea to put callback routines in a DLL, rather than inside the application (see Chapter 2). If you do want to put the callback routine in your EXE (as is done for demonstration purposes in the following example), you must compile your application with the switches that will instruct the compiler to load DS correctly on entrance to the callback routine (i.e., –GEd).

Finally, remember that in order to avoid reentrancy problems, the callback routine should not issue Windows calls, except for Toolhelp and the few reentrant APIs (PostMessage, PostAppMessage, OutputDebugStr, DriverCallback, timeGetSystemTime, timeGetTime, timeSetEvent, timeKillEvent, midiOutShortMsg, and midiOutLongMsg). Most commonly, a callback routine uses PostMessage (which is reentrant) to post a user-defined message to the application, which in turn performs the required action.

TERMINATION NOTIFICATION EXAMPLE

The following program starts a non-Windows process via WinExec. The program allows only one such non-Windows process to be run at a time. Thus, when the non-Windows process is started, the "Start Process" menu option is disabled. After the process is started (and has sufficient time to initialize), the program registers a notification callback routine to wait for the process to terminate. At termination (either normal or abnormal), the "Start Process" menu option is re-enabled.

The notification callback routine that waits for the non-Windows process to terminate ignores all notifications except NFY_EXITTASK, which is received when any task in the system terminates. When a NFY_EXITTASK notification is received, the GetCurrentTask API is used to get the `hTask` of the termination task (the task that is running the notification routine). If the terminating task is our WinOldAp, a user-defined message is posted to our application. When our application receives the user-defined message, it unregisters the notification callback routine and re-enables the "Start Process" menu item.

Note that when NFY_EXITTASK is called, the low-order byte of `dwData` contains the program's exit code. In our case, however, this is WinOldAp's exit code. WinOldAp usually returns the least significant byte of the non-Windows process's exit code as its own exit code. However, if you terminate WinOldAp before the non-Windows process completes (i.e., System Menu, Settings, Terminate, OK), WinOldAp returns zero as its exit code. Furthermore, if WinOldAp itself got started but could not start the non-Windows application, it will return an exit code > 0x80.

Finally, note that while we discussed notification in the context of waiting for a non-Windows process to terminate, the same techniques can be used to be notified of the termination of a Windows task, as well as for all the other notifications supported by Toolhelp's notification mechanism.

MAKEFILE

```
all: mlproces.exe runme.exe

runme.obj: runme.c makefile
    cl -AS -G2 -Ox -W3 runme.c

mlproces.res: mlproces.rc mlproces.h makefile
    rc -r mlproces.rc

mlproces.obj: mlproces.c mlproces.h makefile
    cl -c -DSTRICT -AS -GA2 -GEd -Ox -W3 mlproces.c

mlproces.exe: mlproces.obj mlproces.def mlproces.res makefile
    link mlproces,,,libw slibcew toolhelp, mlproces.def
    rc mlproces.res
```

MLPROCES.C

```
// Multi-processing under Windows 3.1 by using a DOS process
// An example of using Toolhelp's notification
//
// from Modifying Windows by Asael Dror

#include <windows.h>
#include <toolhelp.h>
#include "mlproces.h"

HINSTANCE hInst;                                  // current inst
HWND hWndP;

        // handles to WinOldAp for non-Windows process window
HINSTANCE hInstWinOldAp;
HWND hWndWinOldAp;
HTASK hTaskWinOldAp;

                                                // application E.P.
int PASCAL WinMain(HINSTANCE hInstance, HINSTANCE hPrevInstance,
            LPSTR LPCmdLine, int nCmdShow)

  {
  MSG msg;
```

```c
    if (hPrevInstance)                              // one inst only!
        return(FALSE);

    if (!InitApplication(hInstance))                // init app
        return(FALSE);

    if (!InitInstance(hInstance, nCmdShow))         // init instance
        return(FALSE);

                                                    // msg loop
    while (GetMessage(&msg, NULL, 0, 0))            // get any msg/any wnd
        {
        TranslateMessage(&msg);                     // xlate virt keys
        DispatchMessage(&msg);                      // dispatch message
        }
    return(msg.wParam);
    }

BOOL InitApplication(HINSTANCE hInstance)           // init app
    {
                                                    // reg main wnd class
    WNDCLASS wc;

                                                    // fill wnd class str
    wc.style = NULL;
    wc.lpfnWndProc = MainWndProc;                   // wnd proc
    wc.cbClsExtra = 0;
    wc.cbWndExtra = 0;
    wc.hInstance = hInstance;                       // class owner
    wc.hIcon = LoadIcon(NULL, IDI_APPLICATION);     // def app icon
    wc.hCursor = LoadCursor(NULL, IDC_ARROW);       // std cursor
    wc.hbrBackground = (HBRUSH)(COLOR_WINDOW + 1);  // wnd bkg clr
    wc.lpszMenuName = "MainMenu";
    wc.lpszClassName = "mlproces";                  // wnd class name

    return(RegisterClass(&wc));                     // reg wnd class
    }

                                                    // instance init
BOOL InitInstance(HINSTANCE hInstance, int nCmdShow)
    {

    hInst = hInstance;                              // save in static var

    hWndP = CreateWindow (                          // main wnd for inst
            "mlproces",                             // class name
            "Win16 Multiprocess",                   // title bar text
            WS_OVERLAPPEDWINDOW | WS_VISIBLE,       // "normal" & vsbl
```

```
                CW_USEDEFAULT,                  // default x
                nCmdShow,                       // default y,
                                                // show as req
                CW_USEDEFAULT,                  // default width
                CW_USEDEFAULT,                  // default height
                HWND_DESKTOP,                   // no parent
                NULL,                           // use class menu
                hInstance,                      // inst of mod wnd
                NULL);                          // not used
    if (!hWndP) return(FALSE);
    UpdateWindow(hWndP);                        // send WM_PAINT msg
    return (TRUE);                              // OK
    }


LRESULT __export CALLBACK MainWndProc(
                        HWND hWnd,              // window handle
                        UINT message,           // message
                        WPARAM wParam,          // param
                        LPARAM lParam)          // param

    {

    switch (message)
        {
        case WM_DESTROY:
            PostQuitMessage(0);                 // bye bye, rc = 0
            break;

        case WM_COMMAND:
            switch (wParam)
                {
                case IDM_START_PROCESS:
                                                // gray menu
                    ModifyMenu(GetMenu(hWnd), IDM_START_PROCESS,
                            MF_BYCOMMAND | MF_GRAYED,
                            IDM_START_PROCESS, "&Start Process");
                    DrawMenuBar(hWnd);
                                                // start process
                    hInstWinOldAp = (HINSTANCE) WinExec("runme",
                            SW_SHOWNORMAL);

                                    // give it a chance to start
                    SetTimer(hWnd, IDT_WAIT_FOR_PROCESS,
                            WAITTIME, NULL);
                    break;

                default:                        // def proc & ret
                    return (DefWindowProc(hWnd, message,
```

```
                                     wParam, lParam));
              }
        break;

        case WM_TIMER:
           if (wParam == IDT_WAIT_FOR_PROCESS)
              {
              if (hWndWinOldAp = FindWindow(NULL, "DOS Process"))
                 {                          // if found
                 KillTimer(hWnd, IDT_WAIT_FOR_PROCESS);
                                            // save its hTask
                 hTaskWinOldAp = GetWindowTask(hWndWinOldAp);

                 // register notification callback routine
                 NotifyRegister((HTASK)NULL,
                    (LPFNNOTIFYCALLBACK)
                    MakeProcInstance((FARPROC)NotifyRTN, hInst),
                    NF_NORMAL);
                 }
              }
           else return (DefWindowProc(hWnd, message,
                                        wParam, lParam));
        break;

        case WM_USER:
                          // msg from notification callback routine
           NotifyUnRegister(NULL);          // unregister notification

                                            // ungray menu
           ModifyMenu(GetMenu(hWnd), IDM_START_PROCESS,
                    MF_BYCOMMAND | MF_STRING,
                    IDM_START_PROCESS, "&Start Process");
           DrawMenuBar(hWnd);
        break;

        default:                                     // def proc & ret
           return (DefWindowProc(hWnd, message, wParam, lParam));
        }
     return(NULL);
     }

                              // notification callback routine
BOOL __export CALLBACK NotifyRTN(WORD wNFYID, DWORD dwData)
  {
  if (wNFYID == NFY_EXITTASK)               // if exit task
                                            // and if it's our task
     if (hTaskWinOldAp == GetCurrentTask())
        {                                   // then post a message
```

```
            PostMessage(hWndP, WM_USER, 0, 0);
            return TRUE;                    // we handled it
            }

    return FALSE;                           // let someone else handle it
    }
```

MLPROCES.H

```
#define IDM_START_PROCESS       100

#define IDT_WAIT_FOR_PROCESS    300
#define WAITTIME                1500

LRESULT __export CALLBACK MainWndProc(HWND, UINT, WPARAM, LPARAM);
BOOL InitApplication(HINSTANCE);
BOOL InitInstance(HINSTANCE, int);
BOOL __export CALLBACK NotifyRTN(WORD, DWORD);
```

MLPROCES.RC

```
#include <windows.h>
#include "mlproces.h"

MainMenu    MENU    PRELOAD
            {
            MENUITEM    "&Start Process", IDM_START_PROCESS
            }
```

MLPROCES.DEF

```
NAME            MLPROCES

DESCRIPTION     'Wait for non-Windows process to terminate'

EXETYPE         WINDOWS

STUB            'WINSTUB.EXE'

CODE PRELOAD MOVEABLE DISCARDABLE
```

```
DATA PRELOAD MOVEABLE MULTIPLE

HEAPSIZE        1024
STACKSIZE       5120
```

RUNME.C

```c
// a non-Windows (DOS) process

main(void);

#include <stdio.h>

main(void)
   {
   unsigned int VMID;
   int i;

   __asm
      {
      mov ax,1683h
      int 2Fh              ; Get VMID using DPMI
      mov VMID, bx
      }
                           // show that we are running
   for (i = 0; i < 2000; i++)
      printf ("non-Windows process in VM %i ", VMID);

   return(0);
   }
```

Figure 7-3 shows the "scheduler" and its non-Windows process running.

MODIFYING WINDOWS

Figure 7-3
Appearance of the screen while the MLPROCES program waits for the non-Windows process to terminate

Chapter 8

Dynamic Link Interceptors

HAVING arrived at this stage of the book, you now probably agree that Windows' best features are its flexibility and extendibility. If we do not like the way a particular window procedure behaves, we can change that behavior by using the various techniques discussed in previous chapters. But what if we want to change something much more fundamental about Windows, such as the Windows API itself? This is possible, and not even too difficult, thanks to the fact that Windows is basically a collection of Dynamic Link Libraries (DLLs). Taking advantage of this, we can write *Dynamic Link Interceptors* (DLIs), which are DLLs that are called in place of the original DLL. In addition to performing whatever function it was designed to do, the DLI can call the original DLL for "default processing." DLIs are important for creating debugging tools and profilers. However, due to their ability to redefine the API, their usefulness goes much further. We will look at some of the uses for DLIs at the end of this chapter, after we understand how they actually work.

To understand DLIs, you must have a good understanding of DLLs. If you simply glanced through Chapter 2, this may be a good time to go back and reread it carefully.

There are many techniques for writing DLIs, but they can all be classified into one of three categories:

1. Link-time DLIs

2. Patching DLIs

3. Replacement DLIs

We will take a brief look at the first category (which is very simple to implement) and the second category (which uses too much hacking), and then explore the last category in more detail.

Link-Time DLIs

This is the "official" and well-known way to write a DLI. It is composed of three stages:

1. Write a DLI that exports the same functions as the DLL we want to intercept. There is no need to write all of the DLL's exported routines, just the ones we want to intercept.

2. Create an import library for the DLI.

3. When you link the application that should use the DLI, list the DLI's import library *before* the DLL's import library in the list of libraries the linker uses to resolve external references. This way, references by the application to exported routines in the DLL that are also exported by the DLI will be resolved to the DLI.

If the DLI needs to call a DLL routine that is defined both in the DLI and in the DLL, it can do so by using different internal and external names. Calling the original DLL can be done before, after, or instead of the DLI's code.

While this technique is "clean," it has one *major* drawback: it requires that *you* do the linking! This makes the technique usable only when it's your application that needs to use the DLI, and you have the source code!

How can we implement DLIs for applications for which we do not have source code, or even create a global DLI that will be used by *all* applications? The next section discusses a number of ways in which this can be achieved.

Patching DLIs

There are three common ways to write DLIs using the patching approach:

1. Patch the application on disk.

2. Patch the application in memory.

3. Patch the DLL in memory.

Patching the Application on Disk

This technique is similar to the Link Time DLI, but it does not require the application's source code. As we discussed in Chapter 2, when an application uses implicit dynamic linking, the linker includes fix-up information in the application's EXE file. This fix-up information includes (among other things) the name of the DLL containing the APIs that the application calls (dynamically links to).

Imagine that we created a DLI that exported all the functions of a DLL and used the Link Time DLI technique discussed above. In this case, the application's fix-up information would indicate that calls are to be made to the routines in the DLI. Since in reality we were *not* the ones who linked the application, the application's header actually contains the DLL's name rather than the DLI's in its fix-up information. We can, however, "fix that" by patching the application's header. For example, if we create a DLI for GDI, calling the DLI "GDX", and have GDX export all the routines found in GDI, we can patch the EXE header of an application to resolve external references to GDX instead of GDI. It's that simple!

Patching the Application in Memory

One of the ways to perform application patching in memory is by replacing calls to the DLL with calls to the DLI as the application is being loaded into memory (though this technique, like the application patching on disk, will not trap explicit dynamic link calls, only implicit calls). Using this technique, calls from the application are changed to call the DLI, which performs its job, and in turn may call the DLL. The patching can be done, for example, by setting up a Toolhelp notification callback routine and looking for the application's segment loading. When a segment is being loaded, its calls to the DLL are changed to calls to the DLI instead. The information as to where the application calls the DLL is contained in the application's EXE header.

Patching the DLL in Memory

This technique is based on patching the DLLs rather than the applications that call them. Using this technique, the first instruction in every exported routine that we want to intercept in the DLL is replaced with a jump to the corresponding function in the DLI. Thus, all calls to the DLL's routine will jump to the corresponding DLI routine. If the DLI needs to call the original DLL routine, it must perform the job that was done by the patched code, before jumping back in.

While the patching techniques do work, and are used by some commercial software utilities, they are definitely not "clean." Patching applications or a DLL's code is not good programming practice and may not work in future versions of Windows that utilize protection mechanisms. There are additional ways to write DLIs based on some bugs (or limitations) in the way Windows 3.*x* keeps track of loaded modules. However, those techniques are so "dirty" that they are better not described.

The question remains: Is there a "clean" way to write DLIs when we do not have the source code, using only "legal" and documented APIs? The official word from Redmond is *no*!

"There is no clean, supported way to intercept a library's exported function for all modules in the system unless you have source control over all modules, an unlikely situation!" (*Mechanics of Dynamic Linking*, Microsoft Developer Network, Microsoft Corporation, January 1993.)

However, there is a way to perform just that, as we shall see in the next section.

Replacement DLIs

Here is how the "replacement DLI" technique (which has never been published except in the *Windows Developer Letter*) works. First we rename the original DLL to be intercepted. Then we create a new DLL (the DLI) that has the same filename as the original DLL and exports the same functions. At run time, when our DLI is loaded and initialized by Windows, we explicitly load and initialize the original, intercepted, DLL. Whenever an application tries to call a function in the original DLL (implicitly or explicitly), it will actually be calling our DLI. The DLI in turn can call the corresponding function in the DLL for default processing using explicit dynamic linking (or do whatever we want it to do, instead of, or in addition to, that function). Basically, it's quite simple! (It may actually be possible to perform this with implicit dynamic linking, but this would require relying on some of Windows' special "features" involving module names that are different from their filenames.)

The DLI can explicitly load and initialize the DLL using the LoadLibrary API, get the addresses of routines within the DLL with the GetProcAddress API, and then call the routines directly.

DLI Implementation

Now to the nitty-gritty. We will demonstrate a DLI for the SHELL.DLL of Windows 3.1. SHELL.DLL is a good example because it exports only a few APIs, allowing us to keep the example relatively short.

Since a DLL's initialization routine needs to be written in assembly language, and since our example has little more than an initialization routine, it is written entirely in assembler. This also lets us see exactly what's happening, which is the reason the example program does not even use the high-level language macros from CMACROS.INC

The first thing to do is back up the original SHELL.DLL (just in case). Then rename SHELL.DLL to SHELL@.DLL. This will be the DLL our DLI will call to perform "default processing."

Exported Functions

Before we can start to write our DLI, we need to know which functions are exported by the original SHELL.DLL. A simple way to do this is to use the EXEHDR utility. When we run EXEHRD on SHELL.DLL, the output looks like this:

```
Microsoft (R) EXE File Header Utility  Version 3.00
Copyright (C) Microsoft Corp 1985-1992.  All rights reserved.

Library:                SHELL
Description:            Windows 3.1 Shell API Library
Data:                   SHARED
Initialization:         Per-Process
Initial CS:IP:          seg    1 offset 0010
Initial SS:SP:          seg    0 offset 0000
DGROUP:                 seg   13
Heap allocation:        0100 bytes
Application type:       WINDOWAPI
Other module flags:     Runs in protected mode only
```

CHAPTER 8
DYNAMIC LINK INTERCEPTORS 241

```
no. type address  file  mem   flags
  1 CODE 00000560 001e6 001e6 PRELOAD, (movable), (discardable)
  2 CODE 000007c0 01a5c 01a5c PRELOAD, (movable), (discardable)
  3 CODE 00002340 009e8 009e8 PRELOAD, (movable), (discardable)
  4 CODE 00002da0 013fa 013fa PRELOAD, (movable), (discardable)
  5 CODE 000043e0 00234 00234 PRELOAD, (movable), (discardable)
  6 CODE 00004660 0015e 0015e PRELOAD, (movable), (discardable)
  7 CODE 00004bc0 0023a 0023a (movable), (discardable)
  8 CODE 00004e60 00791 00792 (movable), (discardable)
  9 CODE 00005700 00dbf 00dc0 (movable), (discardable)
 10 CODE 00006690 009e0 009e0 (movable), (discardable)
 11 CODE 00007120 00121 00122 (movable), (discardable)
 12 DATA 00000000 00000 00016 SHARED, (movable)
 13 DATA 00004820 00354 00354 SHARED, PRELOAD, (movable)


Exports:
ord seg offset name
  8   7  0000  WEP exported, shared data
 33   9  0136  ABOUTDLGPROC exported, shared data
 34  10  021a  EXTRACTICON exported, shared data
 21   4  1154  FINDEXECUTABLE exported, shared data
  9   6  0052  DRAGACCEPTFILES exported, shared data
  1   2  15cc  REGOPENKEY exported, shared data
  2   2  15fa  REGCREATEKEY exported, shared data
100   4  0550  HERETHARBETYGARS exported, shared data
 38   5  0000  FINDENVIRONMENTSTRING exported, shared data
  4   2  1628  REGDELETEKEY exported, shared data
  7   2  14dc  REGENUMKEY exported, shared data
 37   5  00ae  DOENVIRONMENTSUBST exported, shared data
 20   4  110a  SHELLEXECUTE exported, shared data
101   8  010e  FINDEXEDLGPROC exported, shared data
 11   6  0094  DRAGQUERYFILE exported, shared data
 13   6  0000  DRAGQUERYPOINT exported, shared data
  5   2  16f4  REGSETVALUE exported, shared data
 39  10  026e  INTERNALEXTRACTICON exported, shared data
 22   9  0000  SHELLABOUT exported, shared data
  6   2  168e  REGQUERYVALUE exported, shared data
 32   9  0829  WCI exported, shared data
102   4  128c  REGISTERSHELLHOOK exported, shared data
 36  10  08dc  EXTRACTASSOCIATEDICON exported, shared data
 12   6  0142  DRAGFINISH exported, shared data
103   4  11ca  SHELLHOOKPROC exported, shared data
  3   2  1670  REGCLOSEKEY exported, shared data
```

EXEHDR shows us the names and ordinals of all exported functions in SHELL.DLL. Those all have to be exported by our DLI, so we place them in the DEF file as exported functions (see the DEF's file listing later in this chapter).

Modifying a Code Segment

Now for the DLI itself (see the listings later in this chapter). To keep things simple (and to demonstrate how to modify a code segment), the example program has only one segment (code) and no data segment. In order to store data in our code segment, we need a data segment alias to the code segment. By using the alias selector we can access our code segment as if it were a data segment. (Otherwise, attempting to write to the code segment would result in a General Protection exception when running in protected mode.) Thus, we have two different selectors to the same memory segment. One selector addresses the segment as code, and the other addresses it as data. This is shown in Figure 8-1.

To get the data selector, we use the undocumented (but safe, because it is used by so many device drivers) AllocCStoDSAlias API. This API is similar to the documented AllocDStoCSAlias API, but works in reverse. It gets a code segment selector and returns a data segment selector that references the same memory segment.

AllocCStoDSAlias

Allocate a data segment alias for a code segment

```
SEG AllocCStoDSAlias (sel);

SEL sel;        // selector of code segment to be aliased
```

Returns:
If successful, returns a selector to a data segment that refers to the same memory as the code segment of `sel`; otherwise it returns 0.

CHAPTER 8
DYNAMIC LINK INTERCEPTORS

Figure 8-1
Alias selectors accessing the same memory segment

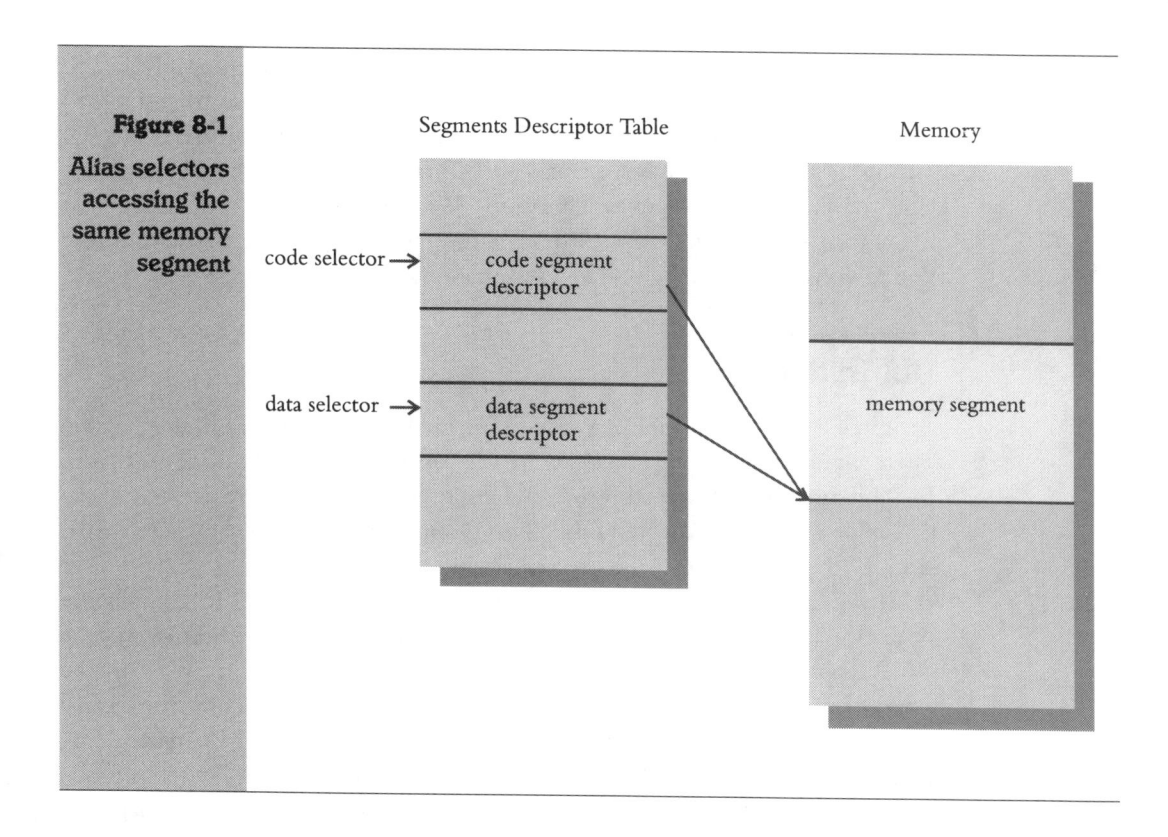

Later, when we do not need the selector anymore, we should free it with the FreeSelector API.

FreeSelector

Free a selector (and its segment descriptor table entry)

```
SEG FreeSelector (sel);

SEL sel;    // selector to be freed (allocated by
            // AllocSelector, AllocCStoDSAlias
            // or AllocDStoCSAlias)
```

Returns:
If successful 0; else `sel`.

An additional point to note is that the code segment is marked FIXED in the DEF file. This is done to ensure that Windows will not discard and reload the segment after we have modified the data. It also ensures that Windows will not move the code segment around and "forget" to update the data segment table to reflect the new memory location. (Windows does not "remember" that there are two segment table entries for the same memory segment, and that these two entries must be updated simultaneously.)

DLI Initialization

At initialization time (LibEntry), the DLI loads (and implicitly initializes) the intercepted DLL (SHELL@.DLL in this example). This is done with the LoadLibrary API. Our DLI then needs to obtain the addresses of all the procedures in the intercepted DLL. This is done with the GetProcAddress API. Both of these APIs were discussed in Chapter 2.

The DLI searches through a table that we have initialized to contain the ordinal number of each exported procedure in the intercepted DLL (except the WEP, as we will see later) and calls GetProcAddress for each ordinal. We store the returned procedure address in the table. Entries in the table containing the ordinal number and the procedure address are created by the `ProcAddr` macro. This macro allocates the ordinal and space for the procedure address. The location at which the procedure address is stored is given the name AddrOf&*FuncName* (for example, `AddrOfDRAGACCEPTFILES`, `AddrOfDRAGFINISH`, etc.).

For each exported function in the intercepted DLL (and hence in the DLI), we define a small procedure that (for now) simply jumps (via an indirect far jump to the address retrieved at DLI initialization with GetProcAddress) to the intercepted procedure for "default processing." The procedure looks like the following:

```
FuncName    proc    far
            public  FuncName
            jmp     cs:AddrOf&FuncName
FuncName    endp
```

Again, to make life easier we use a macro (`DefProc`) to create the procedures for each exported function.

Windows Exit Procedure (WEP)

There is, however, one exception to the above approach: the Window Exit Procedure (WEP). As we discussed in Chapter 2, Windows maintains a use-count for each DLL. Every time a DLL is loaded, its use-count is incremented; and every time the DLL is freed, the use-count is decremented. When the use-count of a DLL is zero, Windows calls the DLL's WEP to perform any cleanup, and then frees the DLL from memory. When the DLI's WEP is called, we need to free (via a call to FreeLibrary) the intercepted DLL, otherwise Windows will free the DLI but leave the intercepted DLL forever "lost in space" (or is it virtual memory?). While the Microsoft documentation explicitly prohibits calling FreeLibrary from a DLL's WEP, I feel that this is a place where the rules should be broken.

Thus, in the DLI's WEP we do not call the DLL's WEP, but instead call FreeLibrary, which will cause Windows to call the intercepted DLL's WEP directly (nested WEPs). The following tables summarize this sequence of events without and with a DLI.

Sequence of Events Without a DLI

Application	DLL

Loaded	if not already in memory then
	{
	load
	initialize
	}
	use-count ++

Call routine	execute code return to caller (application)

Terminated	use-count − −
	if (use-count == 0) then
	{
	WEP
	DLL freed from memory
	}

MODIFYING WINDOWS

Sequence of Events With a DLI

Application	DLI	DLL

Loaded	if not already in memory then
	{
	load
	initialize
	}
	use-count ++	

	LoadLibrary (DLL)	if not already in memory then
		{
		load
		initialize
		}
		use-count ++

Call routine	far jump to DLL	execute code return to caller (application)

Terminated	use-count – –
	if (use-count == 0) then
	{
	WEP
	FreeLibrary (DLL)
		Use-count – –
		if (use-count == 0) then
		{
		WEP
		DLL freed from memory
		}

	DLL freed from memory }	

Note that in the case of SHELL.DLL nothing horrible will happen if you do not use FreeLibrary, since SHELL.DLL is freed only when Windows terminates. One final word of caution: Do not use the `DefProc` macro to call the intercepted DLL's WEP from your DLI's WEP. Doing this will cause the intercepted DLL to perform its cleanup, but will not decrease the use-count of the DLL, and so the DLL will not be freed. If the DLL is later reused, Windows will not reload it (since it has not been freed), and so the DLL will not go through initialization again. This will cause the library to be used after termination cleanup has occurred—dangerous stuff!

DYNAMIC LINK INTERCEPTOR SKELETON EXAMPLE

Here are the listings that make up our DLI skeleton example for SHELL.DLL. For now, this is a skeleton example only; it does not actually change the behavior of the intercepted DLL.

CHAPTER 8
DYNAMIC LINK INTERCEPTORS

MAKEFILE

```
all: shell.dll

shell.obj: shell.asm makefile
    masm shell;

shell.dll: shell.obj shell.def makefile
    link /NOD shell,shell.dll,nul,libw,shell.def
    rc shell.dll
```

SHELL.ASM

```
;
; Dynamic Link Intercepter example
;
; From Modifying Windows by Asael Dror
;

        .286

_TEXT segment word public 'CODE'
        assume  cs:_TEXT,ds:nothing,es:nothing,ss:nothing

        extrn   AllocCStoDSAlias:FAR
        extrn   FreeLibrary:FAR
        extrn   FreeSelector:FAR
        extrn   GetProcAddress:FAR
        extrn   LoadLibrary:FAR


LibEntry proc   FAR

; DLL Entry Point, called for Initialization when DLL is loaded
; On entry:
; DI = instance handle
; DS = DS (none)
; CX = heap size (none)
;
; Preserve: DS, BP, SI, DI
```

MODIFYING WINDOWS

```
        push    si
        push    di
        push    ds

        push    cs
        call    AllocCStoDSAlias        ; alloc a DS alias to CS
                                        ; ax = DS alias to CS
        cmp     ax,0                    ; ax = 0 indicates an error
        je      NoDS

        mov     ds,ax
        assume  ds:_TEXT

        push    ds
        push    offset DLLFileName
        call    LoadLibrary             ; load & init intercepted DLL
                                        ; ax = hInstance
        cmp     ax,32                   ; if hInstance < 32 it's an
                                        ; error
        jb      CanNotLoad

        mov     di,ax                   ; di = hInstance

        mov     si,offset ProcAddrTable

                                        ; get_proc_address loop
NextProcAddr:
        push    di                      ; hInstance
        push    0                       ; lpProcName = 0:ordinal
        push    word ptr[si]
        call    GetProcAddress
                                        ; dx:ax = proc address
        mov     word ptr [si+2],ax      ; save proc address
        mov     word ptr [si+4],dx
        add     si,6                    ; next entry in table
        mov     ax,word ptr[si]         ; get ordinal
        cmp     ax,0                    ; check for end of table
                                        ; (ordinal=0)
        jne     NextProcAddr            ; if not end of table continue
        mov     si,1                    ; OK RC

FreeDS:
        mov     bx,ds
        assume  ds:nothing
        pop     ds                      ; never leave an invalid sel
                                        ; in DS
```

```
        push    bx
        call    FreeSelector            ; free DS alias to CS
ByeBye:
        mov     ax,si                   ; RC in its place
        pop     di
        pop     si
        ret

NoDS:
        pop     ax                      ; life is hell...
        sub     si,si                   ; fail RC
        jmp     ByeBye

CanNotLoad:
        sub     si,si
        jmp     FreeDS

LibEntry endp



DLLFileName db      "shell@.dll",0      ; intercepted DLL
hLibModule  dw      ?



ProcAddr macro  FuncName,Ordinal
        dw      Ordinal
        ddrOf&FuncName dd    ?          ; intercepted DLL proc address
        endm


ProcAddrTable   label   word
        ProcAddr        REGOPENKEY,1
        ProcAddr        REGCREATEKEY,2
        ProcAddr        REGCLOSEKEY,3
        ProcAddr        REGDELETEKEY,4
        ProcAddr        REGSETVALUE,5
        ProcAddr        REGQUERYVALUE,6
        ProcAddr        REGENUMKEY,7
       ; ProcAddr       WEP,8                       ; only Windows calls it
        ProcAddr        DRAGACCEPTFILES,9
        ProcAddr        DRAGQUERYFILE,11
        ProcAddr        DRAGFINISH,12
        ProcAddr        DRAGQUERYPOINT,13
        ProcAddr        SHELLEXECUTE,20
        ProcAddr        FINDEXECUTABLE,21
        ProcAddr        SHELLABOUT,22
```

MODIFYING WINDOWS

```
        ProcAddr        WCI,32
        ProcAddr        ABOUTDLGPROC,33
        ProcAddr        EXTRACTICON,34
        ProcAddr        EXTRACTASSOCIATEDICON,36
        ProcAddr        DOENVIRONMENTSUBST,37
        ProcAddr        FINDENVIRONMENTSTRING,38
        ProcAddr        INTERNALEXTRACTICON,39
        ProcAddr        HERETHARBETYGARS,100
        ProcAddr        FINDEXEDLGPROC,101
        ProcAddr        REGISTERSHELLHOOK,102
        ProcAddr        SHELLHOOKPROC,103
        dw              0                       ; end of table


DefProc macro   FuncName
FuncName proc   far
        public  FuncName
        jmp     cs:AddrOf&FuncName              ; jump to intercepted DLL proc.
FuncName endp
        endm


        DefProc         REGOPENKEY
        DefProc         REGCREATEKEY
        DefProc         REGCLOSEKEY
        DefProc         REGDELETEKEY
        DefProc         REGSETVALUE
        DefProc         REGQUERYVALUE
        DefProc         REGENUMKEY
;       DefProc         WEP                     ; we have our own
        DefProc         DRAGACCEPTFILES
        DefProc         DRAGQUERYFILE
        DefProc         DRAGFINISH
        DefProc         DRAGQUERYPOINT
        DefProc         SHELLEXECUTE
        DefProc         FINDEXECUTABLE
        DefProc         SHELLABOUT
        DefProc         WCI
        DefProc         ABOUTDLGPROC
        DefProc         EXTRACTICON
        DefProc         EXTRACTASSOCIATEDICON
        DefProc         DOENVIRONMENTSUBST
        DefProc         FINDENVIRONMENTSTRING
        DefProc         INTERNALEXTRACTICON
        DefProc         HERETHARBETYGARS
        DefProc         FINDEXEDLGPROC
        DefProc         REGISTERSHELLHOOK
```

```
        DefProc         SHELLHOOKPROC

WEP     proc    far                             ; Window Exit Proc
        public  WEP
        push    cs:hLibModule
        call    FreeLibrary                     ; free intercepted DLL
        mov     ax,1                            ; OK RC
        ret     2
WEP     endp


_TEXT   ends
        end     LibEntry                        ; LibEntry is DLL's entry point
```

SHELL.DEF

```
LIBRARY             SHELL

DESCRIPTION         'A DLI for SHELL.DLL'

EXETYPE             WINDOWS

STUB                'WINSTUB.EXE'

CODE PRELOAD FIXED

EXPORTS
        REGOPENKEY              @1
        REGCREATEKEY            @2
        REGCLOSEKEY             @3
        REGDELETEKEY            @4
        REGSETVALUE             @5
        REGQUERYVALUE           @6
        REGENUMKEY              @7
        WEP                     @8
        DRAGACCEPTFILES         @9
        DRAGQUERYFILE           @11
        DRAGFINISH              @12
        DRAGQUERYPOINT          @13
        SHELLEXECUTE            @20
        FINDEXECUTABLE          @21
        SHELLABOUT              @22
        WCI                     @32
        ABOUTDLGPROC            @33
```

```
EXTRACTICON              @34
EXTRACTASSOCIATEDICON    @36
DOENVIRONMENTSUBST       @37
FINDENVIRONMENTSTRING    @38
INTERNALEXTRACTICON      @39
HERETHARBETYGARS         @100
FINDEXEDLGPROC           @101
REGISTERSHELLHOOK        @102
SHELLHOOKPROC            @103
```

Pitfalls and Problems

Like writing directly to the screen, or like TSRs in the old days (yes, nested DLIs are possible!), DLIs are uncharted waters. It may sound like a dangerous approach, and there are potential problems. However, the tremendous flexibility and power offered by this method are well worth the dangers.

One pitfall to keep an eye out for, is any program that knows the DLL intimately and relies on non-exported properties. Another possible pitfall is performing recursive calls—for example, a DLI for a display device driver that calls a GDI function that calls the display device driver.

A common problem to look out for has to do with DLLs that contain resources. In this case, your DLI will have to include those resources or provide appropriate substitutes.

Finally comes the issue of debugging your DLI. Debugging a DLI for an application's DLL is (almost) like debugging any other DLL. However, if you are creating a DLI for one of Windows' own DLLs, such as the SHELL.DLL, you have to be careful. If your code has a bug, Windows will not boot. A system-level debugger such as the Windows kernel debugger discussed in Chapter 3 is essential.

DLI Applications

Now that we know how to write a DLI, let's take a look at what we can do with DLIs.

We can use DLIs to profile programs, i.e., to figure out which function they call, at what frequency, and how long it takes for each function to execute. For example, if we are designing display hardware for Windows, we can check which display driver functions are used most frequently so we can optimize our hardware and driver for those particular functions.

CHAPTER 8
DYNAMIC LINK INTERCEPTORS

DLIs are a natural for parameter validation. A DLI can be used as part of the development process to verify all parameters and to verify the freeing of all acquired resources.

Although most Windows APIs are documented, some are not. Many applications have DLLs that contain undocumented functions. We can use DLIs to figure out what those functions do by checking the sequence of calls and the parameters passed and returned by them.

Furthermore, DLIs can be very useful in debuggers. A debugger that uses a DLI can provide such services as conditional breakpoints on APIs calls or thorough parameter validation for such calls. If all you want to do is break on a specific API call, this can be done simply by inserting an INT 3 instruction in the DLI's procedure for the function you want to break on, just before the jump to the DLL. Now run Windows under a system-level debugger, and you will hit a breakpoint before the actual API is executed.

The most important use for DLIs is probably to change the behavior of a procedure in a DLL. For example, the SHELL.DLL DragQueryPoint API returns a 0 if the drop location is not in the client area of the window. Suppose we want to change this API so that it will always return 1 instead. In this case, we may also want to "fix" the drop point to be 0,0 rather than the actual drop point, which is outside the client area. To do this, we simply replace the default procedure in the DLI program above for the DragQueryPoint procedure with code that duplicates the parameters passed to the procedure and calls the intercepted procedure (via an indirect far call). On return, we check the returned value. If it is 0, we change the drop point coordinates to 0,0 and return a 1 instead. This is done using the modified code shown in the following listing.

SHELL.ASM

```
;
; Dynamic Link Intercepter example
;
; From Modifying Windows by Asael Dror
;

        .286

_TEXT   segment word public 'CODE'
        assume  cs:_TEXT,ds:nothing,es:nothing,ss:nothing

        extrn   AllocCStoDSAlias:FAR
        extrn   FreeLibrary:FAR
```

MODIFYING WINDOWS

```
        extrn   FreeSelector:FAR
        extrn   GetProcAddress:FAR
        extrn   LoadLibrary:FAR


LibEntry proc   FAR

; DLL Entry Point, called for Initialization when DLL is loaded
; On entry:
; DI = instance handle
; DS = DS (none)
; CX = heap size (none)
;
; Preserve: DS, BP, SI, DI


        push    si
        push    di
        push    ds


        push    cs
        call    AllocCStoDSAlias        ; alloc a DS alias to CS
                                        ; ax = DS alias to CS

        cmp     ax,0                    ; ax = 0 indicates an error
        je      NoDS

        mov     ds,ax
        assume  ds:_TEXT

        push    ds
        push    offset DLLFileName
        call    LoadLibrary             ; load & init intercepted DLL
                                        ; ax = hInstance
        cmp     ax,32                   ; if hInstance < 32 it's an
                                        ; error
        jb      CanNotLoad

        mov     di,ax                   ; di = hInstance

        mov     si,offset ProcAddrTable

                                        ; get_proc_address loop
NextProcAddr:
        push    di                      ; hInstance
        push    0                       ; lpProcName = 0:ordinal
        push    word ptr[si]
        call    GetProcAddress
                                        ; dx:ax = proc address
```

```
        mov     word ptr [si+2],ax      ; save proc address
        mov     word ptr [si+4],dx
        add     si,6                    ; next entry in table
        mov     ax,word ptr[si]         ; get ordinal
        cmp     ax,0                    ; check for end of table
                                        ; (ordinal=0)
        jne     NextProcAddr            ; if not end of table continue
        mov     cx,1                    ; OK RC
FreeDS:
        mov     bx,ds
        assume  ds:nothing
        pop     ds                      ; never leave an invalid sel
                                        ; in DS

        push    bx
        call    FreeSelector            ; free DS alias to CS
ByeBye:
        mov     ax,si                   ; RC in its place
        pop     di
        pop     si
        ret

NoDS:
        pop     ax                      ; life is hell...
        sub     si,si                   ; fail RC
        jmp     ByeBye

CanNotLoad:
        sub     si,si
        jmp     FreeDS

LibEntry endp


DLLFileName db      "shell@.dll",0      ; intercepted DLL
hLibModule  dw      ?




ProcAddr macro  FuncName,Ordinal
        dw      Ordinal
AddrOf&FuncName dd      ?               ; intercepted DLL proc
                                        ;address
        endm
```

MODIFYING WINDOWS

```
ProcAddrTable   label   word
    ProcAddr        REGOPENKEY,1
    ProcAddr        REGCREATEKEY,2
    ProcAddr        REGCLOSEKEY,3
    ProcAddr        REGDELETEKEY,4
    ProcAddr        REGSETVALUE,5
    ProcAddr        REGQUERYVALUE,6
    ProcAddr        REGENUMKEY,7
    ; ProcAddr       WEP,8                   ; only Windows calls it
    ProcAddr        DRAGACCEPTFILES,9
    ProcAddr        DRAGQUERYFILE,11
    ProcAddr        DRAGFINISH,12
    ProcAddr        DRAGQUERYPOINT,13
    ProcAddr        SHELLEXECUTE,20
    ProcAddr        FINDEXECUTABLE,21
    ProcAddr        SHELLABOUT,22
    ProcAddr        WCI,32
    ProcAddr        ABOUTDLGPROC,33
    ProcAddr        EXTRACTICON,34
    ProcAddr        EXTRACTASSOCIATEDICON,36
    ProcAddr        DOENVIRONMENTSUBST,37
    ProcAddr        FINDENVIRONMENTSTRING,38
    ProcAddr        INTERNALEXTRACTICON,39
    ProcAddr        HERETHARBETYGARS,100
    ProcAddr        FINDEXEDLGPROC,101
    ProcAddr        REGISTERSHELLHOOK,102
    ProcAddr        SHELLHOOKPROC,103
    dw              0                        ; end of table


DefProc macro   FuncName
FuncName proc   far
    public  FuncName
    jmp     cs:AddrOf&FuncName        ; jump to intercepted DLL proc
FuncName endp
    endm


    DefProc         REGOPENKEY
    DefProc         REGCREATEKEY
    DefProc         REGCLOSEKEY
    DefProc         REGDELETEKEY
    DefProc         REGSETVALUE
    DefProc         REGQUERYVALUE
    DefProc         REGENUMKEY
    ; DefProc         WEP                    ; we have our own
    DefProc         DRAGACCEPTFILES
```

CHAPTER 8
DYNAMIC LINK INTERCEPTORS

```
        DefProc     DRAGQUERYFILE
        DefProc     DRAGFINISH
        ; DefProc     DRAGQUERYPOINT     ; we have our own!
        DefProc     SHELLEXECUTE
        DefProc     FINDEXECUTABLE
        DefProc     SHELLABOUT
        DefProc     WCI
        DefProc     ABOUTDLGPROC
        DefProc     EXTRACTICON
        DefProc     EXTRACTASSOCIATEDICON
        DefProc     DOENVIRONMENTSUBST
        DefProc     FINDENVIRONMENTSTRING
        DefProc     INTERNALEXTRACTICON
        DefProc     HERETHARBETYGARS
        DefProc     FINDEXEDLGPROC
        DefProc     REGISTERSHELLHOOK
        DefProc     SHELLHOOKPROC


WEP     proc    far                         ; Window Exit Proc
        public  WEP
        push    cs:hLibModule
        call    FreeLibrary                 ; free intercepted DLL
        mov     ax,1                        ; OK RC
        ret     2
WEP     endp

; This DLI routine calls the SHELL DragQueryPoint and then if the
; drop point is outside of the window's client area, the drop point
; is changed to 0,0 in the client area

DRAGQUERYPOINT proc    far
        public  DRAGQUERYPOINT
                                            ; dup params
        mov     bx,sp                       ; (bx does not have to be
                                            ;  saved, but bp does)
        push    word ptr ss:[bx+8]
        push    word ptr ss:[bx+6]
        push    word ptr ss:[bx+4]
        call    cs:AddrOfDRAGQUERYPOINT     ; call intercepted DLL
        cmp     ax,0
        jne     backtoapp                   ; if drop in client then exit
        mov     bx,sp
        les     bx,dword ptr ss:[bx+4]      ; get POINT address
        sub     cx,cx
        mov     word ptr es:[bx],cx         ; x = 0
        mov     word ptr es:[bx+2],cx       ; y = 0
        mov     ax,1                        ; indicate drop is
```

```
                                        ; in client area
backtoapp:
    ret     6                           ; return to app throw params
DRAGQUERYPOINT  endp


_TEXT   ends
    end     LibEntry                    ; LibEntry is DLL's entry point
```

The following program is a drop-client for drag-and-drop, that displays the name of the dropped file at the dropped location. At WM_CREATE message time, the program registers itself as a drop client (by calling DragAcceptFiles). When a file (or files) are dropped on the window, the program will receive a WM_DROPFILE message. At that time, the DragQueryFile API is used to retrieve the number of files dropped on the window and their filenames. DragQueryPoint is used to retrieve the drop point.

You can see how the above DLI works by running the program with and without the DLI installed. With the DLI installed, when you drop file(s) on non-client areas of the window, their name(s) will appear starting from location 0,0 in the client area. Figure 8-2 shows the program's output.

MAKEFILE

```
all: droponme.exe

droponme.obj: droponme.c droponme.h makefile
    cl -c -DSTRICT -AS -GA2 -Ox -W3 droponme.c

droponme.exe: droponme.obj droponme.def makefile
    link droponme,,,shell libw slibcew, droponme.def
    rc droponme.exe
```

DROPONME.C

```
// Drag-and-Drop Client
//
// from Modifying Windows by Asael Dror
//

#include <windows.h>
```

CHAPTER 8
DYNAMIC LINK INTERCEPTORS

```
#include <shellapi.h>

#include "droponme.h"

HINSTANCE hInst;                                        // current instance

                                                        // application E.P.
int PASCAL WinMain(HINSTANCE hInstance, HINSTANCE hPrevInstance,
            LPSTR LPCmdLine, int nCmdShow)

  {
  MSG msg;
  if (!hPrevInstance)                                   // if first instance
     if (!InitApplication(hInstance))                   // then init app
        return(FALSE);

  if (!InitInstance(hInstance, nCmdShow))               // init instance
     return(FALSE);

                                                        // msg loop
  while (GetMessage(&msg, NULL, 0, 0))                  // get any msg/any wnd
     {
     TranslateMessage(&msg);                            // translate virt keys
     DispatchMessage(&msg);                             // dispatch message
     }
  return(msg.wParam);
  }

BOOL InitApplication(HINSTANCE hInstance)               // init app
  {
                                                        // reg main wnd class
  WNDCLASS wc;

                                                        // fill wnd class str
  wc.style = 0;
  wc.lpfnWndProc = MainWndProc;                         // window proc
  wc.cbClsExtra = 0;
  wc.cbWndExtra = 0;
  wc.hInstance = hInstance;                             // class owner
  wc.hIcon = LoadIcon(NULL, IDI_APPLICATION);           // def app icon
  wc.hCursor = LoadCursor(NULL, IDC_ARROW);             // standard cursor
  wc.hbrBackground = (HBRUSH)(COLOR_WINDOW + 1);        // wnd bckgnd clr
  wc.lpszMenuName = "MainMenu";
  wc.lpszClassName = "DropClass";                       // window class name

  return(RegisterClass(&wc));                           // register wnd class
  }
```

MODIFYING WINDOWS

```c
                                            // instance init
BOOL InitInstance(HINSTANCE hInstance, int nCmdShow)
  {
  HWND  hWnd;                               // window handle

  hInst = hInstance;                        // save in static var

  hWnd = CreateWindow (                     // main window
          "DropClass",                      // class name
          "Drag-and-Drop client",           // title bar text
          WS_OVERLAPPEDWINDOW | WS_VISIBLE, // normal & visible
          CW_USEDEFAULT,                    // default x
          nCmdShow,                         // default y,
                                            // show as requested
          CW_USEDEFAULT,                    // default width
          CW_USEDEFAULT,                    // default height
          HWND_DESKTOP,                     // no parent
          NULL,                             // use class menu
          hInstance,                        // inst of mod for win
          NULL);                            // not used
  if (!hWnd) return(FALSE);
  UpdateWindow(hWnd);                       // send WM_PAINT msg
  return (TRUE);                            // OK
  }


LRESULT __export CALLBACK MainWndProc(
                          HWND hWnd,        // window handle
                          UINT message,     // message
                          WPARAM wParam,    // param
                          LPARAM lParam)    // param

  {

  WORD nFiles, i, cszFileName;
  HDC hDC;
  char szFileName[MaxFileSpecLen + 1];
  POINT pt;
  TEXTMETRIC tm;

  switch (message)
     {
     case WM_CREATE:
     DragAcceptFiles(hWnd, TRUE);           // accept file-drops
     break;

     case WM_DROPFILES:                     // files were dropped msg

                                            // if drop in client area
```

CHAPTER 8
DYNAMIC LINK INTERCEPTORS

```c
            if (DragQueryPoint((HDROP)wParam, &pt))
            {                                       // then:
                                                    // get no. of dropped files
                nFiles = DragQueryFile((HDROP)wParam, -1, NULL, 0);
                hDC = GetDC(hWnd);                  // get window's DC
                GetTextMetrics(hDC, &tm);           // for text height

                                                    // for every dropped file
                for (i = 0; i < nFiles; i++,
                    pt.y += tm.tmHeight + tm.tmExternalLeading)
                {
                                                    // get file specs
                    cszFileName = DragQueryFile((HDROP)wParam, i, szFileName,
                                            sizeof(szFileName));
                                                    // display it
                    TextOut(hDC, pt.x, pt.y, szFileName, cszFileName);
                                    // and advance to next screen line
                }
                ReleaseDC(hWnd, hDC);
            }
            DragFinish((HDROP)wParam);              // free drag-and-drop structure
            break;

        case WM_DESTROY:
            DragAcceptFiles(hWnd, FALSE);   // no more drops
            PostQuitMessage(0);
            break;

        default:                                    // default proc & ret
            return (DefWindowProc(hWnd, message,
                            wParam, lParam));
    }
    return(0);
}
```

DROPONME.H

```c
LRESULT __export CALLBACK MainWndProc(HWND, UINT, WPARAM, LPARAM);
BOOL InitApplication(HINSTANCE);
BOOL InitInstance(HINSTANCE, int);

#define MaxFileNameLen (8 + 1 + 3)
#define MaxPathLen 66
#define MaxFileSpecLen MaxFileNameLen + MaxPathLen
```

DROPONME.DEF

```
NAME            DROPONME

DESCRIPTION     'A drag-and-drop client'

EXETYPE         WINDOWS

STUB            'WINSTUB.EXE'

CODE PRELOAD MOVEABLE DISCARDABLE
DATA PRELOAD MOVEABLE MULTIPLE

HEAPSIZE        1024
STACKSIZE       8192
```

Figure 8-2

The output of the drag-and-drop client program

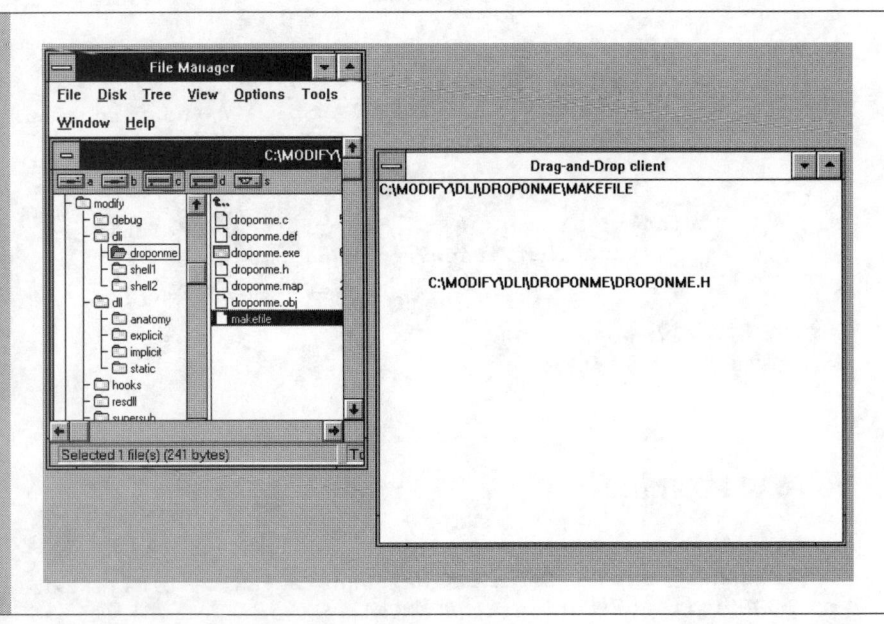

Index

A

AllocCStoDSAlias API, 242-243
ANATOMY.DLL initialization and termination example, 72-73

B

Beeping button examples,
    using superclassing, 100-105
    using subclassing, 107-110
Benchmarks, 216-217
BLTTIME.EXE example program, 211-216
BOSS.DLL for Solitaire example,
    initial version, 112-116
    with termination, 123-126

C

Callback routines, 75-78
    asynchronous operation, 78
    DS setup, 76-78
    reentrancy issues, 78
CallMsgFilter API, 146
CallNextHookEx API, 133-134
CallWindowProc API, 98, 100
Call window procedure hook, 144-145
CDERR.H error codes, 3
Classes of windows, 98
ClassFirst API, 217
CLASSLST.EXE example program, 218-223
ClassNext API, 218
CloseDriver API, 171-172
COLORDLG.H include file, 3
COMMDLG.DLL for common dialogs, 3
CommDlgExtendedError API, 3-4
Common dialogs,
    adding help, 11-13
    customizing via parameters, 4-6
    dispatcher example with help, 13-17
    hooking, 17-19
    message hooking example, 19-25
    modification warnings, 39-40
    registering messages, 12-13
    resource modification, 30-31
Common User Interface (CUI), 2
CommonDialogHookCallbackRoutine, 18
Computer Based Training (CBT) hooks,
    applying, 157
    codes for, 158-159
    timing issues, 160
Control Panel drivers program, 190-191
Controls, creating, 2
CONTROL.INI modifications, 190
CreateWindow API, 98

D

DBGOUT.EXE example, 91-94
DBWIN utility, 85
Debug hook, 161-162
Debug Options variable, in WIN.INI, 89
DebugBreak, 95
Debugging, 82-95
Debugging terminal, advantages of, 94
Debugging version of Windows, 82-94
    problems revealed by, 83-85
    replacement DLLs in, 83
    vs. retail version, 82-83
DebugOutput API, 89-90
DEF file, 52-53
DefDriverProc API, 170
DefProc macro, 244
Device Driver Kit (DDK), 83, 169
Device drivers,

263

MODIFYING WINDOWS

constraints, 167
installable, 168-197
overview of, 166-167
standard, 167-168
virtual, 168-169
See also Installable device drivers
Dispatcher example program,
    initial version, 6-11
    with help, 13-17
DLGS.H include file, 3
DragQueryPoint API, 253
DriverProc callback routine, 169-170, 198
DROPONME.EXE example program, 258-262
DRV_CLOSE message, 175
DRV_CONFIGURE message, 180-181
DRV_DISABLE message, 175-176
DRV_ENABLE message, 174
DRV_EXITAPPLICATION message, 176-177
DRV_EXITSESSION message, 177
DRV_FREE message, 176
DRV_INSTALL message, 179
DRV_LOAD message, 173
DRV_OPEN message, 174
DRV_POWER message, 177-178
DRV_QUERYCONFIGURE message, 180
DRV_REMOVE message, 181
Dynamic Link Interceptors (DLIs),
    link-time, 237
    patching, 237-239
    replacement, 239-262
    See also Replacement DLIs
Dynamic Link Libraries (DLLs),
    advantages, 73-75
    converting to installable device drivers, 197-198
    entry points, 69
    explicit linking, 58-60
    exported routines, 69
    exports, 52-55
    imports, 55
    initialization routine, 70-71
    instances of, 65-67
    mechanisms, 68-69
    structure, 69-71
    termination routine, 71-72
    vs. EXE files, 119
Dynamic linking, 51

vs. static, 58
Dynamic run-time linking, 58

E

ENABLEHOOK flag, 17
ENABLETEMPLATE flag, 31
Entry table, 53
EXEHDR utility, 53-54, 240-242
Explicit dynamic linking, 58-60
__export keyword, 66
EXPORTS statement, 52

F

FAR pointer, 66
FatalExit, 95
Filter function, 131
FreeLibrary API, 60, 245
FreeSelector API, 243-244

G

-GEd switch, 78
-GEe switch, 66
General Protection fault, 83
Get message hook, 145
GetClassInfo API, 99-100
GetDlgItem, 25
GetDriverInfo API, 191
GetDriverModuleHandle API, 192
GetModuleHandle API, 117
GetModuleUsage API, 68
GetNextDriver API, 192
GetOpenFileName API, 5-6
GetProcAddress API, 59, 244
GetWinDebugInfo API, 87-88
GMEM_SHARE flag, 67

H

Hardware event hook, 138-139
Help, adding to common dialogs, 11-13

INDEX

hInstance handle, 67
hModule handle, 67
Hook callback function, 131
    definition, 133
Hooking common dialogs, 17-18
Hooks,
    action codes, 133
    Computer-Based Training (CBT), 157-160
    debug, 161-162
    hardware event, 138-139
    journal, 148-150
    keyboard, 136-137
    mechanisms, 131-135
    message filter, 145-148
    message transfer, 144-145
    mouse, 137-138
    performance issues, 135-136
    shell, 160-161
    system queue, 136
    types of, 136-139
    typical uses of, 130
hTask handle, 67

I

idHook, possible values, 132
IMPLIB utility, 55
Implicit dynamic linking, 52
Import library, 55
IMPORTS statement, 45
Initialization routine of a DLL, 70-71
Installable device drivers, 169-197
    communication APIs for, 171-172
    converting DLLs to, 197-198
    DLL example, 199-203
    driver list example, 192-197
    entry names, 189
    getting information from, 191-192
    identifying, 175
    installing, 188-189
    messages from Windows to, 173-178
    messages from applications to, 178-181
    skeleton example, 182-188
Instance data, 65

INSTDRV.DRV example DLL, 186-188
Interrupt handling, 167
Inter-Process Communication (IPC), 224

J

Journal hooks,
    example program, 151-157
    playback hook, 149-150
    record hook, 148-149
JRNLHOOK.DLL example, 151-157

K

Kernel debugger, 95
    command set of, 95
Keyboard hooks, 136-137
    lparam codes for, 137
KILLERAP.EXE hook example, 140-144

L

LIBW.LIB import library, 90
LISTDRV.EXE example program, 193-197
LoadLibrary API, 58-59, 240, 244
LoadModule API, 58

M

MakeProcInstance API, 77
MAIN.EXE examples,
    explicit dynamic linking, 61-64
    implicit dynamic linking, 55-58
    static linking, 46-51
Message box, 45
Message filter hooks, 145-148
Message filtration, 19
Message registration, 12-13
MLPROCES.EXE example program, 228-234
mmsystem, 89
Module, 65
MOUHOOK.DLL examples,

standard, 142-144
    as a resident DLL, 199-203
MOUMACRO.EXE journal hook example, 151-157
Mouse hook, 137-138
    example program, 139-144
MSGRTN.DLL example, 57-58
Multitasking, 223

N

NBUTTON.DLL subclassing example, 109-110
NEWSOL.EXE example,
    simple version, 112-116
    with termination, 121-126
Non-resident name table, 53
Notifications, 224
    example program, 227-234
    warnings, 226-227
Notifycallback routine, 225
NotifyRegister API, 225
NotifyUnRegister API, 226

O

Object library, 45
ofn structure, 5-7
Open tools, 208
OpenDriver API, 171
OPENFILENAME structure 5-6
OutputDebugStr API, 89
OutputDebugString API, 89
OutputTo variable, in SYSTEM.INI, 85

P

Parameter validation, 253
Patching,
    applications in memory, 238
    applications on disk, 238
    DLLs, 238-239
PostAppMessage API, 120
ProcAddr macro, 244

Profilers, 211
Protection rings, 167

R

Reentrant code, 78, 167
RegisterClass API, 100
RegisterWindowMessage API, 12-13
Replacement DLIs,
    applying, 252-253
    code segment aliasing, 242-244
    example program, 258-262
    overview, 239-240
    parameter validation and, 253
    potential problems, 252
    skeleton example, 246-252
Resident name table, 53
RUN.EXE example program,
    initial version, 7-11
    with help, 13-17
    with hooking, 19-25
    with initial values, 26-30
    with template modification, 32-38
RUNME.EXE multiprocessing example, 228-234

S

SendDriverMessage API, 172
SetClassLong API, 106
SetWinDebugInfo API, 88-89
SetWindowLong API, 111-112
SetWindowsHookEx API, 131-132
SetWindowText API, 25
Shell hook, 160-161
SHELL.DLL,
    DLI replacement, 253-258
    header of, 240-242
    skeleton replacement, 247-252
Solitaire modification example, 112-116
SPY utility, 118
Static linking, 45-46
Subclassing,
    a single window, 111-117
    an entire class, 106-111

INDEX

avoiding side effects with, 118-119
terminating windows and, 120
with multitasking, 118
SUBCLS.EXE example program, 107-110
SUPER.EXE superclassing example, 100-105
Superclassing, 98-105
SYSTEM.INI modifications, 85, 189-190, 198
System message filter hook, 147-148

T

Task message filter hook, 146-147
Terminating subclassed windows, 120
Termination routine of a DLL, 71-72
TimerCount API, 210
Toolhelp,
    callback support APIs, 223-226
    class list example, 218-223
    list-walking APIs, 217-218
    notifications, 226-227
    purpose, 208-209
    standard APIs, 209-211
    termination notification example, 227-234
    TimerCount example, 211-216

U

UnhookWindowsHookEx API, 134
"Unresolved external" error, 90
Unsubclassing, 110-111

Use count, 68
USEDRV.EXE example program, 182-188

V

Virtual device driver,
    debugging, 83
    in kernel debugger, 95
Virtual Timer Device (VTD), 211

W

WH_CALLWNDPROC hook, 144
WH_CBT hook, 158-159
WH_DEBUG hook, 162
WH_GETMESSAGE hook, 145
WH_JOURNALPLAYBACK hook, 150
WH_JOURNALRECORD hook, 149
WH_SHELL hook, 161
WINDEBUGINFO structure, 85-87
Windows Exit Procedure (WEP), 71, 245-246
WinExec API, 223-224
WIN.INI file,
    specifying debug information in, 89
WM_DESTROY message, 32
WM_INITDIALOG message, 15
WM_QUERYSYNC message, 157
WM_QUIT message, 120
WNDCLASS structure, 98-100

Modifying Windows Companion Diskette

The companion diskette (3½") for *Modifying Windows* contains the source (and executable) code of all the examples in the book. It will provide you with the code needed for further experimentation and expansion on the examples from the book. Furthermore, the examples are an ideal starting point for creating your own applications, that utilize the techniques discussed in the book.

Modifying Windows Companion Diskette – Order Form

Please send me the companion diskette for Modifying Windows for $25.00. In California add applicable sales tax. Outside the U.S. and Canada add $5.00 for airmail shipping and handling.

❏ Check enclosed (U.S. funds drawn on a U.S. bank) - made payable to: Wisdom Software, Inc.

Charge my: ❏Visa ❏MasterCard ❏AmEx   Card number: _____ Exp. date:____

Name on card:_____   Signature: _____

Name:_____   Company:_____

Address: _____

City:_____   State:_____   ZIP:_____

Phone:_____   FAX:_____

Mail order form to:
Wisdom Software, Inc., 322 Eureka Street, San Francisco, CA 94114
Telephone/FAX: (415) 824-8482

SPECIAL OFFER
WINDOWS DEVELOPER LETTER
THE TECHNICAL NEWSLETTER FOR ADVANCED WINDOWS PROGRAMMING

FROM THE AUTHOR OF *MODIFYING WINDOWS*

Windows Developer Letter is a unique newsletter for advanced Microsoft Windows developers. It is neither a marketing letter nor an introduction to basic Windows programming. Rather, it is packed with in-depth technical know-how, tips, techniques, secrets, and undocumented knowledge that will turn you into a Windows guru. The sort of knowledge only a few individuals possess, and even fewer are willing to share. The know-how that will give you and your programs a unique advantage in the market. *Windows Developer Letter* is a hands-on newsletter that explains new and complex issues in complete detail, with full source-code examples. No hand waving, no fluff, no ads, no reviews, just the facts – and lots of them.

Each issue of *Windows Developer Letter* takes a detailed look at some of Windows' newest and most advanced features, with special emphasis on 32-bit programming. The *Windows Developer Letter* includes in-depth discussions of Windows architecture and internals.

Written exclusively by developers, for developers, the *Windows Developer Letter* is like no other publication. It provides original and useful information (not reprints of the manuals) that you can not afford to be without. Articles include a discussion and full working source code that show exactly how to use each advanced feature. In addition, each issue includes a diskette with the royalties-free source code for all the examples, so that you can put your new knowledge to work at once, building on the examples to create your own powerful programs. It is this type of innovation and thoroughness that has already earned the *Windows Developer Letter* top praise:

"... a new one-of-a-kind, highly technical newsletter ... designed, and written for the heavy-duty Windows technical guru who is searching for cutting-edge solutions to tomorrow's Windows application problems."
Steve Gibson, *Tech Talk* Column, *InfoWorld*, October 12, 1992

"... an important resource for any serious Windows developer. It's a unique newsletter that presents clear and thorough discussions of little known and unknown features of Windows."
Fran Finnegan, Writer of the *Windows Q&A* Column for *Microsoft Systems Journal*

"*Windows Developer Letter* abounds with programmers' tricks ... has discovered many new techniques that can come in very handy for programmers."
Brian Livingston, *Window Manager* Column, *InfoWorld*, June 21, 1993

Special offer to readers of *Modifying Windows*
Get 12 issues of the *Windows Developer Letter* for only $250.00 (regular subscription rate is $300.00).

No-risk guarantee:
If you liked this book, we are sure you will love the *Windows Developer Letter*. However, if you decide to cancel your subscription at any time, you will receive a refund for all unmailed issues.

OMHMW

SUBSCRIPTION ORDER FORM – Special limited time offer!
Please start my subscription to *Windows Developer Letter* at the special rate of $250.00 (12 issues). In California add applicable sales tax. Outside the U.S. and Canada add $50.00 for airmail shipping and handling.

❏ Check enclosed (U.S. funds drawn on a U.S. bank) - made payable to: Wisdom Software, Inc.
Charge my: ❏Visa ❏MasterCard ❏AmEx   Card number: _____ Exp. date:____
Name on card:_____   Signature: _____

Name: _____   Company: _____
Address: _____
City: _____   State: _____ ZIP: _____
Phone: _____   FAX: _____

Mail order form to:
Wisdom Software, Inc., 322 Eureka Street, San Francisco, CA 94114
Telephone/FAX: (415) 824-8482